CHRISTLY GESTURES

CHRISTLY GESTURES

Learning to Be Members
of the Body of Christ

Brett P. Webb-Mitchell

William B. Eerdmans Publishing Company
Grand Rapids, Michigan / Cambridge, U.K.

Wm. B. Eerdmans Publishing Co.
255 Jefferson Ave. S.E., Grand Rapids, Michigan 49503 /
P.O. Box 163, Cambridge CB3 9PU U.K.

Printed in the United States of America

08 07 06 05 04 03 7 6 5 4 3 2 1

Library of Congress Cataloging-in-Publication Data

Webb-Mitchell, Brett.
Christly gestures / Brett P. Webb-Mitchell.
p. cm.
Includes bibliographical references and index.
ISBN 0-8028-4937-7 (pbk.: alk. paper)
1. Christian education. I. Title.

BV1471.3.W43 2003
268 — dc21
2002035407

www.eerdmans.com

To my parents, Liz and Don Mitchell,
who taught me gestures of love and forgiveness
from a parent to child . . .
To my children, Adrianne Dawn and Parker Isaac,
who teach me the Christly gestures
of love and forgiveness from child to parent
day after day . . .
And to the countless teachers in the body of Christ
who live the gestures of Christ daily
for others to learn from,
I am in your debt . . . .

Contents

Acknowledgments

I write this as a gesture of thanks and thanksgiving, beginning with those of you who helped me discover the subject and write this book over many years. I thank Adrianne and Parker, who taught me the gestures of parenting time and again. To Pam Webb, their mother, I am thankful for her support in caring for our children as I wrote this book. The love of Liz and Don Mitchell, my parents, sustained me over the long haul . . . again. Thanks to Dean, whose gestures of abiding love and Christlike friendship were constant companions.

I am grateful to the many students at Duke Divinity School who have waited patiently for the publication of this book. I am also grateful for those many workshop and conference participants who asked great questions of me as I presented material from this book, refining ideas along the way.

I thank all those educators who read, critiqued, and reread the many drafts of this book. To Bill Myers and Mike Warren, many thanks. George Noblit showed me ethnography *as* education. Wally Hannum and Jim Paul listened well, asking questions to pull the material out of me that was in me all along. My ability to employ the craft of stories came over many years from many conversations with Richard Rodriguez.

Sr. Stefanie Weisgram, OSB, and Sr. Aggie Zwilling, OSB, of St. Benedict's Monastery in St. Joseph, Minnesota were soul mates. Stef read and edited this manuscript many times before it was given over to the publisher. Aggie provided continuous examples of gestures of hospitality.

Thanks to Reinder Van Til of Eerdmans for editing and pulling together the manuscript into a better book.

Thanks to all the Benedictine and l'Arche communities, and all the churches where I have been either congregant or pastor, who helped me see, taste, touch, smell, and feel the gestures of charity.

Finally, thank you to all those God-given friendships that reveal the life-giving gestures of Christlike love among us all.

Introduction

We are about to open a school for God's service, in which we hope nothing harsh or oppressive will be directed.[1]

The School of the Church

I begin this book with this simple, marvelous quote from the *Rule of St. Benedict* because it captures splendidly what I have come to understand as both the place and purpose of education in the church: the church, the body of Christ, is a school in which we are what Michael Casey calls the receivers of the *magisterium* of Christ — for God's service:

> We are pupils in the school of the Lord's service, or, as the medieval Cistercians loved to say, we belong to the school of Christ. . . . It means that as individuals and as members of a group, we are to learn Christ. What other desire is at the heart of the vocation of every fervent Christian man and woman?[2]

In other words, the church in its entirety is a school of Christian discipleship, a place and a people created and called by God, infused with the Holy Spirit,

1. Anthony Meisel and M. L. del Mastro, eds., *Rule of St. Benedict* (New York: Image Press, 1975), p. 45.

2. Michael Casey, *Sacred Readings* (Liguori Press, 1996), p. 36.

where we are to learn Christ, to follow Christ, and to be more like Christ in our daily lives. Or, to paraphrase Joan Chittister, the church is the place and people where we learn and practice the way of "Jesus-life."[3]

I propose in this book that the purpose of education in the church is as follows: Christians live out of the true vision given to them by the grace of God in the writings of the Apostle Paul; the church — amid all the dynamics, controversies, and agendas within congregations and parishes — is the figurative body of Christ on earth and is thus the context of educating all Christians; therefore, the church *is* education — from the intentional or formal programmatic activities of Sunday schools, youth groups, and catechetical instruction to Kerygma and Disciple Bible studies.[4] And the church is Christian education in its worship and prayer and healing services; in all its ritualistic rubrics throughout the church year; in its plethora of meetings and seminar conferences; in its extended retreats and seminars; in its pastoral counseling sessions and administrative board meetings; in its musical and dramatic performances and visual art exhibitions; in its fellowship hour with coffee and juice and its potluck dinners — all of this "stuff" of church culture may be considered the church *as* education.

Being members of Christ's body, we are each called to perform the gospel, literally the Good News, with what I would like to call Christly gestures. Performing gestures of faith in Christ's name is to follow, imitate, and participate in the "Jesus-life," in which every one of our words and deeds is an action of our bodies, hearts, and minds, as we are infused by the power of the Holy Spirit to love one another as we love and serve God in Christ. When our lives are shaped according to God's will and Christ's way in the body of Christ, then our gestures may be instruments of God's gift of grace through faith, which is to incarnate Christ in our very lives.[5]

Remembering Where We Come From

I was not raised to understand education in the church in this way — either as a child and young person or later as I was taught in seminaries. I was

3. Joan Chittister, *Wisdom Distilled from the Daily* (New York: Harper Collins, 1991), p. 101.

4. I understand that Christian education can have a pejorative connotation, especially for "us Protestants" and our Sunday school tradition. I understand Christian education as a shorthand way of saying "this is how we Christians educate." See Thomas Groome, *Christian Religious Education* (New York: Harper & Row, 1980), p. 24.

5. Michael Casey wrote something similar to this, stressing that *Lectio divina* helps us encounter Christ, initiating us into the way of Christ. See Casey, *Sacred Readings*, p. 39.

taught to understand education in what John Westerhoff called a schooling-instructional paradigm, where there are a time, place, and practice considered "education" in the hectic life of a church. Christian education was typically held in a certain set of rooms, with certain kinds of curriculum (paper), activities, and media aids (film projector), held during an hour that was set apart from the other distinct activities of the church, such as worship, preaching, choir rehearsals, counseling, administration, biblical studies, history, theology, and philosophy. Being educated in the church, be it Sunday school, youth group activities, Vacation Bible School, or adult Bible studies, was a one- or two-hour activity held once a week.

Doris Betts explains this phenomenon well in this simple story: There was a day in King Solomon's court when a guard brought to him a child, along with a throng of grumbling citizens, some claiming to own part of the child while others claimed not to desire any part. One of the "grumbling citizen" groups was a collective of Sunday school teachers, who said, in unison:

> Oh King, that *is* our child . . . at least one-seventh is ours. Once a week we'll offer this child spiritual nourishment, but (you understand, Oh King) full-time children would track in mud where we worship.[6]

In the modern world, the church often has "dibs" on many Christians for only one-seventh of the weekly schedule, and even then, only for a "fifty-minute hour" at best, usually on Sunday mornings, with perhaps a weekly meeting on a weekday night. And for some, their schooling in the church is often boring compared to their regular schooling, for example, the public school in the United States. To quote one of David James Duncan's characters in *The Brothers K*, "After a hard week of *real* school, the last thing a person needs first thing on [Sunday] is some goody-goody mom or dad grilling them on the [Sunday school] lesson."[7]

Furthermore, in the instruction in Sunday school and Bible studies in the Protestant churches — and often in catechetical instruction — the pedagogy has often been similar to what Paulo Freire called the "banking concept" of education: one was given information pertinent to the context with the student sitting and receiving education via a teacher's lecture, repetitive drilling exercises, rote memorization, and homework. In many cases, the student then regurgitated this material on tests and worksheets, depending on the

6. Doris Betts, "A parable: Whose child is this?" *News and Observer*, January 15, 1997, p. 11A.

7. David James Duncan, *The Brothers K* (New York: Bantam, 1993), p. 65.

context. Freire called this process of education "dehumanizing," since there was no connection between a person's life and the knowledge accumulated. While reading, listening to lectures, studying, and memorizing have their worthy places in education in general, such approaches may ultimately fail because they do not create a connection with the rest of one's life.[8] In other words, someone needs to connect the dots for students between what is learned in the culture called "school" and the culture called "life."

The problem with the material learned in such conventional Sunday schools (Protestant) and catechetical instructions (Catholic) was three-fold: first, the reason their content (e.g., the Bible, church history, and theology) did not and still may not make a connection with our lives in the growing complexity of today's world is that we have reduced the great ongoing story that we Christians are part of to objective tidbits and consumable "factoids." Not enough can be said about the need to make the learning process relevant to the lives of both teacher and learner. Paulo Freire's "liberating" social literary theory argues that education begins when we start to literally name the things that cause oppression or joy in our lives rather than beginning with a set of words that have no relevance to our context.[9]

Second, by using the educational material in a way that discounts the person's life, we assume that a person is a blank slate to be written on rather than a life already being lived. This can fail to inspire a dialogue with students, thus "killing off the passions" of students because they become passive learners as they are fed a steady diet of facts, according to Parker Palmer.[10]

Third, the current approach to learning in the church is directed toward the individual and not necessarily toward the community as a whole. As I will discuss later in this introduction, Christian education and worship in particular are beholden to the viewpoint that some people are in search of the community for what it can bring to them rather than seeking a community in which they give of themselves — where each person's life is open to the other, without hesitation.[11]

In many ways, this same critique can be directed at the modern public schools, from reading and writing to history and math courses. Only the content differs because of the differing contexts. Knowledge gained through such methodological practices is largely dissociated from actions that inform what we believe outside the classroom, in the context where we live.

8. Parker Palmer makes a similar critique in *To Know as We Are Known* (New York: Harper, 1983), p. 33.

9. See Paulo Freire's *Pedagogy of the Oppressed* (New York: Continuum, 201).

10. Palmer, p. 35.

11. Jean Vanier, *Community and Growth* (Mahwah, NJ: Paulist Press, 1979), p. 5.

Theoretical criticism of how we conceive and practice education in the church has increased in the last few decades; many short-term remedies have addressed the increasing apathy toward the education-as-Sunday-school pattern. And news of the Sunday schools' demise is commonplace, bandied about by religious educators at many denominational conferences. Blaine Fister says:

> "The Sunday school is dying." "It is dead!" "Let's bury it and start anew!" The funeral orations have been preached for many years. A national magazine once labeled it "the most wasted hour of the week." But the Sunday school refuses to die. There is scarcely a church in the country without a Sunday Church School. New churches are still being built with the Sunday school as the forerunner for gathering the new congregations. There are extremely large Sunday schools with thousands of members, and small Sunday schools struggling to keep going. It exists, and has no intention of folding up or dying.[12]

Thomas Groome says that he has spent past years on many bandwagons in search of promising solutions to teaching the gospel, only to be disillusioned again and again. Citing Dietrich Bonhoeffer, Groome says that there is no "cheap grace" in teaching religious education well.[13] Yet new models of education continue to arise quickly and die even more quickly as the Sunday school model of education in the church is considered less and less effective in passing on the educational understanding of the Christian faith to the lives of the next generation of Christians.[14] John Westerhoff observes in *Will Our Children Have Faith?:*

> No longer can we assume that the educational understandings that have informed us, or the theological foundations that have undergirded our efforts, are adequate for the future.[15]

Likewise, Michael Warren has seen how catechesis as it is taught in the Catholic Church today is failing to teach a gospel-based way of living life in communities. He decries the fact that Christianity is no longer a particular way that influences the actual patterns of our lives. Warren writes that cate-

12. In Robert Lynn and Elliot Wright, eds., *The Big Little School* (Nashville: Abingdon Press, 1980), p. 1.

13. Groome, p. xiii.

14. See John Westerhoff, *Will Our Children Have Faith?* (New York: Seabury Press, 1976), and Charles Foster, *Educating Congregations* (Nashville: Abingdon, 1994), p. 20.

15. Westerhoff, *Will Our Children Have Faith?*

chesis is an activity in a classroom but not in the home or in other interactions among those in a community of Christian faith. Thus catechesis has become an intellectual activity that is bound inside a classroom, with no life outside the classroom, meant for a short period of time in one's life and not for the duration of a lifetime.[16]

There has been an ongoing discussion for years among educators in the church — a Luther-like *Tischreden* — raising questions about the future of Christian education. Along with Palmer, Westerhoff, and Warren, two other Christian educators who have in recent years seen and systematically addressed the gradual breakdown — if not failure — of church education are Chuck Foster and Thomas Groome. In *Educating Congregations,* Foster has gone so far as to say that churches have simply not acknowledged the diminishing capacity of their education:

> These churches are no longer capable of building up communities of faith adequate to the contemporary challenge of praising God and serving neighbor for the sake of the emancipatory transformation of the world.[17]

Foster then gives five clues about the flaws in the current way of educating Christians in both Protestant and Catholic contexts. First, there is a loss of communal or corporate memory, in which basic knowledge of the Bible, church history, and theology — that is, the identity of the church itself — has been lost among generations of Christians. Many people are not as loyal to the faith communities in which they were raised. For Foster, this is not only a loss to a congregation but to the generations of Christians in the past and our sense of identifying with the disciples of Jesus.[18]

Second, Foster points to the irrelevance of the way we teach the Bible, which leads to the irrelevance of the Bible itself. He specifically points to the problem of learned clergy and theologians keeping much of the information on how to read Scripture and think theologically away from the laity.[19] Biblical scholars and theologians, who know how to read and interpret Scripture and engage in theological reflection capable of opening up the deeper, more relevant questions concerning people's lives, need to make that knowledge

16. Michael Warren, *Faith, Culture, and the Worshiping Community* (Mahwah, NJ: Paulist Press, 1989), p. xii.

17. Foster, p. 21.

18. Foster, p. 24.

19. To remedy this situation, Lilly Endowment, Inc., has generously granted Duke Divinity School $10 million for the "Learned Congregation" project to learn better how to teach laity such practices as interpreting the Bible and discussing theological issues.

and those "tools" readily accessible to congregation and parish laity. It is not uncommon in some churches to see laypeople who have little or no direction from a pastor or a Christian educator lead a Sunday school class or Bible study, reading word for word from the curriculum's teacher guide. This uninformed layperson may then put down the Bible and simply ask the class, "What do you want to learn about?" The laypeople may then discuss relevant issues of the day, using the Bible to support their viewpoints along the way, in a rather capricious fashion.

Third, Foster points to the subversion of the Christian education goals in the church. Clearly, there is more attention paid to the psychological or emotional and therapeutic needs of the learner, alongside marketing mechanisms for selling curriculum, in today's approach to Christian education than to salvation and justification. The question is: Are we more caught up in education-as-entertainment than education-as-transformation?

As an example of education-as-entertainment, consider "J.C.'s Place," the largest gathering of Christian teenagers in the Minneapolis-St. Paul area. What is its draw? An emotional, personal, one-to-one relationship with Jesus Christ. The charismatic Nate Ruch — "Pastor Nate" to the kids of "J.C.'s Place" — said in an interview: "We don't do video games, we don't play pin the beard on Moses. Our product is a relationship with Jesus. We just try to provide an emotional anchor and an outlet for expression in those volatile teen years."[20] Teenagers gather around and sing, some swaying, others stretching out their arms, while some hug and others get down on their knees in praise: "I can't live without you" is not addressed to their latest crush but to God as they "pour their hearts, and souls, into praising God."[21]

Foster understands that the current trend is to focus on either the above education-as-entertainment or on the attempt to reframe what is most pleasing, emotionally speaking, to the individual learner. For example, Foster writes that there has been great emphasis on meeting each student's personal needs and wants, thus learning by behavioral objectives.

James Loder's theory of transformation has wedded modern psychological theories, such as those of Piaget and Freud, with theological convictions, primarily those of Kierkegaard. Loder argues for a kind of education that is an individualistic transformation of the self, induced by a crisis of one kind or another in a person's life. This crisis opens the self up to both the "dark night of the soul" and out of that darkness the possibility of discovering

20. Kristin Tillotson, "Giving it up for God," *Minneapolis Star Tribune,* May 23, 2000, p. E1.

21. Ibid.

the grace of God in the person's life. Such a moment of revelation gives him the capacity to meet the crisis anew and bring it to a point of resolution.[22]

On the other hand, we have enrichment education activities or *programs* for teaching and learning. Foster says:

> A program is a list of events to be performed, a plan of activities to be completed. It emphasizes entertainment rather than learning, consumption rather than transformation. It tends to embody the values and structures of the shopping mall. People are offered a wide range of choices.[23]

This could also be called the "cafeteria approach" to education: just choose one of the above programs that fits your needs. Alongside the programs approach is the enrichment education approach, where we create an environment, broadly speaking, that reflects the values and spirit of the Christian community in its most desirable form, with the hope that students will take on the thinking and lifestyle of a Christian community.[24] With the programs or enrichment education approaches, topics and themes are interchangeable. Foster claims that traditional teachings of the church, such as sin and salvation, faith and doubt, are trivialized or simply lost in the feeling that students, young and old alike, want topics that are more relevant to their lives in the world. It is impossible in such a milieu to create a significant teacher-student relationship or craft a series of lessons over a sustained period of time with the same community of learners.

Fourth, Foster cites the cultural captivity of the church in North America to the perpetuation of modern cultural stereotypes that some would call racist, sexist, ageist, and classist — to name a few critical agendas for the church. In North America, both Protestant and Roman Catholic churches are welcoming people who are not necessarily white, Anglo-Saxon, heterosexual, or middle class, yet many of the examples in the church's curriculum hark back to a 1950s and 1960s American worldview.

Finally, the change in what is considered "family" has also affected Christian education. No more can one assume, for example, that family life is ordered by congregational life. Rather, whatever constitutes family life often orders congregational life, including, in some instances, determining even the time schedule for worship.[25]

22. See James Loder, *Transforming Moment* (New York: Harper, 1981).

23. Foster, p. 29.

24. Ibid., p. 28.

25. A frequent claim by some pastors is that they have had to change the time of

Another aspect of the current problem is determining how we conceive of church education in the first place. Are we to understand Celtic spirituality-as-formation education? Is service in the community education? Is education an intense, intentional community of peers, such as Disciple Bible or Kerygma groups, where people commit themselves to a basic and rigorous study of Scripture over a period of months, with the added possibility of becoming open and vulnerable to each other? Is Christian education possible simply in being within a church environment, through the socialization and enculturation with other Christians, with a campfire's glow encircling us at a retreat center?

Groome, in his important book *Christian Religious Education,* says that there is little agreement about the nature of educational activity in the church, let alone in the world at large:

> Small wonder then that there is nothing like a universally agreed upon definition of the enterprise. Actually, for such a complex activity there never could be anything like one precise and exhaustive description. There are, of course, a myriad of definitions available, some well known and others less.[26]

Groome tells of his "baptism" into the multiple understandings of Christian "education" in the preface. Entering his first "religion" class in 1966, he had prepared three fine lectures and gone in to teach a class of thirty-five juniors in a Catholic boys' high school in Ireland. The class was a catastrophe. Working out of the pedantic lecture-school desk model failed miserably with this class of younger students. Groome soon learned that what the students desired more than anything was a dialogue: to talk with and listen to one another, including the teacher. Slowly a pattern developed over the pedagogy — namely, a dialogue — and the curriculum: religious topics and life issues of interest to the group. One student's question, "What *are* you doing in this class?" stymied Groome. He didn't know how to name the activity he was performing. The question led him, years later, to consider what he calls "educational praxis," in which education is a dialogue between students and teacher, in contrast to what Paulo Freire called the "banking concept" of education.[27]

And yet it is possible to come up with solutions to some of life's prob-

worship on Sunday morning to fit with soccer schedules for the children. As for the quotes around "family," there is, in the United States, a shift in terms of the boundaries and definition of what a family is, which also affects our instruction in the life of the church.

26. Groome, p. 20.

27. See Groome's preface to *Christian Religious Education.*

lems in the context of studying the Bible together in a Sunday school classroom without touching life outside the classroom context, and vice versa. Consider the following story told by Joe Murray about a Sunday school discussion:

> We had a good discussion in Sunday school. We read Scripture, we recounted stories. One told of a lottery winner who had used part of his millions to build a baseball stadium for his college and to fund scholarships. Someone else recalled a preacher's message that money is the worst thing you can put your trust in. . . . It was an inspiriting lesson. I'm glad I went. Afterwards, some of us got together for lunch at the country club.[28]

This simple story points to a larger, more complicated, and thus intricate problem not only in the way we educate in the church but, more fundamentally, in how we understand what Christian education is. I agree with Westerhoff's basic summary statement about the problem we are facing in educating Christians: that the educational approach and theological arguments that have propped up our efforts are inadequate at best — and failing at worst. Like Parker Palmer, I am discouraged to see the domination of the conventional schooling-paradigm in many churches as the primary way people understand Christian education: that the rich, intricate knowledge of the church's story is often reduced to informational tidbits, and the life of the learner is largely ignored in many instructional formats. While a good deal of church history and biblical interpretation is available on the Internet and various Web sites (e.g., long-distance learning), it is probably again a passing on of information with little or no guarantee of how it will affect a person's life.[29] I concur with Foster's "five flaws" of our current approach to education. Furthermore, Groome is also correct: there is no "one-size-fits-all" definition of

28. Joe Murray, "Tossing around money at Sunday School," *News and Observer* (Raleigh, North Carolina), August 7, 1997, p. 21A.

29. I am aware that this is an issue that is thickly nuanced, to say the least. For example, at St. John's Seminary in Collegeville, some courses are taught via the Internet for a portion of the time, but once a month or so the class of students gather together at St. John's. Such a method of learning allows some students who live far away and do not have the luxury of moving to a seminary a chance to get graduate courses. But there is little to no way to know if a person's life is affected in what she or he is learning. Likewise, if a student attends a theological seminary, sitting in a class of one hundred students for an introductory course, with a preceptorial group of thirty or more students that meets once a week, it is not clear that such an educational approach is so much different from long-distance learning via the Internet.

or approach to Christian education, which is why it is elusive at best, and damning at worst, to claim universal agreement about what it is.

For the purposes of this book, I come to this *Tischreden,* this open table discussion of what is wrong with Christian education, with the following three questions: First, what is the purpose of educating Christians today? Second, where is that education to be found in the life of a congregation or parish? Third, simply, how do we educate today?

Three Primary Questions to Consider

The opening question about the future of Christian religious education or catechesis is this: Is Sunday school a failure or a success? The answer often is that it depends on the kind of Christian produced by these standard educational practices.[30] For example, if education is considered by the schooling paradigm, then it would appear successful if the students were to know a great deal about the church and the actions of being a Christian. But if education is viewed in the prism of certain transformational changes in a person's life, then a student's accumulation of historical, biblical, and theological tidbits may not be considered an adequate education if that knowledge fails to show us how we should live as Christians.

Let me explain the genesis of this question. While I agree with Groome that there are multiple ways of understanding or answering the question of Christian education's identity, we will be helped in answering it by looking at the context, the *polis,* the nature of the social organism — the polity of the community in which the question is asked. In other words, to paraphrase Tip O'Neill, "all education is local." Thus the goal of education is determined, in large part, by those who live, work, and worship in that context because education depends on that context, that body politic, for its definition and our understanding of it.

Because our understanding of education is context-dependent, it is also a political entity. For example, as Lawrence Cremins and other historians of education in the United States have pointed out, the purpose of education in America is to make a good citizen, one who supports American democracy and becomes a cog in the machinery of the capitalistic enterprise that is modern — or postmodern — America.[31]

30. In part, I started to ask this question after the first class I took with Dr. James Loder of Princeton Theological Seminary, who asked a similar question: "Do you have to be a Christian to teach Christian education?"

31. Ivan Illich, *Deschooling Society* (New York: Harper & Row, 1971), pp. 1-36.

While religious educators have argued about strategies, proposed new approaches, and defined the goals of Christian education,[32] I want to ask this question: What is the immediate context of education? Given some of the criticisms of the schooling paradigm, which emphasizes reading, writing, and memorization, one could suggest that the church is more like an academic environment. Other approaches suggest that the church is a spiritual oasis in a desert-world. This leads us to the first of our three primary questions: What is the purpose of educating Christians today in the context of a church? In this book I propose that the purpose is to teach us to be truthful, charitable, and faithful members, one of another, in the body of Christ. This is a rather large, general context, and I may be guilty of staking claim to a context so broad that what it would mean to educate in this context is almost incomprehensible.

However, I understand that every time we bring up the notion of "community" (e.g., teaching the church to be "community") we open ourselves up to a multitude of explicitly uttered, generalized meanings of that magical term — with a subterranean swamp of implicit assumptions. To say "Christian community" puts some parameters on the term; yet that is still quite broad and may thwart any chance of becoming "community" because we're constantly debating what or where or when it *is*.

Community is another context-dependent term: that is, understanding the meaning of membership in a community depends on the community in which one lives. For example, if someone says "Benedictine community," since I have lived tangentially to both St. John's Abbey and St. Benedict's Monastery in central Minnesota, I have some idea of the kind of community being mentioned. Similarly, if one refers to "l'Arche," since I have lived in this Christ-centered community with people with developmental disabilities in London, I have an idea of the kind of community to which they refer. That is why the name of the community to which we Christians have been created, called, and sustained is important: we need such specifics to understand not only what community is but, more importantly, whose community we are referring to: Christ's community — Christ's living body on earth.

32. Groome refers to the church as "'the community of those who confess Jesus Christ as Lord and Savior, who ratify that by baptism, 'who point toward the Kingdom of God as preached by Jesus, by proclaiming in word, celebrating in sacrament and living in deed the Kingdom already and the Kingdom promised.' The Church is to be a sacrament, an efficacious sign, of the Kingdom of God in Christ" (*Christian Religious Education*, p. 46). Parker Palmer does not refer to the body of Christ when discussing his notion of community. Chuck Foster does not refer to the church as the body-of-Christ-as-community in his book.

And the mystery of this community — the body of Christ — is that we are not called to create it from the wild scraps of our imagination in an *ex nihilo* flourish. Because of Paul's promise, that we are members of Christ's body, "for in the one Spirit we were all baptized into one body — Jews or Greeks, slaves or free — and we were all made to drink of one Spirit" (1 Cor. 12:13), it is not a body that we can create or co-create. If we could, this community would be our bodies, not the body of Christ. We were baptized into this mystical yet organic body that already existed before we came into this world. Our task is to discover and reveal, with God's magnanimous and undeserved gift of grace, the body of Christ present around and among and in us, with the educational goal of promoting the body's growth in building itself up in love (Eph. 4:16).

John Howard Yoder says that the church has the very character of a *polis,* that is, a structured social body. It has its ways of making decisions, defining membership, and carrying out common tasks.[33] How we Christians understand what education is depends on the *polis* of the body of Christ. A shortcoming in some theoretical approaches to education is the attention to what kind of persons we are as individual members of the body of Christ. In other words, the focus of our educational theories has long needed to be on "us" and "ours" in the life in the church instead of on "me" and "mine."[34] One critique, then, of the church's education today would be of the presence of the illusion of "radical individualism" or selfishness.

Immanuel Kant provided the intellectual foundation for the shift to radical individualism. According to Stanley Grenz, Kant believed that "through observation, experimentation, and careful reflection, human beings could discover the truth of the world. [Kant] believed that the burden of discovering truth is ultimately a private (and not communal) matter" between the autonomous knowing self and the world, through "the creative power of the active mind." In such a discovery, an individual is set to know what is universal. Little is needed from others in communities — such as the church — in this pursuit of knowledge.[35]

33. John Howard Yoder, *Body Politics* (Nashville: Discipleship Resources, 1992), p. viii.

34. Granted, this is an extraordinarily difficult argument for a seminary professor to make. The very notion of "grades" in modern academic studies in the United States is based primarily on the individual's receiving a grade based upon the individual's work. There are few options for assessing one's work as a group; when I have offered the option to classes, the students turn it down.

35. Stanley Grenz, *A Primer on Postmodernism* (Grand Rapids: Wm. B. Eerdmans Pub. Co., 1996), p. 80.

Even prior to the Enlightenment, the Renaissance humanism movement produced the "individual": no longer were persons connected to villages or even families if they so chose; nor were they part of the past's narrative or its traditions. People were disconnected from a community greater than themselves; their "idea" of who they were came from their particular, inherited social identity. In this view we are all "unique individuals," capable of thinking for ourselves, disconnected from a past, and free to choose to which circumstances we would be slaves. Our lives no longer need to follow anyone else's "script," or be narrated by a story larger than our own. A man or woman can give him- or herself permission to be as bold as he or she wishes to be.[36]

This high view of the individual is common among modern educators. Stanley Aronowitz and Henri Giroux observe that educators such as John Dewey share the belief in the goodness of the Enlightenment ideal of individualism: (1) the capacity of individuals to think critically; (2) the capacity of the individual to exercise social responsibility for him- or herself; (3) the capacity to remake the modern world in the interest of the Enlightenment dream of reason and freedom. A central ideal is "an abiding faith in the ability of individuals to situate themselves as self-motivating subjects within the wider discourse of public life."[37]

The problem is not necessarily simply being an individual. Joan Chittister reminds us that we should cherish each person and not try to reduce a human being to the "least common denominator" or turn individuals into homogenized groups. Rather, we should celebrate the uniqueness in everyone as being created in the image of God.[38] I agree with Chittister that the problem may not be individualism per se but self-centeredness; for the church has failed to teach people a sense of the "we-ness" in the life of the church, family, and any other social setting.[39] Extreme self-centeredness leads one to ask of the community, "What can you do for me?" rather than asking first, "What do I have that I can give to a community?" Again, according to Jean Vanier of l'Arche, it is the posture of looking at "the community for myself," without the transition to or understanding of

36. Alasdair MacIntyre, *After Virtue,* 2nd edition (Notre Dame: University of Notre Dame Press, 1984), p. 220.

37. Stanley Aronowitz and Henri Giroux, *Postmodern Education* (Minneapolis: University of Minnesota Press, 1991), p. 60.

38. Joan Chittister, *Wisdom Distilled from the Daily* (New York: Harper Collins, 1991), p. 111.

39. Ibid., pp. 116, 119.

> "myself for the community" when each person's heart is opening to all the others, without any exception. This is the movement from egoism to love, from death to resurrection; it is the Easter, the passover of the Lord. It is also the passing from a land of slavery to a promised land.[40]

This celebration of the self was made popular through the work of Sigmund Freud, as well as other human developmental and psychoanalytical theorists, but is also intrinsic to the American dream.[41] Among religious educators, C. Ellis Nelson saw the problem with the primacy of individuals as a "holiness" of individualism. He points out that Thomas Jefferson believed that individuals have the "right" to abolish a government and institute a new government if the government becomes destructive of the unalienable rights of "life, liberty, and the pursuit of happiness."[42] Rodney Clapp understands that kind of praise of individualism as "hyperindividualism":

> The common Western framework of values about marriage, divorce, acceptable popular entertainment, and so forth has broken down. In an even more general sense, people no longer feel bound by the authority of any one community consensus.[43]

In this book I want specifically to expand the focus from the individual learner, whether student or teacher, to an ecclesial — or body-of-Christ — consciousness, to move from thinking about "myself," alone in relationship to God, to an understanding that each one of us can and must do something for the rest of the community of Christ's body. "That's what community, that's what family is all about. Alone we may be little but together we can be something," says Chittister. The focus is to take care of others as well as self.[44]

The second question I am raising is this: What do we educate or form in the context of the body of Christ, as revealed in our congregations and par-

40. Vanier, *Community and Growth,* pp. 5, 6.

41. Consider the work of Jean Piaget, Erik Erikson, Lawrence Kohlberg, James Fowler, Anna Freud, Melanie Klein, and Bruno Bettelheim, to name but a few. Each of these theorists focuses on the individual in the group rather than on the person as part of a thriving, living community. It was not until the emergence of family therapy in the 1940s and '50s that the larger system of which a person is part came to be theoretically an option.

42. C. Ellis Nelson, *How Faith Matures* (Louisville: Westminster/John Knox Press, 1989), p. 21.

43. Rodney Clapp, *Families at the Crossroads* (Downers Grove, IL: InterVarsity Press, 1993), p. 24.

44. Chittister, *Wisdom,* pp. 117-120.

ishes? In the above theories of Christian religious education, the focus — either explicit or implicit — of what we cultivate is the enlightened mind. Grenz says that in the Age of Reason, reason itself is more than the human faculty called the mind. Borrowing from the Greco-Roman Stoic position, the argument of the Enlightenment is that there exists a "fundamental order and structure [that] lies within all of reality and is evidenced in the workings of the human mind. The philosophers assumed that there was a correspondence of sorts between the structure of the world and the structure of the human mind which enabled the mind to discern the structure inherent in the external world."[45] René Descartes defined human beings as "thinking substance and the human person as an autonomous rational subject."[46] And it was in France that the Enlightenment so shaped the culture that the 1800s were clearly celebrated as the "Age of Reason." The Enlightenment philosophers' great faith in human reason was always proved through the new sciences, be they biological or social.

Descartes gave expression to a dualistic understanding of the body and soul that continues to be influential today: mind versus body. Descartes assumed that the ego, located in the mind, says, "I am what I am," and knows that "who I am" is distinct and exists only in a tenuous relationship with the body. Our minds are within the body and serve as a pilot of a large vessel. There is a certain kind of unity between the two, or else we would not be able to experience pain. But all of the sensations of hunger, thirst, and pain are nothing more than confused modes of thinking, arising from the union or fusion of mind and body. In the end we are left with a dualism: body, matter, and nature are on one side, and soul, mind, and spirit are on the other side; the body is mechanical, while the mind is volitional.[47]

When Descartes defines "what I am" as a "thing that thinks," he understands it as the mind, the "thing which doubts, understands, affirms, denies, wills, refuses, and which also imagines and feels." One can even feel cold or hot without a body. Descartes even tried to locate the mind in the pineal gland in the body, though it was hard to figure out how it interacted with the rest of the body.[48] He says:

> I [am] a substance whose whole essence or nature consists only in thinking, and which, that it may exist, has no need of place, nor is dependent on any

45. Grenz, p. 68.

46. Grenz, p. 64.

47. See Dale Martin, "The Corinthian Body" (Durham: unpublished manuscript, 1996), p. 6.

48. Samuel Stumpf, *Socrates to Sartre* (New York: McGraw Hill, Inc., 1975), p. 255.

> material thing: so that "I," that is to say, the mind by which I am what I am, is wholly distinct from the body and is even more easily known than the latter, and is such, that although the latter were not, it would still continue to be all that it is. By body I understand all that can be terminated by a certain figure; that can be comprised in a certain place, and so fill a certain space as there from which to exclude every other body; that can be perceived either by touch, sight, hearing, taste, or smell.[49]

Joseph Dunne calls the Enlightenment the "canonization of reason," marking a clear dichotomy between tradition, which is understood as based on myths and legends, and reason, which lives on some "unprejudiced, neutral ground." Indeed, there is no prejudice or bias in the Enlightenment worldview, because the mind is able to know a reality with no contingency. Such knowledge is achieved through our capacity to use our minds to reason critically, aided by the belief in the rational control of dates, single meanings, universal claims for truth, objective interpretation, and a sensation-based doctrine of perception. Human nature and the world are no longer fixed but malleable, foldable, bendable.[50]

Since Robert Raikes created Sunday school in the 1780s, what many Christian educators and theologians have focused on transforming and shaping is the mind and the spirit. And often our Christian instruction and our worship have followed the course of sharpening critical thinking with little or no regard for the heart (or spirit) and body of the believer, let alone the character.[51] Much of the curriculum in Sunday schools and catechesis classes focuses on sharpening the mind's capacity to know more *about* God, Christ, the Holy Spirit, the history of the church, and theological propositions — with faith being subject to human reason.

Wendell Berry disagrees with Descartes's false dualism of mind versus body:

> I would like to purge my own mind and language of such terms as "spiritual, physical, metaphysical, and transcendental" — all of which imply that the Creation is divided by fault lines into levels that can readily be peeled apart and judged by human beings. I believe that the Creation is one continuous fabric comprehending simultaneously what we mean by "spirit"

49. Descartes, quoted in Martin, *op cit.*

50. Joseph Dunne, *Back to the Rough Ground* (Notre Dame: University of Notre Dame Press, 1993), pp. 111, 112.

51. I have heard theologians say "Clear writing reflects clear thinking," with little or no regard to the character of the writer him- or herself, let alone what the body is doing.

> and what we mean by "matter." The distinction between physical and the spiritual is, I believe, false.[52]

Berry further decries the dualism of mind-versus-body because it inevitably reduces physical reality to being a place of either pleasure or hurt. In modern parlance, the body is now commonly understood as a machine: for example, the heart is no longer the emotional center of our life but an organ that pumps blood as if it were a fuel pump in a car. And if the body is a machine for living and working, then it follows that the mind is the machine for thinking.[53] And even the mind has been reduced to being more or less like a computer for the machine-body. No longer do we contemplate with our minds the sense, emotions, memories, traditions, communal life, and known landscapes, the ability to know right from wrong when speaking to somebody, says Berry. Knowledge is formal, informing speech and action; but knowledge has been reduced to information, which now means data.

> The difference . . . between information and knowledge is something like the difference between a dictionary and somebody's language.[54]

In recent years there has been an influx of new ways of perceiving how we learn, which incorporate different modes of expression, as well as a rise in the interest in all things "spiritual." For example, Howard Gardner has written brilliantly and extensively on his theory of multiple intelligences, in which he argues that there is more than one way to learn and more than one kind of intelligence. Rather, there are at least seven primary modes of communication and, thereby, intelligences. Each one of these intelligences is a "product" of both a certain construction of the human brain in which certain parts are more developed in different people (e.g., the area controlling language versus the area controlling spatial imaging) and of being in an environment in which that natural "intelligence" is given freedom to express itself and be nurtured. There is a mathematical intelligence; a verbal intelligence; a spatial or artistic intelligence; a musical intelligence; a physical or athletic intelligence; an interpersonal intelligence; and an intrapersonal intelligence. What Gardner's theory offers the church is an understanding that there are certain ways we know the world and God. We thus need to take into consideration *all*

52. Wendell Berry, "Health is Membership," *Utne Reader,* Sept.-October, 1995, pp. 59-62.

53. Wendell Berry, *Another Turn of the Crank* (Washington, DC: Counterpoint, 1995), pp. 93, 94.

54. Berry, *Another Turn,* p. 96.

of the ways people learn. So while the "chalk and talk" lecture, memorization, and verbal method of the academy may work for some students and teachers, many others learn best through music, or art, or physical movement, or a multitude of combinations of the above options.

Also emerging in the life of the Protestant churches — but something that has been a mainstay of the Catholic Church — is a rise in the interest of all things "spiritual." John Westerhoff wrote critically of Christian education:

> We have become increasingly concerned with the transmission of information and training in skills. We have become enamored of computerized instruction and behavioral modification. The "back to basics" movement in Christian education has emphasized the acquisition of abstract knowledge about beliefs and behaviors, the memorization of "facts," and obedience to authority.[55]

Westerhoff decries our ability to turn to the Bible and make it into an object of our investigation rather than a subject intended to engage us.[56] Or we fail to interpret or exegete Scripture ecclesiologically, which is a failure to understand that the Bible is the church's book, an essential part of what it has inherited.[57]

Westerhoff and the Catholic writer Michael Warren, as well as Protestants such as Howard Rice and Kathleen Norris, have led a movement that has given the church an interest in spirituality. In *Amazing Grace,* Norris says that immersing herself in the life of Benedictine monasteries greatly improved her spiritual life, after the spiritual impoverishment she had settled into after too much mystery-killing rationality. She claims that the Protestantism she was raised with had "all the mystery scrubbed out of it by a vigorous and slightly vinegary reason."[58]

What still seems to be lacking is a discussion of the human body when we talk about educating Christians in the ways of the body of Christ. The body is not alone, adrift from mind and spirit, air, food, drink, clothing, shelter, and companionship; nor is it a cadaver. Berry reminds us that the body is an organism that "lives and moves and has its being, minute by minute, by an inter-involvement with other bodies and other creatures, living and unliving, that is too complex to diagram or describe."[59] And the body is under the in-

55. John Westerhoff, *Spiritual Life* (Louisville: Westminster/John Knox Press, 1999), p. 17.

56. Westerhoff, p. 24.

57. Michael Casey, *Spiritual Readings,* p. 41.

58. Kathleen Norris, *Amazing Grace* (New York: Riverhead Books, 1998).

59. Berry, *Another Turn,* p. 95.

fluence of thought, feeling, and the Spirit of God. In this book, I will lift up the importance of the body in educating Christians — parallel to and an equal partner with the mind and spirit. To that end, gestures — a rich fusion of body, mind, and spirit — will be my focus toward how we educate in the body of Christ.

The third question I bring to the table discussion is this: *How* should we educate in the church today? Groome cites twin approaches to current church education: socialization and education. He says that theologians and educators such as Horace Bushnell, George Albert Coe, C. Ellis Nelson, John Westerhoff, and Berard Marthaler (and I would add Michael Warren and Jerome Berryman) are all of the socialization or enculturation school of educating Christians, that is, Christian formation begins and ends with being part of a culture — the church — which teaches a person to be a Christian. Bushnell argues that, rather than waiting for a conversion later in life, one should grow up Christian, never knowing himself or herself to be otherwise. Coe believes that the whole social network of a person's reality is the primary educator, whereas Nelson says that the "natural agency" for communicating Christian faith is the church. Warren and Westerhoff, agreeing with Marthaler and Mary Boys, both see worship, the liturgical life, as an embodiment of the community's life and thus responsible for forming, maintaining, and transmitting the faith to the next generation of Christians.[60]

On the other side of this question is the approach of intentional, formal instruction — or catechesis. Instructional pedagogy of this persuasion has reflected the practices of modern secular education: though there is a change in the content, the instruction is bound to a certain time, in a certain classroom, with a specific group of students, usually grouped according to age, grade, or experience. At an early age the focus has been on artistic, hands-on projects. For example, a session in the primary grades begins with a gathering moment of stories and songs. There will be a short prayer, followed by the recitation of a Bible verse, an explanation of the verse, and then an art project or activity. Many homes are littered with small precut, predrawn biblical action figures on popsicle sticks, paper praying hands with simple prayers written on them, paper stickers our children drew on with crayons, and paper plates with various Bible verses that our children have brought home and hung on the refrigerator (often art projects for the sake of art projects). The period is concluded with another song, sometimes in a circle, and then a snack.

60. See Groome, pp. 118-120; Michael Warren, *Faith, Culture, and the Worshiping Community,* p. 71; Mary Boys, *Educating in Faith* (Kansas City: Sheed and Ward, 1989), p. 196.

Beginning in the adolescent years, there are fewer art projects and more small-group discussions between teachers and students: the teachers come to the class with formula questions, usually based on a Bible verse, that may or may not be geared to the lectionary schedule. In these classes, students are asked to reflect on the assigned story within the greater context of the biblical narrative, which is what Groome calls "shared Christian praxis," based on the social-literary work of Paulo Freire. The desired result is the opening of a new way of seeing and understanding life's circumstances through the lens of the Bible in the church. This mode of learning — action and reflection — continues through young adulthood and is used in adult Bible studies as well, such as Disciple Bible Studies and Kerygma.[61] It is also used in the context of modern secular education, with the addition today of computer-generated learning via on-line services. The only distinction between the way we teach in church and the way we teach in secular places is the content of the message.

Along with Westerhoff, Warren, Nelson, and Groome, I believe that the church needs a heightened awareness of the socialization, or enculturation, approach to educating Christians in the traditions, rituals, and storied life of the faith. According to Groome, "becoming Christian requires the socializing process of a community capable of forming people in Christian self-identity. We 'become Christian together.'"[62]

61. A word about Disciple Bible Study. I understand the significance of this course of study in the life of the church, especially the United Methodist Church in America. Disciple Bible Study course participants usually meet for thirty-four weeks, making a commitment to meet once a week, with homework assignments as they learn the Bible, with only a few absences allowed.

While I affirm the kind of learning that goes on in these sessions, I wonder about certain portions of the program. For example, after thirty-four weeks of intense study and coming to know each other, then what? I've witnessed people receiving pins and diplomas and having parties at the end of the sessions; then what was learned dissipates because there is nowhere in the common life of a congregation or parish for the participants to go to sustain what they've learned — except Disciple Bible II, III, and IV. Furthermore, Disciple Bible Study has the capacity of creating a clique in a church because many members are not able to faithfully remain in such a sustained, intense program for thirty-four weeks. In other words, there is an "in-group" and there is the rest of the congregation. Without a community to sustain, maintain, and nurture what habits were learned in Disciple Bible Study, these habits will go by the wayside, and Disciple Bible becomes but a sweet memory. Finally, Disciple Bible Study focuses on a certain kind of learning, basically verbal and linguistic, reading and writing. What about those people who are not intellectually capable of learning that way, e.g., people with learning disabilities or mental retardation, or people with Alzheimer's? And what about those who are excluded because they are too young or too old? Is there another way of educating that embraces everyone?

62. Groome, p. 126.

While I agree that there is a call for some kind of purposeful, instructional moment in educating Christians, the shaping of how we think and feel, the focus must be on how we know and intuit the movement of God in our lives. I will seek to wed the two poles of this dialectic — socialization and intentional education — by proposing that we not instruct *out* of the context of the church's life and our being in the world, but that by teaching *in* context we show what it is to be a Christian in the world. Rather than moving out of the context of education, be it worship, administrative meetings, or service to others in the world, education happens best in the context where a Bible-based, theology-imbued lesson on gestures is to be taught and learned.

The church is the context in which we are educated by God's Spirit, who lives among us in the very community in which we are born, live, and die. Everything we say and the gestures we exhibit in the name of Christ, as well as the gestures others perform in the name of Christ, educate us in the ways of Christ. Because God is integrally part of the "when, why, where, what, and who" of Christly education, the entirety of our life in the church is open to being educated in the ways of God.

The Outline of This Book

While there have been many abstract theological and educational reflections on the church-as-education, which are popular and numerous among religious educators and others in Christian ministry, such discourses often remain just that — abstract.[63] Recent Catholic and Protestant religious educators, such as Groome, Nelson, Foster, Westerhoff, Mary Boys, Craig Dykstra, Gabriel Moran, Maria Harris, Jack Seymour, and Michael Warren, have placed more emphasis on the church in its entirety as a place of education rather than relying on what is called the "schooling-instructional paradigm," also known as "chalk-and-talk." These educators all struggle with the competition of separate programs and activities called "Christian education" within the larger community of Christian faith, which gives Christian education its distinctive shape and edge.[64]

I now add my voice to this important conversation. In Part I, I will reframe the very context of educating Christians. Gerhard Lohfink says that, in being the body of Christ, the church has a kind of bodiliness to it: "It is vis-

63. See Stanley Hauerwas's article on gestures in *Christian Existence Today* (Durham: Labyrinth Press), pp. 101-110.

64. See Boys, *Educating in Faith*, p. 131.

ible, palpable, tangible. It is socially organized. . . . Because the Church is a sacrament of salvation it must be as physical as its sacraments."[65] Part of what is intriguing in this understanding of the context of education is that within the body there is also the vision of the kingdom of God, which is what Groome believes is the ultimate, the *metapurpose,* of Christian religious education: "The overarching framework and end toward which our more immediate educational purpose is directed and within which it can best be understood . . . is the Kingdom of God in Jesus Christ."[66]

Part II focuses on the gestures of the body of Christ. Because we are part of the body of Christ — physically, intellectually, and spiritually — we are called to perform certain gestures that embody the gospel in our daily lives. How do we perform the Scriptures so that the Spirit of God is working within us? Citing Galatians 2:20 ("I live now, not I, but Christ lives in me") and Gregory of Nyssa, Michael Casey says that not only are we to consciously speak, act, and present ourselves as "'other Christs,' but Christ works in us."[67] As we perform the gestures of Christ's body, is it not Christ working in us? That is why I call these "Christly gestures."

Part III centers on the unique pedagogy of Christly gestures in the context of Christ's body. I understand this pedagogy as a pilgrim catechesis: catechesis (from the Greek *katechein)* means to literally re-sound, to echo, or to hand down, implying gestures of speaking, hearing, and physically "handing down" the traditions of the church.[68] I call this a pilgrim catechesis because the process of learning is a journey, often over the same material in the Bible or other theological sources, but at different times and places in our lives. Casey reminds us that there are varying levels of penetration: repeating certain passages in the Bible, repeating certain gestures, means that "we pass through the same territory several times during life. Each time we will find ourselves aware of different aspects of what we are reading or doing." As our perceptions change with time and experience, we will have a different understanding of the text and the accompanying gestures: "This means there is always more richness waiting to be uncovered in the Bible."[69]

I hope that the theme of this book — discovering and learning to be the body of Christ by the grace-filled gestures we perform — will be useful to a broad audience. Because I will address issues concerning many within

65. Gerhard Lohfink, *Does God Need the Church?* (Collegeville: Michael Glazier Press, 1999), p. 207.

66. Groome, p. 34.

67. Casey, p. 38.

68. Groome, p. 26.

69. Casey, p. 47.

Christ's body, I intend this book to be used not only by students and teachers of Christian religious education in our seminaries and divinity schools, but also by congregations and their lay leaders and directors of educational programs. This is where I have learned — and continue to learn — what it is to be a member of Christ's body through the gestures we perform daily.

Thus I will include my own personal narratives as well as those of others who perform Christly gestures. I hope that these stories will be interesting embodiments of the theory that illustrate what I am trying to say; but it is also possible that the greater theological "point" may best be seen as we follow one story's thread carefully, seeking to envision the entire fabric of the woven narrative. Regardless of my intentions, and in keeping with what I have suggested above, there is more than one way to learn or teach in the body of Christ, given the wide range of educational styles.

This leads me to one more caveat. I have been labeled a "scholar-activist" by some. Some readers will be interested in the more scholarly theological arguments I lay out in this book; but some readers, especially those who are educators in a congregation, may want to get right to the chapter that describes how performing Christly gestures in the body of Christ might look in their congregation. I have woven both the academic and pragmatic threads through the text.

In the end, in the process of teaching and learning the performance of Christly gestures, I hope to be faithful to the Latin root of "education," *educare,* which means to bring up, rear, or train (or *educere,* which means to lead, draw out, bring along).[70] Thus education in general, whether it be education-as-formation and enculturation, or education-as-pedantic-practice, or education-as-gestured-performance, focuses on drawing someone out of himself or herself into a larger world of ideas and feelings, and in that process focuses on forming that person to be a directed human being in a specific context. I hope to offer a way of educating in which a person's character is created, shaped, and nurtured in the gestured ways of Christ.

Groome says: "Education is an activity of leading out."[71] What I intend to do in this book is to lead Christians out of the socialization/enculturation versus intentional/formal "education" dialectic into a consideration of the how, what, and where of religious education, its parameters, actions, and future *in* the body of Christ. In the real hustle and bustle, the chaos and calmness, of daily life, I am interested in education that is both deeply intense in its

70. *Webster's New World Dictionary, Second College Edition* (Englewood Cliffs: Prentice-Hall, Inc., 1978), p. 444.

71. Groome, p. 5.

focus on gestures that are critical in Christ's body and as steady and calm as the instructions of God, whose discourses permeate us like the dew (Deut. 32:1, 2). Watching water wear away rock near riverbeds and lakesides, one can see rocks being sculpted by the water — slowly but surely, nuanced, and not grandiose. I am interested in promoting an education in which we are called to create an ongoing awareness of what each member needs while serving the needs of others in Christ, recognizing that the whole of the church is greater than all of its parts. There is a sense of interdependence in the entire structure, according to an already given plan, which is flexible, able to grow, but neither chaotic nor infinitely negotiable.[72] For we are all held together by the trajectory that gave birth to the body of Christ — that is, the kingdom, the reign of God's love.

72. Yoder, *Body Politics,* p. ix.

PART I

THE BODY OF CHRIST

Prologue to Part I

"What is your experience of community?" asked Terese Vanier, Jean Vanier's sister and a member of the l'Arche Lambeth community in London. I hesitated because it was a question that had bothered and fascinated me for some time. I was not sure what my experience of "community" was because I wasn't sure whether I had had one or not.

"Community" is one of those terms that I have come to know as "context-dependent." It depends on the genesis of the "community" in which it finds its context, and what goals best describe or define it. Politicians talk about America as a "community," and they usually mean a group of practices attached to democracy and capitalism. Psychologists, sociologists, and anthropologists mean something more universal and foundational when they use "community," for example, that every community shares a common language, a common goal, a common place or land, with a certain kind of commitment and loyalty, and a common beginning and end. One hears media talk of the "gay community," the "disability community," the "African-American community" — with the errant assumption that these are monolithic, homogeneous gatherings of people who all share the same agenda and list each other on some super-Rolodex. Administrators of institutions of higher education, as well as secondary and primary schools, refer to their teachers, students, and staff as "community"; they mean something different perhaps from how it is used in the above situations. The hallways and classrooms of churches, the pastor's sermon, the liturgical responses during worship, and the church's newsletter — all use the word "community" almost blithely, assuming and hoping that we all have a common definition, hidden or explicit, of what we mean when we use it. Many theologians and religious educators use the concept of community in their writings without necessarily defining what they are referring to.[1] Even Wendell Berry, a master storyteller of community in America, uses the term "community" generally and broadly, having to defer to the people, places, and things that make up the community to be sure they are part of that social organism.[2]

Since Terese Vanier asked me that simple, probing question, I have spent much time reading, writing, teaching, and struggling to get a handle on the almost amorphous nature of community. I have spent even more time actually in so-called "intentional" Christian communities of people who self-consciously identify themselves as a community, where members have pointed out to me where they see, hear, taste, and touch — and are touched by — a community of Christ's love. (I struggle with using the concept "intentional community" to designate something other than a congregation or parish, for it suggests that churches aren't intentional while these small alternative communities are.) Nevertheless, I have lived in and been touched by community in London's l'Arche Lambeth, as well as the Community of the Ark (a l'Arche community) in Washington, D.C. Likewise, I have served l'Arche as a board member in Spokane, Washington, and am part of an effort to create a l'Arche community in North Carolina. I have also lived in and been touched by those who understand themselves as a community at St. Benedict's Monastery in St. Joseph, Minnesota. The sisters of St. Benedict's Monastery have lived in the area since it was founded in the 1800s, meeting daily for prayer and worship, work, and "holy leisure." Among the sisters I have witnessed hospitality that has forged friendships among the most unlikely people, as these sisters have created hospitals, sent missionaries, and served the needs of the faraway and nearby poor.

However, I've also been shaped and nurtured by the churches in which I was raised and nurtured (Congregational, Baptist, United Methodist, and Presbyterian), and by the Presbyterian Churches (USA), which I have served as a pastor for both short and long stints. And I have found glimmers of something like a community shine in the theological seminary where I work.

1. For example, consider that Groome's *Christian Religious Education* refers to community without defining how he is using the term "community." John Westerhoff has written much *about* Christian community without defining what it is. Michael Warren, in his book *Faith, Culture, and the Worshiping Community,* does not define community. Chuck Foster writes *about* community in *Educating Congregations,* with a chapter on "Building Community" without defining exactly what community is.

2. See Wendell Berry's *Home Economics* (San Francisco: North Point Press, 1987); *Sex, Economy, Freedom, and Community* (New York: Pantheon Books, 1993); *Another Turn of the Crank* (Washington, D.C.: Counterpoint, 1995). These three books, along with many others, are about community and the nature of community.

With that personal background, and in dialogue with the apostle Paul's writings, I intend to define the *telos,* or purpose, of educating Christians in the dynamic, fluid act of discovering, naming, becoming, and being a member of the mystical reality of Christ's living body on earth. It is in large part the revelation that we are, by our baptism and God's gift of grace, sustained and nurtured by the Eucharist, by being members of Christ's body.[3] We are not called to build anew the body of Christ from nothingness. Rather, drawing on the theological vision of Paul — as described in Romans, Colossians, Ephesians, and his first letter to the Corinthians — I understand that the purpose of educating all Christians is that they take their rightful, God-given place in Christ's body. And inherent in this body, bred in the marrow of our existence as Christ's body, is the vision of the kingdom of God in Jesus Christ.[4]

Given Paul's writings and the theological history of the church, I further understand that all who are baptized are one in Christ; for being baptized into Christ we have clothed ourselves with Christ, writes Paul to the Galatians: "There is no longer Jew or Greek, there is no longer slave or free, there is no longer male and female; for all of you are one in Christ" (Gal. 3:28). I understand by this that in the body of Christ there is a great diversity of people, who bring with them other narratives and "social constructions" from their lives. Yet in the body of Christ there is also a oneness, a unity, a sense of solidarity.

Those to be educated in the ways of Christ's body include men and women, rich and poor, young and old, and people with different ethnic histories; those who are considered "normal" and those labeled "disabled;" gay, lesbian, transgendered, and straight people; people from rural, urban, and suburban settings. The variety of people is magnificent. Yet amid the diversity Christians find their solace in being members of the one body of Christ, their "community," their "home" and "household," their educational context.

One other important aspect of the body of Christ that I will address in these chapters is its porousness: as human skin allows moisture and air in and out, so the "skin" of Christ's body is porous, letting the Holy Spirit in and out, as well as the waters of baptism and of footwashing. "Wherever two or more are gathered in my name, I am there," Jesus promised. Such is church: two or three in a soup line at a homeless shelter; a room of fifty children in a pre-

3. I thank John Westerhoff for this point of clarification. In one draft of this book, I argued out of the assumption that our task, as Christians, was to make congregations and parishes members of Christ's body. That was to get it backwards: because of our baptism, we are *already* members of Christ's body.

4. Groome, *Christian Religious Education,* pp. 43-51.

school program with teachers tagging along; a congregation of one hundred or one thousand in worship and prayer — all are places of education in the body of Christ.

In the next two chapters I will outline the parameters of the body of Christ, using Paul's letter to the Romans as the overarching theme of these two chapters. Chapter One, "The Church, the Body of Christ," will focus on the very nature of the one body of Christ itself (Rom. 12:4, 5); Chapter Two, "Gifts and Services," will explore the various gifts, roles, and services that are part of our being members of Christ's one body (see Rom. 12:6-8).

CHAPTER ONE

The Church, the Body of Christ

So we who are many, are one body in Christ.

Romans 12:5

In proposing that the church in its entirety *is* education, I mean that anywhere Christ's Spirit chooses is a "teaching moment," a time and place to be taught about being a disciple of the "Jesus-life." With the entirety of Christ's body as our "classroom," our vision of the very nature of what education is may be challenged and changed as follows: first, it expands the "walls" of the Sunday school classroom or catechetical instruction to focus on the life *within* and *among* the members of Christ's body. On the one hand, practices such as Sunday school, youth groups, and worship provide a context — a time, a place, and some sense of order within which we may understand the movement of God among us. Joan Chittister reminds us that a community's customs, such as monastic practices and worship, are created to weld a community of faith together, uniting people to bring a certain mindfulness to their lives, even in the most mundane activities.[1] On the other hand, educating Christians via the members of Christ's body means that education can take place wherever and whenever the Spirit of God wills to build up the body of Christ in love. It can take place among people in catechetical instruction, in homeless shelters, during mission trips to Guatemala, in youth group events, during worship, at administrative board meetings, in small confessionals, and

1. Joan Chittister, *Wisdom Distilled from the Daily,* p. 171.

in pastoral counseling sessions. As Jean Corbon says, "No closed door can prevent the risen Lord from pouring out his Spirit to 'convert' hearts and 'convert' everything into his glorious body."[2]

Second, the "timing" of the lessons to be learned may be according to a schedule in a lesson plan that we educators have constructed for an evening with young people, or an adult Bible story, or a large intergenerational event. No doubt we, more than God, need the structure of such learning processes to live our lives decently and in order. Yet, with the movement of God's Spirit flowing freely wherever and whenever God chooses, education may happen late at night in a conversation with a friend who is distraught, or with a daughter ready to celebrate an achievement in life, or in silent moments of prayer in the wilderness — in those serendipitous moments of life just around the corner from the next step on our pilgrimage.

Third, try as we may to put time and place limits on what "education" in the church is, we are often faced with the discovery of great educational moments in our lives that occur outside the prescribed, normative boundaries of education. Since the Holy Spirit often acts from the borders, we might call it a "border pedagogy" among the disenfranchised in life, such as the poor and disabled. "Teachers" of the Christian faith may be discovered in memories and stories of those who have long since died yet are still part of the body of Christ. Since the body of Christ includes those who are visible and present as well as those in distant lands, it also includes lingering stories of those who are members of the communion of saints. The stories of the German Holocaust or a family's Christmas traditions embodied by a dying family member may be instructive of how we are to enjoy each day of life. And there are the incredibly diverse, rich stories of the saints of the church who may have met challenges similar to those we meet today and whose story could guide our modern pilgrimage.

Fourth, in the body of Christ there are no individual learners or solitary teachers; no need for competitive learning unless competing against oneself for some goal; no need to struggle alone in a Don Quixote moment. Living as a member of Christ's body is to learn to live cooperatively with our friends as well as our enemies, with known acquaintances as well as complete strangers. We are linked together in ways that are more meaningful than we can comprehend. Such is the mystery behind the unity in the one body of Christ.

Fifth, the learners and teachers in Christ's body are an amazingly diverse gathering, more splendid and chaotic than any of us might have chosen. Yet God has chosen us all to be members of this one body. Nowhere in Paul's

2. Jean Corbon, *The Wellspring of Worship* (Mahwah, NJ: Paulist Press, 1988), p. 71.

description of the body of Christ are there standards regarding who can and cannot learn and teach in the body. Women and men, rich and poor, people of all ethnic heritages, disabled and nondisabled, young and old — all these categories and their descriptive characteristics and associated narratives become secondary in the body of Christ. What does matter is the desire to follow the call of God in Christ as we continually learn to love one another. That is why an adult with mental retardation could be a great teacher of patience to other members. It also underscores the necessity of welcoming strangers, such as children, to a church's worship in order for us to visit and revisit the practices of hospitality.

To further broaden our understanding of education in this body, I will begin with a cursory explanation of the function of narrative in discovering, revealing, sustaining, and nurturing the body of Christ. The *story* of the body of Christ serves as a great rule guiding our perception of the boundaries of the who, what, how, and where of this educational context. I am using the word "rule" here much as the Benedictines understand the *Rule of St. Benedict.* The *Rule* is a guide to the Gospels, not an end in itself. St. Benedict called it "a little rule for beginners" in the spiritual life, "not a handbook for the elite, or the literati, or the accomplished," as Joan Chittister says.[3] So too with Paul's description of the body of Christ: while his description of the body is authoritative in the life of Christians, it is open-ended and general enough to welcome a host of interpretations concerning how the body looks, sounds, and feels as it functions in a church.

Following this description of the function of narrative in shaping us and the boundaries of the community-as-Christ's-body, I will focus on some biblical and theological references about how some ancient people to whom Paul wrote letters — in Rome, Corinth, and Colossae — perceived the body as *polis.* These are important references because they bring to our attention essential characteristics of the ancient body of Christ as our primary community of origin.

Finally, using Romans 12:3-5, I will highlight the theological significance of this passage as it pertains to the very nature of the community in which we've been called to live. The reflection will be by no means exhaustive; rather, I am turning to the biblical-theological characteristics as a guide toward mapping out the nature of the communal gathering of Christ's body in our congregations and parishes, which become evident in the sacramental practices of baptism, the Eucharist, and gestures of hospitality.

3. Chittister, p. 11.

How Story Shapes Community, and Vice Versa

A basic assumption of this book is that we Christians are dependent on stories for our very lives. Indeed, Christian life has a narrative structure — with a beginning, a middle, and an end. Consider the Apostles' or Nicene creeds: they begin with the claim that God is Creator of heaven and earth, then focus on the life of Jesus, and end with a note of praise for the life that is to come. The story we live as Christians is not our own story: rather, we are born and baptized into a story that preceded and will follow our presence in the world. In the in-between, our story is sustained and nurtured by the gospel of God, which we re-create and re-narrate as we live in and as Christ's body. It is in God that our story continues to find its meaning, hope, and purpose.

The Story That First Creates, Cradles, and Names Us

Genesis starts with "In the beginning God created the heavens and the earth," and the Gospel of John begins with "In the beginning was the Word, and the Word was with God, and the Word was God." For Christians, it is obvious that before we were born into this world, there always was and is and will be God. God is our beginning, our present, and our future. Before we even know ourselves, we know and are known by God. We are born into a living and changing community whose story reaches far back into time, of which we are but the most recent beneficiaries. We are born into a community as receivers of the story of the community that is responsible to care for us as we are learning the language of the tellers. Acknowledging such dependence on the story of the community we are born into reminds us that we cannot make it on our own in this world, that we are in need of all the intermediaries possible. We have little choice about the stories we pass down along the generations, like the genes that make up our physical bodies. Soon enough we will be tellers of the story, re-enacting the story, adding our experiences to the ongoing story, relating times of great joy and dramatic sorrow for others to learn.

To understand in more concrete ways how God's story first narrates us, consider baptism. At our baptism we recognize that we don't know who we are until God calls us into being. God's initiative precedes our faith and the incredible knowledge of whose we are.[4] In baptism we are given our name and identity, "children of the Most High," as are the many who are visible and

4. John Baillie, *The Theology of the Sacraments* (New York: Charles Scribner's Sons, 1957), p. 89.

those among the "cloud of witnesses" who preceded us and are thus invisible, save in the corporate story that is echoed among the stories of the faithful. In Reformed theology, this naming is not of our own doing; it is something that happens *to* us, much like God's gift of grace. We cannot do anything in order to receive it, for it is a free gift of God (Eph. 2:8). Those who preceded us in this faith community, who remind us that we need Christ, reiterate such a dependency on grace.

This movement of story, being something we are born into, will shape our understanding of what education is among the members of Christ's body. Unlike modern secular education, the education of Christians is not about learning something new while dismissing the old as antiquated, nor about the celebration of "my uniqueness," nor about the Enlightenment project's notion of "self-esteem," in which "I" am the beginning of the story, nor about teaching me to be a good citizen for the good of the state. It is more than learning disconnected sets of knowledges through the use of mind, divorced from body and spirit.

Richard Rodriguez has written that there is such an anti-intellectualism in America — with the rejection of the wisdom of the elders of the past, of authority, of the many artifacts and old sayings of "this is what we used to do" — that we have been lulled into the suffocating illusion that we have "stumbled upon experience, we have discovered sex and evil, that we are somehow innocent of history." In doing so, we fail to understand the ways that we are connected to one another, preferring instead the misguided sense of individualism that says we can "make it on our own." The education of Christians in Christ's body is about teaching people something old: the story of God's chosen people of Israel, of his son Jesus Christ, and of the lives of the Christians who preceded us. But it is more than learning *about* a narrative; its purpose is to teach a people to perform the gestures that embody the narrative of God and God's people. In doing so, we are cultivating the very character of the members of Christ's body.[5]

The Narrative Structure of Life

Being born into a plethora of stories, with their intriguing casts of characters and twisting plots, we come to understand that our very life has a narrative structure — as we all have a beginning, a middle, and an end. For example,

5. See Richard Rodriguez, "On Borders and Belonging," *Utne Reader* (March/April, 1995), p. 79.

when we celebrate a birthday we remember our beginning; likewise, at a funeral we mark the passing of life, remembering God's promise of life everlasting. The narrative provides unity in our otherwise scattered life as we share our story of life with and among the storied community of people who know us from our birth to our death. The stories of our early years are linked to the stories that abound throughout our daily life. Stories shared with others link what precedes us to what follows us, for stories tell us whose we are and are a map for the pilgrimage of our life.

For example, read a daily newspaper's obituary: there is often just such a narrative of life, in which the tidbits of a person's beginning, middle accomplishments, and end of life are carefully selected for the public to read. Obituaries note the relationships with significant family members and friends, as well as the organizations and churches attended; they sum up and remember a person's life in a few short phrases. Furthermore, stories abound around us and are powerful in determining our daily lives because we depend on them: they can either reconcile us or cause divisions; they can shape and guide us to our future or stop us cold in our tracks. Stories can be told, played, sung, gossiped, moved, danced to, woven or painted — we crave them in any form.

The very way people understand not only their lives but the lives of those around them is shaped and nurtured by the primary stories they inherit and hold in common. A person's life story is told through the composition of the many stories that unfold and draw us in, like a spider going deeper into a web. Consider the parable of the Prodigal Son, a story that draws some of us into it as either one of the children or the parent. We see our family life — and perhaps our life with God — fully displayed, and given hope, depending on where we are in our own life stories at any given time.

The Teleological Function of Story

The teleological point of a story is served well by a greater story that guides our life. We live life in the light of a possible shared future — the promise of the Celestial City of God in *Pilgrim's Progress.* The end point of a story lures us forward and perhaps constrains us, establishing the necessary borders for life. Such story-borders are necessary because what occurs among the other "cast of characters" in life stories is often unpredictable, save for what is constant in life, which is God. Our lives "make sense" only with the knowledge of the end point of the story of the church in which we live.

How dependent are we on the *telos* of our stories and their conclusions? MacIntyre says:

> Deprive children of stories and you leave them unscripted, anxious stutterers in their actions as in their words. Hence there is no way to give us an understanding of any society, including our own, except through the stock of stories which constitute its initial dramatic resources.[6]

For example, Christians' life stories are absorbed into the narrative of God's people who preceded them — yet whose stories live on within the community of saints. In some Benedictine monasteries, such as St. John's Abbey and St. Benedict's Monastery in central Minnesota, it is common during prayers and worship to read, on the anniversaries of their deaths, the names of those sisters and brothers who have died years before. For example, on the dining room tables at St. Benedict's Monastery, for thirty days after the death of a sister, a small picture of the sister and a small votive candle call those dining to remember her. Often the sisters also look through a book of stories about those who have died, those who were and still are members of this community. This is why sharing stories and memories is significant in educating us in the body of Christ. For the church is a place of great memory as we tell and retell the stories on all occasions, from worship to daily prayers. Inside and outside the church, such stories may serve as a kind of compass on the sea of competing stories that can cause a riot in our daily lives. Or stories function as verbal, linguistic maps, plotting out for those who follow a certain narrative where the hazards and "points of interest" are in the life of a community. Simply put, we need to know whose we are, and the truthful story of God's love is essential to help us traverse this new terrain as we are formed and re-formed in God's image.[7]

Anthony Giddens understands that human communities exist "in so far as they are created and re-created in our own actions as human beings."[8] Narratives grow out of our own actions, which are themselves narrative-driven. In this regard, a story serves a dual function: to constitute the community while also providing the reason for change or renegotiation of a people's way of living among themselves. Giddens refers to this movement of story as a "double involvement" of individuals in institutions: "We create society at the same time as we are created by it. Institutions . . . are patterns of social activity reproduced across time and space." Giddens challenges the static nature of many sociologists' view of a community's life, arguing that such sociologists

6. Alasdair MacIntyre, *After Virtue,* 2nd edition, pp. 204-216.

7. Stanley Hauerwas, *The Peaceable Kingdom* (Notre Dame: University of Notre Dame Press, 1983), p. 27.

8. Anthony Giddens, *Sociology* (Orlando: Harcourt Brace Jovanovich, 1987), p. 11.

fail to understand the dynamic nature of human beings. For while some people may repeat a traditional pattern with little change from how they first experienced it, others seek to employ some improvisation, what is called in music a "variation on a theme," often depending on the circumstances of the time, place, and people.[9] Communities are not corpses that remain in one place and in one shape all the time. Living communities are always changing because people change.

Re-Creating the Story That First Created Us

While we are born into and inherit our community's story, which shapes every aspect of our lives, we are also now part of the unfolding story, adding another reason for telling or re-creating the story. It will be the responsibility of the next generation to continue to tell the story, so that it will not forget what we have been liberated from and delivered into, and will have a sense of what salvation history means to us Christians. For example, in the death of the firstborn in Egypt and the beginning of the Exodus, God decreed that on that "same night is a vigil to be kept for the Lord by all the Israelites throughout their generation" (Ex. 12:42). To this day, the Passover Seder is celebrated by Jews, as they eat certain foods and recite particular verses of Scripture, remembering symbolically the events of that period. Thus the truths of Passover become alive again and again for the generation performing the Seder.

Alasdair MacIntyre understands that every tradition is "embodied in some particular set of utterances and actions and thereby in all the particularities of some specific language and culture." He also understands that there will be some "invention, elaboration, and modification of the concepts" by those who are the inheritors of a story that can constitute a community and its storied traditions. Nonetheless, we who inherit the stories need to be reminded that understanding the traditions of a culture such as Christianity involves knowing the culture as a "native inhabitant knows it, and speaking, hearing, writing, and reading the language as a native inhabitant speaks, hears, writes and reads it," making one more an anthropologist than a "sometime" theologian.[10]

To know oneself, one cannot but make claims about the kind of world in which selves are able to exist. Not God, nor world, nor selves are properly

9. Giddens, pp. 11, 12.

10. Alasdair MacIntyre, *Whose Justice? Which Rationality?* (Notre Dame: University of Notre Dame Press, 1988), pp. 373-374.

known as separate entities but are enmeshed in relationships that require concrete display.[11]

Having shown the primacy of story in determining our community life, I want to now show, through a closer examination of Paul's account of the church as the body of Christ, both how and why the story found in the Pauline letters is our context, directing the church in its overarching educational mission or lesson plan, showing us who we already are and are becoming: members of Christ's body on this earth. The issue of *why* is equally important because we depend on this story to know *how* we are to live together as Christ's body. It is also a key to knowing the purpose of educating Christians in the context of church, and to laying out the methodology that is integral to that education.

Considering "Body Politics"

In considering how the church came to be called the "body of Christ," John Calvin writes the following:

> We understand that all these things could not be brought about other than by his [Christ's] cleaving to us wholly in spirit and body. But Paul graced with a still more glorious title that intimate fellowship in which we are joined with his flesh when he said, "We are members of his body, of his bones and of his flesh." Finally, to witness to this thing greater than all words, he ends his discourse with an exclamation: "This," he says, "is a great mystery." It would be extreme madness to recognize no communion of believers with the flesh and blood of the Lord, which the apostle declares to be so great that he prefers to marvel at it rather than to explain it.[12]

To reflect on how the church is a community uniquely narrated as Christ's body, let me begin by acknowledging that "Christ's body" is one of many metaphors and images attached to the church in the New Testament. These metaphors reveal the different ways Christ's followers may live in community with one another. Thus we remain dependent on an interpretation of the Christ narrative to shape the practices of being church. As we reflect on the origins of the church, let me be clear that the very establishment of the

11. Hauerwas, *The Peaceable Kingdom,* p. 26.

12. Calvin, *Institutes,* 4.17.9, ed. John T. McNeill, trans. Ford Lewis Battles (Philadelphia: Westminster Press, 1960), p. 1369.

church begins with Jesus Christ himself, who inaugurated the church when he preached and lived the Good News. We are members of God's household, whose foundation is the apostles and prophets, "with Christ Jesus himself as the cornerstone. In him the whole structure is joined together and grows into a holy temple in the Lord, in whom you also are built together spiritually into a dwelling place for God" (Eph. 2:20-22).

Furthermore, as Jean Corbon writes, the very liturgy of the church "burst from the tomb," becoming the liturgy that could finally be "celebrated — only when the river returned to its fountainhead, the Father. The liturgy begins in this movement of return," for liturgy always turns us, his people, toward God in Christ.[13] In great part, the liturgy of the church outlines its parameters and practices in the celebration of the sacraments, the preaching and explication of God's Word, and the praying of God's people.

God's Spirit was made manifest in the early days of the church on the day of Pentecost. Since then, we have used some Old and New Testament sources for describing the church, God's gift to us. For example, the church is a flock of sheep of which God foretold he would be the shepherd (Is. 40:11; Ezek. 34:11); we the sheep, though watched over by human shepherds, are led to and from the pasture by Christ himself, the prince of all shepherds (John 10:11-16). Or the church is a cultivated field, where the holy roots of ancient olive trees are the prophets, and in which the reconciliation of Jews and Gentiles has been brought about; it is a choice vineyard, planted with Christ as the true vine and Christians as fruitful branches (John 15:1-5; Is. 5:1). Christian evangelism is a planting in which we are told that while Paul planted, "Apollos watered . . . God gave the growth" (1 Cor. 3:6).

Theologians such as Karl Barth argue that this body is not quite like our human bodies, regardless of anyone's philosophical or theological construction. This is Jesus Christ, the risen Son of God, the new Adam, in whom we encounter God through fellowship and communion with other Christians. Barth understands that Christ's body is not a human body per se but is a kind of reflective realism: that is, the church as Christ's body *reflects* some attributes of the human body in certain ways but is *not* a human body in some very important ways. Following Barth's line, Janet Soskice argues that theological models such as "body of Christ" must be understood contextually. That is, "body" is a way of talking about Christ's activity. "Body of Christ" reappears more often than any other vision of what the church is in Paul's letters. Soon speaking of the church as Christ's body became a part of the Christian community's common vocabulary, embellished over generations of Christians

13. Corbon, *The Wellspring*, p. 39.

and giving each generation a context for Christian reflection. There is not to be a rigid definition but a consideration of the various ways "body of Christ" is used within the church's tradition and Scripture.[14] What matters is how naming the church as Christ's body is being used and to what end. Ronald Rolheiser reminds us that Paul never tells us that the body of believers replaces Christ's body, nor that it represents Christ's body, nor even that it is Christ's mystical body. God is still here, just as real and physical as God was in Jesus Christ. If it is true that we are members of Christ's body, then God's presence in the world today depends very much on us.[15]

For example, what are we to make of Paul's example of the ear saying to the eye, "I do not belong to the body because I am not an eye" (1 Cor. 12:16)? Are we to consider it an account of friction within the Corinthian church, in which Paul used the language of his time and tradition to explain both the reality of living in the body of Christ and in the presence of Christ himself?[16] I propose that this is a way of talking about the experiences within the body of Christ, in which one group of people, because of their place and function within the body, were exclusionary of another group of people. Paul quickly reminds the members of this body that they are to act contrary to their "natural inclination," that is, members of the body who seem to be weaker are to be deemed indispensable and treated with greater respect (1 Cor. 12:22, 23). We should practice such respect because we are members of Christ's body, and this is the way of Christ, which we know through his earthly ministry, in which God was among us. Christ is still with us as we mediate him to the world. The power of God flowing through us is how God acts through those who are being changed to Christ's image.[17]

Gerhard Lohfink cautions us that, while saying that we are the "body of Christ" does not mean that that is equal to his Word, his life, his purity, and his total surrender, yet we would be wrong to think that this is a narrow theological example. Rather, Paul calls us members of Christ's body on "a broad textual basis, a long list of passages that speak of the baptized's being 'in Christ.'"[18] Thus the references to being "Christ's body" and being "in Christ" were and are an educational agenda for how members are not only to live with one another but also to understand their place before the omniscient God of creation.

14. Janet Soskice, *Metaphor and Religious Language* (Oxford: Clarendon Press, 1985), pp. 153-54.

15. Ronald Rolheiser, *Holy Longing* (New York: Doubleday, 2000), pp. 79-80.

16. See Soskice, p. 152.

17. Rohlheiser, p. 80.

18. Gerhard Lohfink, *Does God Need the Church?* p. 259.

Where did Paul come up with the idea of the church being the body of Christ? It was certainly, in part, a gift of God; but it was also in common usage in the ancient world as a metaphor for the church — as were the metaphors of sheep, buildings, and pilgrims. Some scholars argue that Paul uses the human body as a metaphor for society because it was an ordinary practice in ancient rhetoric. Paul wrote his description of the church as the body of Christ in a certain context, depending on the congregation to whom he was writing and its circumstances at the time. The metaphors embodied in a particular culture do not stand free of time, society, and geography; they are to be interpreted in the context of the Christian community for whom they were intended, and in which they continue to be read and practiced.[19] Scholars such as Dale Martin and Peter Brown, among others, have done exhaustive scholarly work in describing the many features of how the "body politic" was understood among the ancient Greeks and Jews of Paul's day and may have contributed to Paul's vision of the specific "body politic" of Christ's body.[20]

First, the social bodies in ancient Greece were considered a microcosm of the universe at large. Furthermore, the Greeks assumed that human bodies themselves were made of the same stuff as the world around them, such as air, earth, water, and fire. Thus they considered the congregation and its members a microcosmic synthesis of a larger body of Christ: members' lives are made of the same "stuff" as Christ himself.

Second, the Greeks believed that the social *polis* was hierarchically arranged, taking its cues from the physical body, with the head as the primary seat of knowledge. Plato believed that the human head is spherical because that is the shape of divinities, and that the head, being the most divine part of the body, ruled the rest. In fact, the ancient world considered the body to be a

19. It is to be understood that reading is itself a practice learned in and by a community; for the Christian community reads Paul's letters both as a community and for the benefit of the community in which they are read.

20. See Peter Brown, *The Body and Society* (New York: Columbia University Press, 1988), p. 306. Brown writes about the similarities between the rhetoric of ancient Jewish societies and Paul's imagery of Christ's body. See also Dale Martin, "The Corinthian Body." In this manuscript Martin writes that the body, according to ancient Jewish and Greek sources, was first a microcosmic reflection of the universe, as the body of Christ in our churches is a microcosm of the larger body of Christ; second, the body is hierarchically arranged, as is true in the body of Christ with Christ as the head of the body; third, the body is beautifully balanced, as is Christ's body, in which the lesser parts are more highly honored than the ones to whom we would usually give higher honor; fourth, the body has permeable boundaries, in which the spirit and air can flow freely, as is true with Christ's body; fifth, in regards to pollution in the body, the body of Christ has those who are designated to heal the body.

mere vehicle for the head, designed to carry it and keep it from rolling around on the ground. Likewise, in Paul's description of the body, the mind of Christ is the central mind for Christians: "For who has known the mind of the Lord so as to instruct him? But we have the mind of Christ" (1 Cor. 2:16).

Third, there is the idea of balance and the harmony of the various parts of the physical body, and thus of the body politic. Dale Martin says that, in the ancient Greeks' notion of beauty, one should be neither too thin nor too fat, neither too soft nor too hard, neither too warm nor too cold. One's disposition should be neither too rash nor too cowardly, neither slow nor reckless, neither pitied nor envied. Rather, one should be kind, affectionate, humane, and prudent. Likewise, in Paul's description of Christ's body, he claims that God has arranged the parts of the body and their functions so as to give "the greater honor to the inferior members that there be no dissension within the body" (1 Cor. 12:24, 25).

Fourth, there are permeable boundaries in all bodies, physical and social alike. Because our physical and social bodies are a part of the universe we live in, we are constantly influenced by the elements in it. Physically, it is through the pores of the skin that our bodies breathe and sweat, sustaining our internal organs in their important balance. If a system is porous, it is not a system with firm boundaries but is open to elements of nature. Paul understood that Christ's body is porous as the Spirit of God moves freely within this social body: "To one is given through the Spirit the utterance of wisdom, and to another the utterance of knowledge according to the same Spirit" (1 Cor. 12:8).

Fifth, one of the elemental substances that enters and leaves a body is air, or spirit. For the ancient Greeks, *pneuma* (spirit) was the "stuff" of life itself, making it possible for the human body to move and have sensation. Likewise, it is the Holy Spirit who makes it possible for us not only to live as Christ's body but also to move and proclaim that "Jesus is Lord only by the Holy Spirit" (1 Cor. 12:3).

A final issue regarding the similarities between the ancient Greeks' and Paul's understanding of the body is that of pollution. If the body is porous, with water flowing in and out of the physical body, and ideas flowing in and out of Christ's body, there is the possibility of pollution and contamination making an impact on the entirety of the body. As interconnected in the body of Christ, we are dependent on those who are "healers" in the body (1 Cor. 12:28), through God's powerful and merciful gestures of grace. Mindful of the dialogue in Paul's letters concerning time, place, language, and customs, we will now explore in greater depth Paul's narrative of the body of Christ, which is fundamental to knowing what we are teaching as we learn the gestures of Christ.

The Body of Christ

"Paul's message is counter-intuitive and counter-traditional," says John Howard Yoder about Paul's articulate yet broad description of the body of Christ. Yoder claims that when Paul called the church the body of Christ, he meant that the church should function as a social organism, a *polis:* "To be political is to make decisions, to assign roles, and to distribute powers, and the Christian community cannot do otherwise than exercise these same functions going about its business as a body."[21] Indeed, this *polis* is not only radical for our time in the church's life, but it was also unique in the culture in which Paul was raised and educated, and to which he preached.

To better understand this "counter-traditional" gathering, I will review portions of Paul's letter to the Romans as the overarching narrative in his description of the church as Christ's body. I wish to interpret these passages in order to learn more about the nature of our place, time, and people — as well as the gestures of this particular body.

It is important to understand that Paul was not the founder of the church in Rome, as he was the church in Corinth; it already existed before he wrote them this letter. But, like other churches, it was a body with a great deal of unrest. Some New Testament scholars believe that Paul was writing to a church that was often split between Gentile and Jewish Christianity, or more precisely, between Christianity and Gnosticism, which took a Jewish-Christian form.[22] In Romans 12, Paul is writing to this church about being the body of Christ, about uniting the many house churches into a stronger whole.[23] Furthermore, he says that, while people have different gifts in the body of Christ, no person should seek to use his or her gifts to exalt himself or herself above the rest. The worship of God is to lead to a transformation of lives and a renewing of minds, so that they are living proof of what the will of God is, regardless of whether their origins are Jewish or Gentile. Such submissive action becomes a formative event for Christians as they become the people God desires.

21. Yoder, *Body Politics,* pp. 48, 55.

22. Willi Marxsen, *Introduction to the New Testament* (Philadelphia: Fortress Press, 1980), p. 94.

23. Marva Dawn, *The Hilarity of Community* (Grand Rapids: Wm. B. Eerdmans Pub. Co., 1992), p. 15.

Analyzing Romans 12

Karl Barth draws us away from the "romantic" notion of the body as an individual human personality, as if it were made up of so many particular cells, to critically understand that this body, the body of Christ, is where we encounter God in Christ through the fellowship and communion that we receive among our neighbors.[24] The church as Christ's body, and thus not Adam's body, is an equally important distinction to make in understanding the uniqueness of this body. Robert Jewett says that in ancient Judaism one's soul was somehow tied into Adam's body, which contained the souls of all God's people. In emphasizing that this is Christ's body, he focuses on a new relationship that is different from the one with Adam and Adam's children: a new unity between persons is established, one that people can better understand as they begin living their lives in this radical Christian community.[25]

Romans 12:1-2

> *I appeal to you therefore, brothers and sisters, by the mercies of God, to present your bodies as a living sacrifice, holy and acceptable to God, which is your spiritual worship. Do not be conformed to this world, but be transformed by the renewing of your minds, so that you may discern what is the will of God — what is good and acceptable and perfect.*

Before outlining Karl Barth's Reformed perspective on the body of Christ, I want to consider the passage preceding verses 3-8. Apparently, it was tempting for the Roman Christians to join other charismatic religions that were abundant in that city at the time of Paul's ministry. Beginning in verse 3, Paul outlines what it means to be in Jesus Christ: living this life as a sacrifice can only be done with the knowledge that we are held firm by God's mercy, which alone transforms our lives. Joseph Fitzmyer writes that spiritual worship is the realization of God's work

24. Karl Barth, *Commentary on Romans* (New York: Oxford University Press, 1968), pp. 442-443.

25. Robert Jewett, *Paul's Anthropological Terms* (Leiden: E. J. Brill, 1971), pp. 456-458.

in which he is claiming for himself the world that belongs to him. It implies the offering to God of the human body and self in an act of obedience stemming from faith.[26]

Paul, then, clearly draws a distinction between world and church in explaining how Christians are to act in this world, and he contrasts this world with the world to come, the kingdom of God. The renewal of one's mind (Greek *nous,* considered to be the seat of intellectual and moral judgment) is not an act of self; we are not strong enough by ourselves to make this act of contrition, but it is brought about by God's Spirit. Fitzmyer adds that the "mind," or the "intellect," is no longer to be ruled by the passions of our bodies, by material things; but, because we are to "have the mind of Christ" (1 Cor. 2:15-16), it is Christ's example that is to rule our lives.[27] Having the mind of Christ and being part of the Christian community frees us from having to set our own agenda or to prove our own importance.

Romans 12:3

> *For by the grace given to me I say to everyone among you not to think of yourself more highly than you ought to think, but to think with sober judgment, each according to the measure of faith that God has assigned.*

Beginning in verse 3, we are reminded that to be "*in* Christ" is to be a member *of* Christ's body. All persons who are members of the body of Christ have been given the gift of grace necessary for them to take their place in the body. This gift is not to point to self but is in coordination with the larger body of Christ — for the common good. The call is to serve one another, and in doing so to serve Christ. Each part of the body is given a measure of God, by God, in order to perform in the community the role each has been given to perform. "Measure" here is like a "dipper which apportions to each person at table his or her own share," says Yoder. It is not to be considered a yardstick that quantitatively measures who gets a bigger share than others.[28]

Faith *(pistis)* is a gift that is given by God in full; and we know it, as we know grace, because Christ's community lives in it. As the church performs in

26. Joseph Fitzmyer, S.J., *Anchor Bible Series: Romans* (Garden City: Doubleday, 1992), p. 640.

27. Fitzmyer, p. 641.

28. Yoder, *Body Politics,* p. 48.

faith and grace, we are shown the faith and grace that are alive in us as well. We do not receive a little bit of faith at the beginning of life and then develop more or receive more as a reward for good behavior. The full measure of faith may not be known until we are placed in circumstances where the practice of faith *(fide quae creditur)* is called for, made concrete, and more fully understood — before even the stingiest member of the body of Christ.

Romans 12:4

> *For as in one body in Christ we have many members, and not all the members have the same function. . . .*

While there is the one body, there are many members, who all have different functions, allowing the presence of Christ to be manifest in ways once never thought possible. Christians are one body as a moral imperative, but this oneness does not diminish the many gifts in the one body; instead, it puts the manifold gifts in a specific context. They are located among a defined people called Christians, and this is where we discover the gifts that are given by God.

Barth writes that the focus is on fellowship in communion with Christ through communion with one another; and it is through this relationship and fellowship, he insists, that we encounter the one true God. This fellowship is unique, as is this body, for it is not an aggregate of individuals, thousands of "me's" and "I's." It is not a very visible concrete thing except when we relate to our neighbor; then we will embark on our "unsearchable search for God."[29]

Baptism is one great teaching aid in the liturgy of the church that combats the notion of the church as an aggregation of many individuals and instead posits the unity of being the body of Christ. Consider 1 Cor. 12:12-13:

> For just as the body is one and has many members, and all the members of the body, though many, are one body, so it is with Christ. For in the one Spirit we were all baptized into one body — Jews or Greeks, slaves or free — and we were all made to drink of one Spirit.

This is more than just a group of people who gather voluntarily; it is more than merely another volunteer agency, social club, or therapeutic support group; it is more than a social clique or private club for those of a certain standing; it is different from a gang on the street corner or parents meeting for

29. Barth, *Commentary on Romans.*

a barbecue in a suburban cul-de-sac. Rather, baptism reveals to us that we are a people created and chosen by the Holy Spirit to be members of Christ's body, a body that preceded our very lives and will continue long after we're dead.

Instead of seeing the church as a collective of independent or interdependent individuals who live in a false individualism amid the world's temptations to be utterly selfish, Paul reminds us that it is an individual organism in which each part is dependent not only on other members but also on the head of the body, Jesus Christ: "We must grow up in every way into him who is the head, into Christ" (Eph. 4:15). This is what the ritualistic, sacramental act of baptism signifies.

In baptism the labels and categories of the world become secondary to our identity in Christ. For example, while the world around us may make presumptions about people's status in society based on their being man or woman, "Jew or Greek, slave or free," in Christ's body such labels are superfluous. In baptism we remember that we are united with Jesus in his death and thereby are resurrected with him. We have crucified our old self and destroyed the body of sin — so that we may no longer be enslaved to sin. Such is the deep hope born out of our baptism into Christ (see Romans 6).

Yet being baptized into this one body does not mean that we lose our whole identity or those attributes that make us who we are. Barth notes that there is a varied peculiarity of this body; and Joan Chittister reminds us that we are not to reduce people to the least common denominators. Being baptized into Christ is not about turning individuals into a homogenized group. Rather, it is bringing the uniqueness in us and around us out of us and into holiness.[30] What the members are and do in this observable, varied, and peculiar body is not of our doing but of God's. We owe our place and presence in this body to our relationship to the "unobservable Oneness of the Body . . . who . . . transcends every individual whether isolated or gathered in one whole."[31]

Romans 12:5

> *So we, who are many, are one body in Christ, and individually we are members one of another.*

The dependence hinted at in the preceding paragraph is clearly mandated here. In the body of Christ, all Christians are related to one another by the

30. Joan Chittister, *Wisdom Distilled from the Daily,* p. 111.
31. Karl Barth, p. 442.

blood of the Lamb of God; "no one stands in isolation; so all their services must be in terms of the body as a singular unit."[32]

As I will discuss below, the implication of this passage will bring conflict to the pervasive Enlightenment ideal of "private versus public" aspects of life, even in the church. Living into an understanding of our part in the larger whole is more than reaching our individual human potential. And while there may be some areas of our lives that are more personal, everything about our lives is in reality open to the life of the church because we are members of the one body of Christ. But this notion of a healthy dependency giving life and love to the body of the church is problematic for us in the modern world because it appears to run counter to the American constitutional understanding of independence that we have cultivated.

Barth, as we have noted, thought Paul made it clear that this is not a body of individual members but of the Other. If we were created in the image of God, doesn't it mean that we were created to have a longing for God? Barth continues to unpack the dangerous romantic illusion of body: there isn't a mass of individuals, not even a corporation or loose conglomerate, but the one body, the individual who is Christ, which confronts us in the problems and challenges and celebrates the simple joys of living with one another. Rather than perceiving the body as self versus others, a "me" against "you" or "them," the challenge is to understand ourselves as being the "one body in Christ, and individually-we-are-members-of-one-another." I have added the hyphenation in the last sentence to crudely emphasize the deep sense of connectedness, whether we like it or not, that is found in our being part of this community. Again, this connectedness is not of our doing but is the reality of the culture that Christ's Spirit cultivates.

The most astounding thing about this body is that it is the body of the crucified Christ — the once crucified but now resurrected and living body of Christ. This insight Paul proclaims in 1 Corinthians 15, where he makes it known that this body of Christ of which we are part is the risen body of Christ, through whom we bear the image of the man of heaven (v. 49). Barth writes that if the crucified Christ is the measure of faith that God has dealt to each in his or her particularity, then we must understand that it is our ethical gesture to be properly humbled before God, a compelling and inevitable demand. Then, in corporate recollection and by God's grace and will, we are bent backward toward the power and dignity of our origin, Jesus Christ, toward the primary ethical act, toward certain Christian gestures.[33]

32. Fitzmyer, p. 646.
33. Barth, p. 444.

Lessons for the Church as Christ's Body

The awesome, timeless, and holy mystery that shines brightly in the life of a church, holding us together even in our most fractious and weak moments, is the truth that we are related to one another because of our relationship with God in Christ simply by being baptized into this body. The magnitude of this truth, which is our reality, engulfs us because it is too great for us to comprehend with our limited cognitive, emotional, and spiritual abilities. But even though we may not be able to understand the magnitude of this gift of grace or the subtle theological nuances of this organic yet ethereal gathering, there is a constant change in our identity simply because we are members of Christ's body. By this I mean that there is a continual change in how we understand our lives, actions, and behavior, as well as our relationships with others and with God. Paul calls this change a "transformation by the renewing of your minds so that you may discern what is the will of God" in Romans 12:2. The reason for this ever-changing identity is that, in God's grace, we are drawn closer to God as we daily aspire to be more like Christ.

There are three communal practices within the body of Christ that continually form and transform Christians as members of the Christian community in their diversity and solidarity: first is the sacramental, ritualistic gesture of *baptism,* in which we are received into the body of Christ; second is the sacramental, ritualistic gesture of the *Eucharist,* in which we receive the body and blood of Christ, which in turn nurtures our relationship with one another and with Christ; third, because of our baptism and the continual nurturance of salvific grace in the Eucharist, we are called to perform gestures of *hospitality* as we receive others into communion in the name of Christ. All three practices involve a set of gestures that, when we perform them, draw us closer to one another in Christ, reinforcing our knowledge of whose we are.

Baptism

Michael Apple says that all education begins as a "process of initiation in which the neophyte accepts a particular social reality as the way that 'life really is.'" The cultivating process that sustains and continually reorganizes a community of people occurs in myriad patterns of people's interactions as they go about their daily lives.[34] Baptism is that initiation process for Chris-

34. Michael Apple, *Ideology and Curriculum,* 2d ed. (New York: Routledge, Chapman and Hall, Inc., 1990), p. 27.

tians: we take neophytes and teach them the way life really is in Christ's body. In other words, in baptism we die to ourselves and are initiated into this holy gathering as we are raised up and received into the active life of Christ's body. Our dying and resurrection with Christ's death and resurrection is echoed in Romans 7:4, where Paul says: "In the same way, my friends, you have died to the law through the body of Christ, so that you may belong to another, to him who has been raised from the dead in order that we may bear fruit for God." Paul Minear says that the church being in Christ means we share in the dying to the law: "Only thus do believers belong to Christ and therefore to one another. To Paul the only means of deliverance from the body of death is the body of Christ."[35] Being baptized into Christ (Rom. 6:3) means we both die to self and are raised from the dead with Christ (Rom. 6:4).

Yoder understands that baptism initiates us into a new people whose distinguishing mark is that all "prior given or chosen identity definitions are transcended."[36] There is the merging of two stories, of two people who were separated — Jews and Gentile, male and female, slave and free. But what is unique about this "new people" is a new "inter-ethnic social reality into which the individual is inducted rather than the social reality being the sum of the individual,"[37] as is the case in the dominant Western fixation on individualism. Yoder points out that the modern world hopes that divisions among human beings can be overcome by summing up our individual parts, leaving significant parts of our lives behind in order to become part of a bland-tasting "melting pot." Instead, we live a new reality that changes our identity completely while preserving what is unique in our lives, a gift of God's grace. This contributes to the extraordinary diversity of Christ's body and shapes our understanding, feelings, and gestures as Christ's body.

Regarding education in this new social reality of Christ's body, baptism sends all new members off on a pilgrimage in which they will learn — and soon teach — myriad new and old gestures that are scripted by the gospel and that embody virtues governing our relationship with those in Christ's body. In a very public way, with water running and candles lit, the sacrament of baptism is *the* moment when we recognize the unimaginable ways that God's grace has already been performed in the education of the person. Furthermore, it is in baptism that the congregation promises that this son or daughter of God will be raised and nurtured in the faith of the church. From the

35. Paul Minear, *Images of the Church in the New Testament* (Philadelphia: Westminster Press, 1960), p. 178.

36. Yoder, *Body Politics*, p. 28.

37. Ibid.

time of our baptism forward, our lives will be constantly changing as we are trained to die to sin and the old self and to live as a people who are raised to a newness of life, shaped by the love that Jesus proclaimed with his life.

The ritual of baptism in our churches invites us all to behold the unity of our lives as we welcome to this body someone whose new name and identity is that of "Christian." As we sprinkle, anoint, or immerse an infant or a grown person with the waters of baptism, perhaps marking the forehead with oil, and as we invite the parents, guardians, godparents, and congregation to raise the child, we are open to seeing how much good baptism does not only for the one being baptized but for the whole body present at that moment. For in baptism we remember our own baptism and the baptisms of others we know and love. We turn around and remind our children of their baptisms, telling stories of that day. For a moment we are swept up with the realization that baptism is one point of unity among the diversity gathered together in the church, a ritual we share not only with one another but with Christ himself.

Eucharist

In the Sacred Heart Chapel of St. Benedict's Monastery there is a large baptismal font, carved out of granite, that has continual running water gurgling into its small pool of water. Young and old, women and men, disabled and non-disabled alike touch the water with their fingertips or cup the water with their hands, tangibly remembering their baptism and drawing forth words of thanks. Around the baptismal font are various plants and flowers, reminding us of the gift of life symbolized by the water, with the Christ candle standing tall at one end of the font. The baptismal font is aligned with the altar, which is directly in the center of this cruciform floor plan of the chapel. According to Sister Mary Anthony Wagner, this alignment was designed on purpose: the baptismal font is directly in line with the altar so that we are visually reminded that we must go through the waters of baptism in order to get to the Eucharist. Baptism and Eucharist are central reminders that we are one of the many who are one in Christ.

If baptism is the communal act in which we are received into Christ's body — the ritual of initiation — then the Eucharist is the act in which we receive the body and blood of Christ. It is a ritual of intensification of what was begun in our baptism: it is a process that continues to grow as it is shaped and nurtured in the sharing of the body and blood of our Lord Jesus Christ. Why is there such power in these sacraments? Calvin says that, because we are flesh, we have a dull capacity and need to be led by the hand "as tutors lead children." Quoting St. Augustine, Calvin says that sacraments such as baptism and the Eucharist are bodily gestures symbolizing "God's promises as painted in a picture and set before our sight, portrayed graphically and in the manner of images."[38] Perhaps it is in our participation in the gestures of baptism and Eucharist that we see most clearly, hear most appreciably, and touch most gently the unity of Christ's body as it is re-membered and re-enacted, each one of us taking our part in the holy mystery of being united as members of Christ's body.

The gestures of the Eucharist have been passed down from generation to generation, beginning with Christ handing down the gestures to his disciples. Paul says: "For I received from the Lord what I also handed on to you. . ." (1 Cor. 11:23). When we eat the bread and drink from the cup, "the new covenant in my blood," we do so with the intention of remembering whose, and therefore where, we are. Christ told us to eat the bread, his body, for us: "Do this in remembrance of me." For "as often as you eat this bread and drink the cup, you proclaim the Lord's death until he comes" (1 Cor. 11:26).

As baptism brings about our birth into communion with the Trinity within the body of Christ, the Eucharist embraces and transforms the entirety of Christ's body, thus transforming our lives. Jean Corbon goes one step further in writing about the way the Eucharist in a sense guides and teaches us to be like Christ in our daily lives:

> [In Eucharist he] makes this participation [in baptism] personal by himself becoming the indefectible energy of the new member. In the reconciliation of sinners and the anointing of the sick he exercises his power to give life from resurrection to resurrection. In marriage and the ordained ministry, he, "the Lord who gives life," enables the Spouse to share her fruitful virginity; more accurately, he communicates to the members of the Church, each according to his or her gift, that "nothing is impossible to God" which he has already made a reality in the Church.[39]

From our baptism to when we receive the bread and wine of the Eucharist, we are learning and rediscovering gestures that draw us ever closer to God and thus to one another. In that process the reign of the Lord becomes a reality, as the richness of life in God is made manifest and irresistible to everyone.[40]

38. Calvin, *Institutes,* p. 1281.
39. Corbon, p. 119.
40. Ibid, p. 120.

Hospitality

In baptism we are all received into the body of Christ. In the Eucharist we receive the body and blood of Christ, which further nurtures us in being the body of Christ with one another. In acts of hospitality we receive others into the body of Christ. For if life in God is made manifest and irresistible to those who believe, a great desire grows in us to share that good news of the new covenant with others in gestures of word and deed. For example, consider the words of blessing in a benediction at the conclusion of worship: "Go out to love and serve the Lord, with gladness and singleness of heart, mind, and body."[41] We do so primarily because we are receivers of the Good News of Christ, who now lives in us and inspires us to do what he would do.

In gestures of hospitality we live out our baptismal vows and we practice the sacrificial loving gestures of Christ that we have been taught in Eucharistic practices. Consider that when we feed the hungry, give drink to the thirsty, welcome the stranger, clothe the naked, care for the sick, and visit those in prison, we do it unto Christ: "Just as you did it to one of the least of these who are members of my family, you did it to me" (Matt. 25:40). We perform such gestures in the name of Christ because of the politics of our baptism, which has initiated us into God's love; for we have died to the sin of selfishness and now live unto God.[42] Such is the politics of the Eucharist: we are sustained and nurtured in the sacrificial love of Christ as we eat the bread and drink the cup of salvation with one another.

In the politics of hospitality we open up our lives to others as God in Christ opened his life to us, receiving us in baptism and nurturing us with his very life.[43] Hospitality is a cornerstone virtue of Benedictine communities in particular, and a virtue that should be performed in the church in general. This is because all guests to a monastery

> should be welcomed as Christ, because he will say, "I was a stranger, and you took me in" (Matt. 25:35). Show them every courtesy, especially servants of God and pilgrims. When a guest is announced the superior or brothers should greet him with charity; and they should pray together in order to be at peace.[44]

41. Presbyterian Church (USA), *Book of Worship* (Louisville: Westminster/John Knox Press, 1993), p. 78.

42. Minear, p. 176.

43. Chittister, *Wisdom Distilled,* p. 128.

44. Meisel and del Mastro, *Rule of St. Benedict,* Chapter 53.

As with the practice of Benedictine hospitality, we are called to enact gestures of Christ each day, going outside of ourselves for someone else at least once a day. Joan Chittister reminds us that in gestures of hospitality we will excite new thoughts, see life with a new perspective as we talk to new people, and give part of ourselves away day after day. Likewise, she warns us that "hospitality is one of those things that has to be constantly practiced or it won't be there for rare occasions."[45] This is exactly why we need to be part of a community that celebrates baptism and reaffirms the Eucharist as constant reminders of why we behave hospitably in the first place — because God first loved us.

45. Chittister, p. 132.

CHAPTER TWO

The Body of Christ: Gifts and Services

Paul graced with a still more glorious title that intimate fellowship in which we are joined with his [Christ's] flesh when he said, "We are members of his body, of his bones and of his flesh."

John Calvin

We have gifts that differ according to the grace given to us.

Romans 12:6

The sacramental, gestured rituals of baptism, the Eucharist, and acts of hospitality are key ingredients in forming and re-forming us into Christ's body. The water, the broken bread, the extending of a helping hand help locate us and remind us of whose we are among the plethora of narratives competing for our attention. In this chapter I continue to look toward Paul's letter to the Romans in guiding our understanding of another important aspect of the body of Christ: the way we have been blessed, as Christ's followers, with various gifts and services, roles and activities, which promise confusion and chaos as well as hope and joy for the many members of Christ's body.

Romans 12:6a

We have gifts that differ according to the grace given to us.

There are four overriding concerns for us as Christ's community. First, we need to remember that the gifts and services we have in life are a result of God's gift of grace. It is not the result of a person's ability to invent something of him- or herself that makes that person a prophet or teacher, a "foot or ear" in this body. Rather, God has endowed us with a purpose in creating and calling us to be part of Christ's body. Therefore, as we discover the daily wonder of being in Christ's body, we discover the gifts and services with which we and others have been endowed by God's grace. And it is among the community of Christians who have known us for a long time, in good and bad times, that we discover our gifts and services.

Second, as John Howard Yoder reminds us, when we realize that we depend on God for the gifts and services accorded to us,[1] it is inappropriate to have selfish pride, which is a danger to the life of the community at large. We are, in some ways, rightly humbled when we realize that our gifts and services come through God's grace rather than being based on human effort in its entirety. *The Rule of St. Benedict* says that it is only by humbling ourselves that we arrive at the "heavenly heights," and we go down by praising ourselves.[2] It seems that such humility is key when we remember that the gift is of God's giving, that we do not attain it by ourselves.

Third, every member of the body of Christ has been given a gift (*charisma* means grace-given) by the Holy Spirit. And every gift is of equal dignity, as Yoder says: "Thus each bearer of any gift is called, first of all, to reciprocal recognition of all the others, [by] giving 'special honor to the less comely members.'"[3] This is a significant insight because it points to the deeper mystery of Christ's body, where all who are baptized — women and men, poor and rich, disabled and nondisabled, gay and straight, young and old, of all ethnic heritages — are bearers of God-given gifts and services for the good of Christ's body. Therefore, one goal of the body of believers in our congregations should be to aid others in discovering, naming, and growing into their gift. By doing so, Yoder suggests, we become a church that embraces a Pauline vision of "every-member empowerment," where there would be "no one ungifted, no one not called, no one not empowered, and no one domi-

1. Yoder, *Body Politics,* p. 51.
2. *Rule of St. Benedict,* Chapter 7.
3. *Body Politics,* p. 50.

nated. Only that would live up to Paul's call to 'lead a life worthy of our calling.'"[4]

With the emphasis of the gift clearly pointing to the Giver of the gift, Yoder reminds us that there is to be a deep acknowledgment to Christ that our gift, role, and service in the body have been given to us by the Spirit of God. This acknowledgment should change our posture from one of independence to one of dependence as we praise the source of all gifts of life. Yoder says that a deep bow of humility will be the result of our recognition that our gifts and services are God-given and not a source of selfish pride in our own accomplishments.[5]

Fourth, as Joan Chittister says, the "art of community life in general lies in the balance of the person and the group. Benedictine spirituality exacts two things: self-giving and self-development (community order and community understanding). Any one of these without the other reveals a person or a group gone askew."[6] Chittister further observes that individual people do not exist for groups; rather, groups exist for people. And it is for the good of the group — the church, Christ's body — that we have been given gifts of grace. The function of a group like the church is to aid people in achieving together what they cannot possibly achieve alone: "Groups are meant to make our highest personal hopes achievable through common search and common effort and common discipline."[7] This is significant for keeping everything somewhat in order as we live among all the multiple gifts and generous services accorded to the body of Christ.

Romans 12:6b-8

> *Prophecy, in proportion to faith; ministry, in ministering; the teacher, in teaching; the exhorter, in exhortation; the giver, in generosity; the leader, in diligence; the compassionate, in cheerfulness.*

Having made it clear that everyone has a gift in the body of Christ, Paul considers some of the gifts in verses 6-8, and the structuring of life in the body of Christ. Each person who is present in the body of Christ has a place and an opportunity to serve God and neighbor, "according to the grace [of God]

4. Ibid., p. 60.
5. Ibid., p. 51.
6. Chittister, *Wisdom Distilled,* p. 109.
7. Ibid., p. 110.

given to us" (v. 6).[8] In Romans 6:23, Paul writes that the greatest gift that we have is Jesus Christ himself. Joseph Fitzmyer says, "All others partake in the gift that is Christ Jesus."[9] Seeing and hearing that the members of the body of Christ must perform in the community, God's Spirit provides the gifts necessary for the building up of the common good, that is, the body of Christ. Each gift is social in nature, with the goal of serving one another as we serve God in Christ. "All *charismas* are graces that move Christians to action on behalf of others. No one is superfluous or to be regarded as a supernumerary," Fitzmyer continues.[10] Indeed, counting what is listed in Romans 12, 1 Corinthians 12, Ephesians 4, and 1 Peter 4, there are eighteen or so gifts of the Spirit in the body of Christ, and this by no means exhausts the various manifestations of these gifts.[11]

The first gift is prophecy, or speaking out in the name of God in "proportion to faith," or in a "right relationship" to faith. We read in 1 Peter 4:11 that "whoever speaks must do so as one speaking the very words of God." It is not by accident or "luck" that God chose the most unlikely people to be prophets. Instead, it was — and is — God's intention to lift up those who have been relegated to the fringes by others more powerful, even in the church today. God instills in them a heart for justice where there is injustice, peace where there is violence, and love where there is hatred.

The second is *diakonia,* or service, and the one who does this service is to put his or her heart and faith in God. In 1 Peter 4:9-11 we read: "Be hospitable to one another without complaining. Like good stewards of the manifold grace of God, serve one another with whatever gift each of you has received . . . whoever serves must do so with the strength that God supplies, so that God may be glorified in all things, through Jesus Christ." In some sense, we serve the needs of others so as not to draw attention to ourselves but to remind both the giver and the receiver of the One from whom all good things flow.

The third is the teacher *(ho didaskōn),* the "one who instructs, either in catechesis or the interpretation of Scripture."[12] We will return to this designation later in the book. Briefly, being a teacher is to be like Jesus Christ, the one who was called "rabbi" by both his followers and detractors. Jesus embodied in his very sinews and nerve endings the kingdom of God, so that every ges-

8. Yoder, *Body Politics,* p. 51.
9. Fitzmyer, p. 646.
10. Ibid., p. 647.
11. Dawn, *Hilarity of Community,* p. 94.
12. Fitzmyer, p. 648.

ture, every touch was holy; he was always teaching us, his followers, the way to live with one another and thus with God.

The fourth is "exhorter," the "spiritual leader" of the community: through consolation and admonition, and with the gift of exhortation, he or she guides the members of the body of Christ. Fifth is the giver who shares personal wealth with those in need, and does so simply. Sixth is the leader, the one standing in front or behind the crowd, the one who presides, directs, or rules, doing so with "diligence." The final gift is for the compassionate one, the one who performs acts of mercy, the one Fitzmyer calls the "Good Samaritan."[13]

There is a similar list of gifts and services in 1 Cor. 12:28-30: "And God has appointed in the church first apostles, second prophets, third teachers; then deeds of power, then gifts of leadership, various kinds of tongues." From this Pauline description came this Trinitarian doctrine: "The gifts are granted by the Holy Spirit, service is performed under the tutelage of Jesus Christ, and God himself 'energizes' the entire process"(1 Cor. 12:4-11).[14] Gifts and services are all accountable to their source of being: God. It is all summed up in verse 11, where Paul reaffirms that all these gifts — speaking in the spirit, uttering wisdom and knowledge, faith, the healing of others, doing miracles, prophesying, discerning the spirits, speaking and interpreting tongues — are manifestations of the Spirit of God allotted to each person individually for the common good, "just as the Spirit chooses." There is little if anything in this description that anyone can boast of as his or her own doing. Instead, all that we do in this body is of Christ's doing, which is Christ's victory.[15]

This connective embeddedness is given flesh and made concrete through the exercise of the God-given gifts that the various members have for the greater good of the body of Christ. Barth is clear that we should not romance our individuality, our peculiarity, for it will be shattered and disturbed, as "only God can disturb it. Yet in this disturbance, we are under the sign of victory and hope."[16]

What makes it possible for the body to bow to God in worship as a gesture of praise and humility, to extend a hand to others in need or receive a hand when we are in need, to proclaim the Good News with the gestures of our mouths, is a certain malleability of all of us as members of his body. Just

13. Ibid., p. 649.
14. Ibid., p. 281.
15. Yoder, *Body Politics,* p. 48.
16. Barth, *Romans,* p. 444.

as the ancient world was attuned to and concerned with the proper formation and understanding of the physical and social body-as-*polis,* even to the point of instructions on swaddling and unswaddling infants in certain places and at certain ages, the body of Christ is about formation, practice, and posture. That is why the focus on gestures is so important, for it is the practice of certain gestures that ensures the proper balance of constitution and control, helping the body in assuming a posture that is required. The danger is that, without enough exercise or learning, during times of not relying on or using the body — both the physical body and the social body — the pattern of living correctly will atrophy or be broken from either no use or misuse. The results are usually calamitous.

Romans 12:9-13

> *Let love be genuine; hate what is evil, hold fast to what is good; love one another with mutual affection; outdo one another in showing honor. Do not lag in zeal, be ardent in spirit, serve the Lord. Rejoice in hope, be patient in suffering, persevere in prayer. Contribute to the needs of the saints; extend hospitality to strangers.*

I have added this section from Romans 12 (and will refer to 1 Cor. 12:31 later) because it points to the primary force, or "glue," that holds the church as Christ's body balanced and harmonized, together and focused on what gives us life abundantly: the love of Christ (v. 9). Charity, or *agapē* love, is the core gift to the body of Christ; it is what marks this body as peculiarly Christian. It is a love that is more than what is shared among friends (filial love) and different from sexual love (*erōs).* Both of these are examples of human love, which is directed toward and seeks contact with another person for his or her own sake. Dietrich Bonhoeffer writes that human love wants to gain, to capture by every means possible, the other person: "It desires to be irresistible, to rule."[17] While human love has its limitations, what Bonhoeffer calls a "spiritual love" serves Christ. While human love desires another person, spiritual love would rather serve. This love of Christ is genuine, not false or eager to capture another person; in Bonhoeffer's view, it loves an enemy as a brother or sister in Christ. This is true because such love originates not in the brother or the sister or the enemy, but in the Word of God: Christ. "Human love can never understand spiritual love," says Bonhoeffer, "for spiritual love is from

17. Dietrich Bonhoeffer, *Life Together* (New York: Harper, 1954), p. 34.

above; it is something completely strange, new, and incomprehensible to all earthly love."[18]

Because this is a love freely given by God in Christ, it cannot help but be genuine and transparent, almost a bit surreal. Human love is an end in itself, whereas Christ-like love gives of itself, freely, for the good of the body of Christ.[19] Being embedded in a community and undergirded by Christ-like love gives us the "eyes" and "ears" to perceive what is evil as we hold fast to what is good. This is a love we learn in order to live with one another, as only members of a household learn to love, "with mutual affection." With Christ as the end of such love, we are given reason enough to be patient in suffering and persevering in prayer. It is Christ-like love that inspires us to contribute to the needs of the saints, both visible and invisible, extending hospitality to strangers. In contributing "to the needs of the saints," understood as truly a gesture of *koinōnia,* we are to share what we have in common with others. This is because to exclude those considered weak and insignificant, "the seemingly useless people, from a Christian community may actually mean the exclusion of Christ; in the poor brothers [and sisters] Christ is knocking at the door."[20] Paul challenges us to be immersed in the stuff of other people's lives, for in their lives we may find Christ. Likewise, we may welcome times of being surrounded by those who love us; in addition to welcoming the stranger, they may reveal to us the Christ who lives in our hearts.[21]

Given the love of Christ, which from our birth has comforted us on each step of the pilgrimage, and the good news that each person has received a gift and service from the Holy Spirit for the good of Christ's body, the next important aspect of church life is the very health of the community itself. Yoder points out that Paul gently offers us a kind of "corrective" in the face of "unbridled enthusiasm," whose presence in a church poses the potential danger of disorder and oppression, namely, when it honors one gift or service more than all others in the body.[22]

I turn now to Paul's first letter to the Corinthians to establish some general guidelines that may prove to be a corrective for disharmony — if not outward aggression and hostile politics — in the body of Christ.

18. Ibid., p. 35.
19. Ibid., p. 35.
20. Ibid., p. 38.
21. Dawn, *Hilarity,* p. 215.
22. Yoder, p. 51.

1 Corinthians 12

Paul founded the church at Corinth on his second missionary journey. New Testament scholars have said that this church was being threatened by many different beliefs — not only outside the church but within the congregation itself. For example, within the church there was a struggle between the "haves and have-nots." Gerd Theissen writes that there were controversies over the Eucharist, which often split the church along socio-economic status lines. Often the wealthy would arrive at church early and begin to eat and drink when they wanted to, breaking the bread more formally later, during the service. But while they were eating and drinking to their hearts' content, if not getting drunk, others were "going hungry" (1 Cor. 11:21). This meal had begun to reflect the social status levels of the Greek and Roman traditions, with the better food and wine going to the host's more honored guests and not to the poor, who received poorer quality food because of their lower status. Paul tried to emphasize that this should be a common meal for the whole church, not one that would create division.[23]

Outside the church, Corinth was a cosmopolitan city that drew people from all over the known Roman Empire with its large port, its Roman officials, and its famous sports center — as well as its reputation for "debauchery and licentiousness," according to Richard Kugelman.[24] Paul's letter makes references to whether or not church members could eat meat offered to idols, and this subject also engaged the issue of how the members should relate socially with non-Christians. In addition to these problems and temptations, the city of Corinth had temples for almost every deity, some of them filled with prostitutes, tempting some to lead a life of immorality.[25]

In this first letter Paul outlines the circumstances in the body that would make it ripe for a crisis, showing the church that it needs a "more excellent" way of getting the chaotic commotion within the church resolved, as if the one body of Christ were a reality (which Paul addresses in 1 Cor. 13), by means of Christ-like love (which he addresses in Rom. 12:9). In both outlining the parameters of the politics in this particular body and identifying what will keep it together — the love of Christ — Paul provides his readers with a way to resolve conflict that appears inherent in such a community.[26]

23. Dale Martin, "The Corinthian Body," p. 116.

24. Richard Kugelman, "The First Letter to the Corinthians," in Raymond Brown, Joseph Fitzmyer, Roland Murphy, eds., *Jerome Biblical Commentary* (Englewood Cliffs: McGraw Hill, 1968), p. 254.

25. Marxsen, pp. 74-75.

26. Yoder, p. viii.

1 Corinthians 12:14-15, 18-25, 31

Indeed, the body does not consist of one member but of many. If the foot would say, "Because I am not a hand, I do not belong to the body," that would not make it any less a part of the body.

But as it is, God arranged the members in the body, each one of them, as he chose. If all were a single member, where would the body be? The members of the body that seem to be weaker are indispensable, and those members of the body that we think less honorable we clothe with greater honor, and our less respectable members are treated with greater respect; whereas our more respectable members do not need this. But God has so arranged the body, giving the greater honor to the inferior member, that there may be no dissension within the body, but the members may have the same care for one another.

But strive for the greater gifts. And I will show you a still more excellent way.

Here Paul describes a certain order within the organism known as Christ's body, and he outlines where the struggles exist and will exist for the church: who does what and who goes where in the body of Christ. There is not just one member but many members. The foot might regard itself as a lowly member of Christ's body since it carries the weight of the body and gets soiled by the ground on which it walks. On the other side, the hand may see itself as being the most effective agent of work, of having the primary job of expressing the body in gestures, and thus might regard itself more highly. While the eye provides vision, considered by most people a necessary sensory skill, the ear's function of hearing is equally necessary. Can we say which of these is more important?

Yoder says that whether it is the hand, the foot, the eye, or the ear in the body of Christ, they all have the following characteristics in common within the body of Christ: first, they are each vital and irreplaceable; second, they possess and exercise their own duty within the body of Christ with dignity; third, they can function fully only when they understand that they are bound to the other members, and that bond is Christ; and fourth, each member can be crippled through no fault of its own when some other part of the body suffers.[27]

The significance of each body part does not come from that part itself but from the movement of the Holy Spirit, which alone can reveal to us the

27. Yoder, p. 49.

significant parts of the body and their concurring relationship with other parts. Hans Conzelmann says that Paul is opposed to the "practice of individuals dissociating themselves from the 'body,' that is, against enthusiastic individualism.'"[28] Yoder suggests some

> long-range cultural-historical sense in which this notion of the gifted dignity of each person is at the root of Western individualism. The hand or the body or the eye is in no sense "individual." It is unique and irreplaceable, yet it can possess and exercise its own dignity, its own life and role, only in its bondedness with the other members. It can be crippled for no fault of its own when some other part of the body suffers.[29]

William Orr and James Arthur Walther argue that Paul wanted to make sure that there was a compensating balance of Christ's body to "eliminate division and establish mutual care."[30]

1 Corinthians 12:27-31

Echoing Romans 12:5, Paul proclaims our true identity — that outside of the body of Christ we do not know whose we are. Paul goes on to explain exactly what God, in his wisdom, has appointed in the church. First are the apostles, whose role is to do missionary work and who have some degree of authority; second are the prophets, who speak for God, whether they want to or not, as the Old Testament prophets demonstrated quite clearly; third are the teachers, who have the responsibility of presenting Christian doctrine and its application in particular circumstances.[31] Unlike what he says in Romans, here

28. Quoted in William Orr and James Arthur Walther, *I Corinthians:* Anchor Bible Series (New York: Doubleday & Co., 1976), p. 286.

29. Yoder, p. 49.

30. Orr and Walther, p. 286.

31. The question that is often raised concerns the listing of the various roles and functions within the body of Christ. Is there a hierarchy that we are to follow or recognize as the church? In Rom. 12:6-8, Paul describes the following order of grace-given gifts: prophets, ministry, teachers, exhorters, givers, leaders, and the compassionate. In Eph. 2:20, the church, the "household of God," is built on "the foundation of the apostles and prophets, with Christ Jesus himself as the cornerstone." In Eph. 3:5-6, Paul writes that "in former generations this mystery was not made known to humankind, as it has now been revealed to his holy apostles and prophets by the Spirit: that is, the Gentiles have become fellow heirs, members of the same body and sharers in the promise in Christ Jesus through the gospel." In Eph. 4:11 there is another listing of gifts: some to be apostles, prophets,

Paul stops naming the various offices of the church and focuses instead on what these people will be able to do, with "deeds of power, gifts of healing, forms of assistance and leadership, and speaking in various kinds of tongues" (1 Cor. 12:28). Then, rhetorically expecting a negative answer to each query, Paul asks if all people possess the gift of healing, of speaking in tongues, of interpreting, and so forth. Then he announces that there is a more "excellent" or more "extraordinary way" of living than that of the Corinthians, and beginning in 1 Corinthians 13:1, he speaks of charity, much as he did in Romans 12:9.

One of the confusing aspects of the Corinthian passage — and about most Christian communities in our modern world — is the way we are to function among the various members of the body of Christ. In 1 Corinthians 12:8-10, there is the scattering of the various gifts of the spirit in the body of Christ, with no sense of order but only God's sense of whimsy: "To one is given through the Spirit the utterance of wisdom, and to another the utterance of knowledge according to the same Spirit. . . ." There have been two different ways of reading this passage. One reading emphasizes that there is a certain hierarchy in which some parts of the body are set higher or gain more respect than other parts:

> The members of the body that seem to be weaker are indispensable, and those members of the body that we think less honorable we clothe with greater honor . . . but God has so arranged the body, giving the greater honor to the inferior member, that there may be no dissension within the body, but the members may have the same care for one another.

Another reading of this passage would consider mutuality or egalitarianism significant. The emphasis in this reading is the promise that there is one body, but within it there is a diversity in what people are called to be and to do. Regardless of which interpretation one leans toward, it seems evident in 1 Corinthians 12 that though there is an order and sequencing among the many parts, this is not what is of most importance. What is intriguing about the imagery is the order or "hierarchy": the blatant paradox in which the less respectable members are treated with greater respect in the body of Christ, implying that those considered lesser members were being treated with little if any respect. Is this another case of the foolish shaming the wise? One can't

---

evangelists, pastors, and teachers, "to equip the saints for the work of ministry, for building up the body of Christ." Clearly, there is no consistent hierarchy of one gift being "higher" or "lower" in rank than others.

help but wonder whether this is a little of God's humor. Indeed, the argument can be made that some gifts are of more value due to the context of the church as Christ's body. The parts of the body of Christ that are highlighted are a matter of the context and fluid circumstances at any given point. For the body of Christ needs to be flexible enough to respond quickly yet with wisdom and compassion to the matters of the overall health of the community of Christ's followers.

Lessons for the Church as Christ's Body

From both Romans and 1 Corinthians we can learn a great many lessons, not only about becoming members of Christ's body but about how we are to live together as Christ's people. Beginning with the waters of baptism, we are initiated into a community of Christ-like love that surrounds and fills our being. The discernment process of our respective Christian communities — given the gift of wisdom and knowledge — names the gifts and services provided to us by God's grace. And with the Eucharist as one of our primary sacramental rituals, a cornerstone of sorts for the entire Christian community, we are engaged in the exciting adventure of teaching, learning, and becoming a part of the Jesus-life in all acts of hospitality.

Christ, the Head of the Body

It is clear that, for Paul as well as for us, the beginning and end point of all community life as the body of Christ is Christ. While Christ's body has many members, it is still Christ's body, Christ's Church, and Christ who alone unites us and makes us all one in him (1 Cor. 12:12). It is Christ, after all, who emptied himself as he took on the form of a servant, being born in our likeness as human beings. It is Christ who not only spoke of God's gift of love for us, but is himself the gift embodied. "All things are to be united in Christ," writes Mary Anthony Wagner. "We who have heard this gospel and believed in it have been sealed in the Spirit" at our baptism.[32]

So how does this truth bear witness in our life as members of Christ's body? This central theological affirmation is significant in terms of leadership in the church in general, and in our individual congregations in particular.

32. Mary Anthony Wagner, *The Sacred World of the Christian* (Collegeville: Liturgical Press, 1993), p. 65.

The head of the church — both literally and figuratively — is Christ. There is a certain hierarchy: Christ is the head, and we are the body. "Hierarchy" is not a new theological conundrum or corporation mentality but a concept that peoples and communities have responded to differently through the ages. To begin with, Paul himself knew what questions about authority would arise among Christians. He distinguished Christ from the rest of the body as its "head," the seat of authority over the entire body:

> And he has put all things under his feet and has made him the head over all things for the church, which is his body, the fullness of him who fills all in all (Eph. 1:22, 23).[33]

Later theologians such as Aquinas understood the church as the body of Christ with different functions and states; he believed that the fullness of God's grace, found in Christ, is variously and widely distributed through the members of the body. Since the gifts of God's grace are so widely distributed, "assigned to different people . . . everything can be clearly and efficiently executed."[34] For Aquinas, there are beauty and dignity in the church when it embraces such order among all the functions of the body:

> Diversity of states and functions in the church doesn't hinder its unity; indeed that is rather perfected by faith, love and mutual ministry to one another. . . . So diversity among the members of the church contributes to its perfection, its efficient function and its beauty.[35]

There was no doubt in Aquinas' mind about the hierarchical ordering of the body: Christ is its head, "its different members having different functions in the whole."[36] Aquinas goes on to liken the Holy Spirit to the heart,

> invisibly giving life and unity to the church, while Christ is likened to the head, standing out in his visible nature as man above all others. So the whole Christ, body and soul, acts first on men's souls, and then on their bodies.[37]

33. See C. H. Dodd, *According to the Scriptures* (London: Nisbet & Co., Ltd., 1952), p. 121.

34. Thomas Aquinas, *Summa Theologiae* (Westminster, MD: Christian Classics, 1991), p. 454.

35. Ibid.

36. Ibid., p. 487.

37. Ibid., p. 488.

Aquinas believed that through the sufferings of Christ we will be led to our "heavenly home," which is God. The body of Christ is present in this time and place, yet is not bound to this time and place; it is bound in Christ. "Christ is the head of the entire gathering, closer to God than the angels and acting on them also."[38]

How, then, do we, the body of Christ, know the mind of Christ? Paul says that we are to live a life transformed so that we may discern what is the will of God — "what is good and acceptable and perfect" (Romans 12:2). This indicates both a nurturing in the community and constant transformation or conversion. Horace Bushnell, the "father" of the Christian nurture approach to education, says: "It is the only true idea of Christian education, that the child is to grow up in the life of the parent, and be a Christian, in principle, from his earliest years." One doesn't wait for the child to sin and then be converted after a mature age; rather, Bushnell argued, the culture should be a nurturing environment for the life of the child and adult.[39]

Along with an environment that focuses our attention on the ways of Christ, Paul also calls us to transformation, or what Benedict called "conversion," that is, incremental moves toward being more like Christ. Paul Wilkes renders the Latin *conversatio morum suorum* as a conversion of manners, "a continuing and unsparing assessment and reassessment of one's self and what is important and valuable in life." Wilkes describes *conversatio's* objective this way: to make each person the self-constituting, good, holy, responsible person God intended him or her to be."[40] Benedict didn't understand conversion to be a traumatic or spectacular turnabout but a continual renewal of self and an openness to the larger community of Christians, through prayer, Scripture reading, worship, and service to others. Conversion in the monastic tradition — in the Christian tradition — is "both active and passive, being and becoming."[41]

Learning to Be Body in the Body of Christ

If Christ is the head, then we are the body. And we learn to become his body both through daily acts that nurture our life together and our small but continual acts of conversion as we are constantly becoming his followers. Wilkes

38. Ibid., p. 489.
39. Horace Bushnell, *Christian Nurture* (Cleveland: Pilgrim Press, 1994), p. 228.
40. Paul Wilkes, *Beyond These Walls* (New York: Image, 2000), p. 45.
41. Ibid., p. 50.

admits that only by continually taking stock of our lives, agreeing to a difficult alliance of our minds and wills, can we ever know the beauty and depth of *conversatio*, or learn the daily gestures needed for living with others.[42] And much of the learning will come when we least expect it. Wilkes says: "It is life's leaven, so small an ingredient, yet absolutely essential."[43]

But how are we to live with one another? This is the key question to ask if we are to understand education as I propose it in this book. A short answer is this: we begin learning to live with each other by getting a good sense of the "lay of the land" in our congregations — their flexibilities and hard edges, their orderliness and divine eccentricities. Wayne Meeks explains that this metaphor of Christ's body is unique because the body's leadership in particular and life in general is not of human origin, as was the case with other social groupings. In other contexts, our place in the body politic has been decided by natural kinship structures, modern employment practices, or democratic elections. In Christ's body, the "typical" method of placing people has been supplanted by a new set of relationships based on a new politic: our place is determined as a "gift" of the Spirit.[44] Thus some people who would not ordinarily be considered "heads" in secular settings become leaders in congregations under this charismatic governance of Christ's body.

For Paul, the more powerful, knowledgeable members of Christ's body are to regard with high esteem those considered weak, because this is the way of Christ:

> And those members of the body that we think less honorable we clothe with greater honor, and our less respectable members are treated with greater respect; whereas our more respectable members do not need this. But God has so arranged the body, giving the greater honor to the inferior member that there may be no dissension within the body, but the members may have the same care for one another. (1 Cor. 12:23-25)

Dietrich Bonhoeffer believed that our act of respecting those who usually receive less respect is the way of Christ. He wrote that the visible church is the body of Christ, for

> the body of Christ can only be a visible body, or else it is not a body at all. This is a result of the Incarnation: God in Christ came into his own as a

42. Ibid., p. 57.

43. Ibid., p. 60.

44. Wayne Meeks, *The First Urban Christians* (New Haven: Yale University Press, 1983), p. 88.

> baby in Bethlehem. Christ's body is both the ground of our faith and continual assurance of that faith as we are caught up into eternity by the act of God as members of the body of Christ.[45]

Christ's eternal presence with us is the key to how we learn to live with one another — with Christ as our model to imitate. Bonhoeffer observes no private-public split for disciples:

> The fellowship between Jesus and his disciples covered every aspect of their daily life. Within the fellowship of Christ's disciples the life of each individual was part of the life of the brotherhood. . . . In the Christian life, the individual disciple and the body of Jesus belong inseparably together.[46]

Jesus underwent crucifixion and death, having taken upon himself the human form, which meant sinful flesh, so that we suffer and die with him: "It is all our infirmities and all our sin that he bears to the cross. It is we who are crucified with him, and we who die with him."[47] Through the sacraments of baptism and the Lord's Supper we come to participate in the body of Christ. No longer do we live our own lives; instead, as Bonhoeffer says, Jesus lives his life in us: "The life of the faithful in the Church is indeed the life of Christ in them."[48] Because of this, we are part of the living temple of God "and of the new humanity."[49]

Hannah Arendt, citing the work of St. Augustine, answers the question of how we are to live with one another by showing that the Christian community was not as interested in things of this world as they were in the world to come, that is, the kingdom of God. As Christ's body, our politics are determined in light of God's dominion rather than the dominion of the nation-state. The early church's emphasis was on the common link or common good of charity, which was fostered among the brother- and sisterhood in the body of Christ.[50] Charity, according to Arendt, provides Christians with a way of living in an other-worldliness:

45. Dietrich Bonhoeffer, *Cost of Discipleship* (New York: Macmillan Press, 1975), pp. 263, 277.

46. Ibid., p. 284.

47. Ibid., p. 266.

48. Ibid., p. 272.

49. Ibid., p. 276.

50. Hannah Arendt, *The Human Condition* (Chicago: Univ. of Chicago Press, 1958), p. 53.

> The . . . character of the Christian community was early defined in the demand that it should form a *corpus*, a "body," whose members were to be related to each other like brothers (sisters) of the same family. The structure of communal life was modeled on the relationships between the members of a family because these were known to be nonpolitical and even antipolitical.[51]

Understanding Christ as head of the body, we have one other way of visualizing being Christ's body with one another: we can change the focus from a "top-down" to a "side-to-side/back and forth" emphasis. Sidney Callahan, citing modern scientific brain research by Gerald Edelman and Giulio Tononi,[52] argues that a dynamic core of the brain produces our human consciousness through an elaborate process of circuitry; in this process an amazing back-and-forth communication between all the complex parts of the body and the brain occurs. A mutual intercommunication of seemingly independent parts of the body produces an integrated harmony, richer than one unit or body part acting alone. Callahan suggests that, as Paul describes the unity of the church through the ancient vision of the body, we might look to this modern research to see how it is possible for

> truly independent and equal entities to operate in their own unique ways, but through mutual communication to achieve a coherent unity without dominance . . . coherence in the kingdom need not be dependent upon ascending hierarchies, exercising ever more executive control and exacting ever more subordination. A more vital way to achieve unity would consist of constant communication and mutual receptivity of all to all in the system.[53]

Callahan closes with these prophetic words: "Jesus told his disciples that authority in his kingdom would not be exercised in the domineering way that power was exercised in the world," through top-down hierarchies of control.[54]

51. Ibid., pp. 53-54.

52. Gerald Edelman and Giulio Tononi, *A Universe of Consciousness: How Matter Becomes Imagination* (New York: Basic Books, 2000).

53. Sidney Callahan, "Towards a Brainy Church," *Commonweal* (January 12, 2001), pp. 8-9.

54. Ibid.

Discerning Body Parts

With Christ as the head of the body, and the members as "limbs" of the body, the next move is to identify who is called to perform which part as a member of Christ's body. In Romans and 1 Corinthians, Paul says that there are various members, imbued with God's grace, who are called to serve the wider community of Christ. But how do we know what gift or what body part we have been called to fulfill?

Paul Minear says that the body of Christ has been given the gift of discernment for the communal solidarity to be found in Christ:

> Such discernment produces mutual courtesy, mutual concern, and an active sharing of resources by those who have with those who have not. This discernment can be produced only by genuine participation in the body that has been broken for others. . . . Therefore the body that must be discerned includes this nuance: it is such an interdependence of the Crucified with his own that a denial of koinonia with them is in fact a denial of koinonia in him.[55]

The nature of the role within the body is guided by this body's narrative, which is remembered by certain parts of the body. For example, Yoder says that within the body of Christ there are those whose roles are to be an agent of memory, such as those called to prophecy in 1 Corinthians 12:10 and in Romans: "We have gifts that differ according to the grace given to us: prophecy, in proportion to faith" (Rom. 12:6). This role is a gift to the body that is monitored by the Holy Spirit.[56]

Brian O'Leary says that discernment may be best defined as "a conscious experience of God's grace drawing one to a course of action or exposing the influence that a projected course of action will have on one's relationship with God."[57] In the discernment process we are striving to find the will of God as we try to respond to God's love and to serve his kingdom. Discernment is that subtle, deep, and stretching experience of discovering God's will for our lives. This can never be exclusively based on an individual's needs and abilities — with God excluded from the equation. Furthermore, once we have come to understand which part of the body we've been called to be, we are

55. Minear, p. 188.

56. John Howeard Yoder, *The Priestly Kingdom* (Notre Dame: University of Notre Dame Press, 1984), p. 28.

57. Brian O'Leary, "Discernment and Decision Making," *Review for Religious* 51 (1992): 56.

called to let obedience to God be our guide. Brother David Steindl-Rast says that obedience is learning to listen "to the Word of God that comes to us moment by moment, listening to the message of the angel that comes to us hour by hour."[58] The holy trick is this: if we yearn to give to God what God wants — our very lives — then chances are that we will soon want what God wants, and God will seem to want what we want.

Discernment is not a solo adventure or a survivor's tale. Rather, we embark on the process of discernment as members of a church, surrounded by family and friends, and in the household of the One who knows us better than we know ourselves. It is through the lives of these very people, in the moments of prayer and service, worship and fellowship, silence and noisy banter, that we receive knowledge of our role in the Christian community. One caveat: Yoder notes that the gifts Paul speaks of are not the specialized skills of a secular vocation per se, nor are they associated with certain physical attributes. Nor do the gifts that we discern in one another's lives have to do with social position. The lists in Paul's letters (Rom. 12, 1 Cor. 12, Eph. 4) are roles within the gathered body. Therefore, one can be a physician, a lawyer, or glassblower — each with his own specialization or guild; but one's professional status is not the same as the gifts of the Holy Spirit, which call for a certain level of accountability, responsibility, and dependence on one another for the upbuilding of Christ's body.[59]

Our Mind, Body, and Spirit as *Christ's* Mind, Body and Spirit

The peculiarity of the discernment process, or what makes it different from job placement searches in secular positions, is this: not only do we seek God's will rather than our own, but what leads us in this discovery of gifts is not just our habits of the mind — carefully thinking out each decision we make — but also our "habits of the heart," our very character. Paul Wilkes says that discernment is not only an act of cognition, an act reserved for the smartest among us: "It is available to those who are able to open their hearts to God. Our minds can sort out the details later, but without this opening, the power of the Holy Spirit . . . cannot enter our lives."[60] Wilkes then quotes the Jesuit Pierre de Caussade: "Their hearts tell them what God desires. They have only to listen to the prompting of their hearts to interpret his will in the existing

58. Steindl-Rast with Lebell, *The Music of Silence,* in Wilkes, p. 119.
59. Yoder, *Body Politics,* p. 53.
60. Wilkes, p. 118.

circumstances. God's plans, disguised as they are, reveal themselves to us through intuition rather than through our reason."[61]

Focusing on the habits of the heart as well as habits of the mind draws us into an important discussion about how we perceive being human within Christ's body in general, and how we perform gestures in particular. For example, consider carefully what Paul tells us about submitting our lives to God. First, he says that our minds are not to be "conformed to this world" but to be transformed, with the express purpose of being able to discern what is the will of God (Rom. 12:2). In pressing on for the prize of the "heavenly call of God in Christ Jesus," we, "who are mature, are to be of the same mind," which, for Paul, is to have the mind of Christ (Phil. 3:12-14).

Second, Paul writes that our individual bodies have become temples established by the indwelling Spirit of God: "Do you not know that your bodies are members of Christ?" (1 Cor. 6:15). When Paul says that we are God's temple, he is reminding us that God's Spirit resides in our bodies (1 Cor. 3:16). He continues that we should shun fornication, for the body is meant for the Lord and the Lord for the body: "Do you not know that your bodies are members of Christ?" It is not only our hope to embody Christ's mind, body, and spirit, but God's desire that we seek to learn the many habits necessary for that endeavor. It is through our bodily senses — tasting, touching, smelling, seeing, and hearing — through the mediation of the body itself, that we know and are known by God.

Third, God's Spirit has transformed our minds, our bodies, and spirits so that we are children of God. The spirit that resides in us, flows through us, and surrounds and comforts us is God's Spirit, who dwells in us now (Rom. 8:9). Paul says: "For what human being knows what is truly human except the human spirit that is within? So also no one comprehends what is truly God's except the Spirit of God" (1 Cor. 2:11). To be a member of Christ in such a way determines the "totality of one's existence vis-à-vis other men [and women]," says Paul Minear. While some see the church as a membership organization, Paul thought that Christ's body has members, that is, men and women whom he has incorporated within himself.[62]

What is important here is the incredible union of body, mind, and spirit in our very being. It is impossible to separate one from the other, even though, for the sake of argument or to make a theological point, people sometimes place one over another, for example, habits of the mind over habits of the heart or body. What I believe has led us to make such separations of

61. Ibid., p. 118.
62. Minear, p. 182.

body, mind, and spirit can be traced from the ancient Greek philosophers such as Plato through the Enlightenment philosophers such as Descartes. Robert Barron points out that, prior to Aquinas, the ideas of Origen, Gregory of Nyssa, Augustine, and Anselm drew greatly from the philosophical work of Plato, emphasizing the sharp distinction between soul and body. We see a similar dichotomy between mind and body in the work of Descartes. Because we have undoubtedly been shaped by the perspectives of these historical philosophers and theologians, we continue to find ourselves attributing parts of our being to habits of the mind versus habits of the heart and body. This separation of mind, body, and spirit appears to run counter to Paul's understanding of human beings: for example, Paul believed that the physical body represents the person's whole self, "inclusive of will and heart, soul and mind," according to Paul Minear.[63]

In searching for theologians who understand the union of our bodies, minds, and spirits with Christ's body, mind, and spirit, I am drawn to Aquinas' appreciation for the togetherness of soul and body precisely because God made us this way — to be in a right relationship with the Creator. Aquinas understood that the soul "is not a thing separate from the body but is rather the 'form' of the body . . . it is the unifying and organizing energy by which a particular conglomeration of bone, flesh, and nerve becomes properly human."[64] Aquinas says:

> Man then is not soul alone. Sensing is one of man's activities, though not peculiar to him, and this shows that individual men are not simply souls, but composed of body and soul.[65]

And of the mind, Aquinas writes:

> Mind is the form of man's body. Active things must have forms by which they act; only healthy bodies heal themselves and only instructed minds know. Activity depends on actuality, and what makes things actual makes them active. Now the soul is what makes our body live; so the soul is the primary source of all activities that differentiate levels of life.[66]

63. Minear, pp. 180-81.

64. Robert Barron, *Thomas Aquinas, Spiritual Master* (New York: Crossroad Pub. Co., 1996), p. 144.

65. Thomas Aquinas (Timothy McDermott, ed.), *Summa Theologiae* (Westminster: Christian Classics, 1989), p. 110.

66. Ibid., p. 111.

Furthermore, we are mind, body, and spirit because we are created in God's image, and God's nature itself implies that all three persons of God are represented within us. Aquinas says:

> For a creature's shaping and conditioning indicate that it *comes from* somewhere; its specific form indicates its maker's *word* as a house's shape indicates its architect's idea. . . . A first image of the Trinity in our minds is found in our activities of thinking out and formulating an inner word from the information we have, and then bursting out from this is a love. . . . A secondary image of the Trinity exists in our powers and dispositions to act. . . . So God's image is to be found in the conceiving of a word that expresses what we know of God and a love flowing from that.[67]

I believe that Aquinas rightly understands that, since we desire to know God and enjoy God forever, we desire to be more like God so that God's image may be found in us.

Wilkes says that it is easy to be "confounded by the contortions of my mind, by the unpredictable events of my life . . . [but I am not a] mindless beast being sucked down by the vortex that is moral indolence and counterfeit self-absorption." So Wilkes places his life in the body of Christ and in so doing focuses not on the impossible but on what is possible in the single act before him at any one time, praying for introspection and alertness, insight and patience, courage and love. In sum, we are able to experience such change in our bodies, minds, and spirits because this is God's will. The writer to the Ephesians argues that, before we were saved through Christ, we were enslaved by following the desires of our mere minds, bodies, and spirits:

> You were dead through the trespasses and sins in which you once lived, following the course of this world, following the ruler of the power of the air, the spirit that is now at work among those who are disobedient. All of us once lived among them in the passions of our flesh, following the desires of flesh and senses, and we were by nature children of wrath, like everyone else. (Eph. 2:1-3)

Without Christ, outside the bounds of this body of believers, left up to our own individualized, fractured minds, bodies, and spirits, our name was "children of wrath." Being left subject to our will, constructing our own sovereigns, we are left in sin. However, being found in Christ, our name has be-

67. Ibid., pp. 144-145.

come "children of God" because of the grace that saves us and seats us with God in the "heavenly places in Christ Jesus" (Eph. 2:4-6). The individualized minds, bodies, and spirits have now been transformed by grace through faith; and we are obligated to serve Christ, "to manifest union with him, to become his instrumentality," according to Minear.[68]

The Death of Radical Individualism in Christ's Body

In the introduction I addressed the centrality of "radical individualism," a social invention that is reinforced by many practices in the world today. Many of us who are part of the "baby boom" generation have also experienced the "me decade." The radical "in-dividual," or "un-divided one," is a single atomistic entity, isolated and claiming that he or she is unique, not part of a community of people who share in a series of intricate relationships with people who know them before they know themselves.[69]

The real problem of radical individualism is selfishness and stridency, which are contrary to life in Christ's body. We are reminded that the reason we are not individuals is the catholicity of this body of Christ, in which the focus is on the many who make up the one body; an often overwhelming characteristic that keeps people forever changing is that they are becoming more like Christ and thus less like themselves. There simply is no room nor desire for individualism in the body of Christ, because we were made to be in relationship, "one with another," says Paul. Stanley Hauerwas says that one does not know him best by talking to him individually — since he is part of a more significant, ever-changing body of relationships. In order to know him, or get a growing sense of who he is, he asks the reader to talk to his friends:

> I am best-known through my friends. This is not a confession of humility, but rather it denotes my increasing theological, epistemological, and moral conviction that theology is done in service to the church and accordingly cannot be the product of the individual mind.[70]

Claiming we are not authors or creators of our own lives and that we may not be in as much control of our existence as we would like to believe, we

68. Minear, p. 181.

69. Rodney Clapp, *Peculiar People* (Downers Grove: InterVarsity Press, 1996), p. 91.

70. Stanley Hauerwas, *Dispatches from the Front* (Durham: Duke University Press, 1995), p. 24.

find that we are part of a history of a community that knows us before we know ourselves.[71] In a similar vein, Wendell Berry says that, of course, we are not the creators of own lives, and that this is not a religious perspective only but also a biological and a social one:

> Each of us has had many authors, and each of us is engaged, for better or worse, in that same authorship. We could say that the human race is a great coauthorship in which we are collaborating with God and nature in the making of ourselves and one another. . . . This is only a way of saying that by ourselves we have no meaning and no dignity; by ourselves we are outside the human definition, outside our identity. "More and more," Mary Catharine Bateson wrote in *With a Daughter's Eye,* "it has seemed to me that the idea of an individual, the idea that there is someone to be known, separate from the relationships, is simply an error."[72]

Richard Rodriguez writes poignantly about community and the difference in how it is understood by Protestants and Roman Catholics. One such case concerns the notion that the pure English Protestants are strangers to community:

> We write of a new community who share with each other daily the experience of standing alone with God. This is the difference between individualistic Protestant and institutional Catholic.[73]

What does this have to do with being Christ's body with one another? In the body of Christ we are constantly looking out for the needs of other people first rather than necessarily thinking of ourselves and our own self-centered needs. This means letting go of petty resentments toward other congregants, making good decisions, and asking God in Christ for help in doing what is right, good, and loving. Perhaps what Paul means by saying that we are members one of another in the body of Christ is that we do not write our own story but are written by the many stories of other people who preceded us, who are with us now, and who will follow us. We must live before we can tell the story; thus we are swept into a story that preceded us but is still living and still told for all of eternity. And the storyteller is none other than God in Christ, who gives us life.

71. MacIntyre, *After Virtue,* p. 221.

72. Wendell Berry, *Home Economics* (San Francisco: North Point Press, 1987), p. 115.

73. Richard Rodriguez, *Hunger of Memory* (New York: Bantam, 1983), p. 110.

Conflict in Love with the Many in the One Body

Conflict and crisis is part of living together in Christ's body. Having ministered to churches that were in great conflict, I was reassured to hear that truth — loudly or subtly — amid the voices of hurt and hatred that came my way. Crisis in churches was what inspired Paul to write some of his epistles in the first place. The Corinthian church, as well as the churches in Rome, Ephesus, and Colossae, were constantly being assaulted by discord and strife, both from inside and outside the church.

Paul wrote certain kinds of letters to bring the dissension and strife to some hopeful resolution. Dale Martin notes that, in ancient Greek society, different kinds of speeches were given to bring about certain results. One kind was *homonoia,* or concord speeches, which were meant to bring peace to any strife or civil disturbance — "as disease must be eradicated from the body."[74] Martin argues that the situation was indeed intense enough in Corinth to warrant such a speech. He offers the example of 1 Corinthians 1:10: "I encourage you, brothers and sisters, by the name of our Lord Jesus Christ, that you all agree and that you allow no schisms to exist among yourselves, but that you be mended together in the same mind and the same opinion." Or consider 1 Corinthians 12:25, where Paul counsels that there "be no dissension within the body, but the members may have the same care for one another." Paul truly wanted the church to remain together, reaffirming and solidifying the hierarchical structure of the society, the *polis* of Christ's body.

The basic problem is that while we are members of the redeemed body of Christ, we are still born into sin. We are sinners, and yet we are created to live in relationship with other people — who are also sinners — in the body. The key to monastic life in a Benedictine community is the truth that life without another person is only half a life. While we have to live with one another to have a full life, human imperfection due to sin will still be part of our reality. Joan Chittister reminds us that, in Benedictine spirituality, community is a very human thing: "We do not expect perfection here, but we do expect growth, in ourselves as well as in others."[75]

Rather than being a "bad" thing, crisis or conflict can lead to our discovering the good we share in common in Christ's body. To paraphrase what Jean Vanier often says, it is necessary for a community to have individuals who are difficult to live with: they make the community "interesting," and they may also reveal the strengths and weaknesses in our churches. And when

74. Martin, "The Corinthian Body," p. 58.

75. Chittister, *Wisdom,* p. 47.

such people are no longer there, mysteriously enough, someone else will come to take their place. In truth, conflict is often important in helping a community understand what it means to live as a community. Conflict also unveils for all to see and hear a community's convictions — as well as certain virtues Christians need to live together.

Parker Palmer says that conflict arises from our ability to confront one another "critically and honestly over alleged 'facts,' computed meaning, personal biases and prejudice [which is] impaired when there is no community." Without openly expressed conflict there is only a haunting silence in which private games are being played. Conflict in the church is a "public encounter, in which the whole group can win."[76] Though crisis for the sake of crisis is a dead-end street, crises may make our communities stronger, if they are bonded together with strong friendships. Palmer says that the true test of a friendship is "the ability to sustain conflict, its capacity to incorporate tension as a creative part of a relationship; indeed, it is in tension and conflict that the transformations of friendship often occur."[77] Our friendship with one another becomes a kind of school itself — a school of charity that makes possible the resolution of crises. Charity wants the best for the other, which means that there are going to be times of joy and times of challenge. "For charity is the love which demands our self, but charity is also the love which promises a self," says Paul Waddell.[78]

Paul says that we are to strive for the greater gifts: "And I will show you a still more excellent way," leading the reader into 1 Corinthians 13, which features a discussion of the "gift of love" (*agapē*), love as charity. The tests of this love-as-charity are the many arguments and conflicts within the context of Christian friendship. Let us take the example of speaking honestly. In Ephesians 4 we read that we are to tell one another the truth "in love." By doing so, we will "grow up in every way into him who is the head, into Christ" (verse 15). We are called to reject our practice of speaking dishonestly, which we do in our attempts to hide truth from one another because we have not known or trusted this love-as-charity. Minear suggests that such things as "anger, theft, laziness, graceless talk and bitterness are primary sins against the body," constituting the "old nature, the body of flesh."[79] But by putting away false-

76. Parker Palmer, "Community in the Academy," an address to the 1987 National Conference on Higher Education.

77. Parker Palmer, *To Know as We Are Known* (San Francisco: Harper, 1983), p. 104.

78. Paul Waddell, *Friendship and the Moral Life* (Notre Dame: University of Notre Dame Press, 1989), p. 121.

79. Minear, p. 218.

hood, "let all of us speak the truth to our neighbors, for we are members of one another" (v. 25).

Aristotle and Plato understood that education, even the talk of it, can happen only in the realm of the *polis* — the body politic — since it maintains the politics of a social order. Educating Christians is a "deliberate and structured intervention in people's lives which attempts to influence how they live their lives in society," says Thomas Groome.[80] Education reinvents the culture in which it is located through the people it produces and reproduces. In these two chapters I have wished to reclaim Paul's image of the body of Christ not as a volunteer organization that one can join as a member; rather, Christ's body *has* members whom God created, Christ calls, and the Spirit infuses and marks for eternity. We are initiated into this body through the sacrament of baptism: "By water and the Holy Spirit, we are made members of the church, the body of Christ, and joined to Christ's ministry of love, peace, and justice."[81] Baptism is a sign to the rest of the world of what God's grace is and will do in our lives together. In mysterious ways we are marked as Christ's own forever.[82]

We are reminded that we also receive Christ's body through the sacrament of the Eucharist, in which we are given the heavenly nourishment, filled with Christ's spirit, and renewed to do his will on this earth. Aquinas says that whereas baptism is given once, the Eucharist is given many times. Baptism makes us sharers in the unity of the church; by receiving the Eucharist, "we signify that we are united to Christ and joined in one body with his members," the very companionship of the saints and the Lord himself.[83] But as Caroline Simon points out, "Christianity is not about flourishing; it is about taking up one's cross."[84]As Christ's body following his way, we take on the form of a servant. In receiving others into the life of our congregations, especially those who are strangers to us, we welcome the Christ who lives in their hearts as well as in ours.

80. Groome, *Christian Religious Education,* p. 15. In his footnotes Groome quotes a passage from Aristotle's *Politics:* "It is clear then that there should be laws laid down about education, and that education itself must be made a public concern. But we must not forget the question of what that education is to be, and how one ought to be educated" (p. 453).

81. *Book of Common Worship* (Louisville: Westminster/John Knox Press, 1993), p. 405.

82. Ibid., p. 414.

83. Aquinas, *Summa,* p. 587.

84. Caroline Simon, quoting Anders Nygren, in *The Disciplined Heart* (Grand Rapids: Wm. B. Eerdmans, 1997), p. 82.

Called to be members, baptized into his body, nurtured by eucharistic practices, we are provided, by God's grace, with talents and services that are discerned by Christ's body. With much love and affection, challenge and conflict, we perfect those gifts as we experience a constant conversion in our becoming more like Christ each day of the year. Minear says that the truth embodied in Christ's body is an "explosive force, designed to shatter all other conceptions of social organization and historical process. But it is clear that this explosive power has not been fully effective even within the church."[85] How is this explosion to be ignited? Minear believes it is through the growth and building up of Christ's body. Growth comes from "holding fast to the head, from whom the whole body, nourished and held together by its ligaments and sinews, grows with a growth that is from God" (Col. 2:19). The body grows as we are engaged in the gestures of allowing the word of Christ to dwell in us richly, teaching and admonishing one another, singing psalms and hymns and spiritual songs with thankfulness in our hearts (Col. 3:15, 16). Growth comes through the practice of compassion, patience, forgiveness, and love — all of those activities of the mind and spirit nourishing the body, but also activities in which the body is held fast to the head and to the heart. This growth involves a renewed dying to self and is also directed toward a particular end: "All things have been created through him and for him" (Col. 1:16).[86]

85. Minear, p. 211.
86. Ibid., pp. 212-13.

PART II

CHRISTLY GESTURES

Prologue to Part II

In the body of Christ, our bodies, minds, and spirits are shaped and nurtured, both for our own good as individual members and the common good of the congregation of which we are members. For we see Christ in each person in this body. In Romans 12, Paul reminds the church of some marks of being a Christian, such as: "Contribute to the needs of the saints; extend hospitality to strangers" (v. 13); "bless those who persecute you; rejoice with those who rejoice, weep with those who weep" (vv. 14-15); "if your enemies are hungry, feed them; if they are thirsty, give them something to drink" (v. 20). In reflecting on these verses, I am struck by both the matter-of-factness and straight talk of Scripture to our daily lives.

New Testament scholars and theologians have openly discussed Paul's letters as a "church manual" of sorts, instructing the reader on how to be church with one another in our daily life as Christians. While Paul was writing to a specific church in a certain time and place, the timeless universality of his letters has been heralded throughout the ages because we continue to hit the same snags and controversies that were commonplace in Corinth, Galatia, Rome, and Thessalonika, to name but a few. Moreover, in reflecting, interpreting, and physically working out these passages in youth groups, adult Bible studies, and seminary classes, I have become more and more convinced that teaching the ways of Christ's body, like the ways articulated in Romans, involves not only habits of the mind and the heart but also habits of the body. Indeed, for some members of Christ's body, instruction in the ways of the Jesus-life is primarily body-oriented.

For example, what does it look, feel, and sound like when we learn to "hate what is evil, hold fast to what is good," or "love one another with mutual affection," or "extend hospitality to strangers" (Rom. 12:9-13)? Because we are composed of body, mind, and God's spirit, there needs to be a movement of all three, in concert, with the intention of purposefulness in love. Philosophers, educators, and theologians have written exhaustively about the "habits of the mind." To know intellectually what it is to hate the evil and hold fast to the good, to offer hospitality to strangers as an act of genuine love, is one piece of the puzzle of performing a charitable act. But two other puzzle pieces come into play. Another piece is to teach this habit to the heart, to shape one's very being — one's character and emotions. The third piece of the puzzle is the body: teaching the habits of hospitality, goodness, and love to our body parts is significant in completing this threefold action of love in Christ's name. Working with our mind and heart, our body needs to engage in such action, embodying love with our mouths, our hands, our very lives — so that such gestures seem almost "natural."

In Part II, I will focus on the gestures of the body of Christ. Careful to address mind and spirit in our gestures, I will also examine the crafting and nurturing of the human body itself, an area that has received little attention in the fields of religious education and theology, let alone courses in modern education in general (except for courses in physical education). Why the body? While for many people religious instruction, like Christian education, has focused on our capacity to think and reflect on how we know God and the world around us, with attention to matters deemed "spiritual" in the life of the church, when it comes to addressing the actions of the body itself — or a kind of bodily knowledge — we in the church remain uninformed. Perhaps this is due to a Cartesian dualistic approach to education in the church.

In this book I also argue for the inclusion of people with disabilities of body, mind, or spirit. Education for some people with physical, emotional, behavioral, visual, auditory, or developmental disabilities often begins with their bodies: the crafting of intentional movement from an array of possible actions. Or in the case of a person afflicted by Alzheimer's disease, we in the surrounding community may become his or her mind as we negotiate the disabled one's body through the gestured motions of Christ's body.

Part II's overarching theme of gestures is based on a definition of Christly gestures. First, in Chapter Three, I will explore how gestures performed become a practice that fuses mind, body, and spirit in Christ's one body. Second, in Chapter Four, I will describe how gestures are corporate — learned, practiced, and performed by members of Christ's body. The community of Christ is re-created by the gestures that embody the story of God's gospel. Some gestures are particular for an individual's grace-given gift and service in Christ's body; others are performed in common and in coordination with other members of Christ's body; and there are some gestures that are performed within the context of worshiping God. Third, in Chapter Five, I will highlight the way Christly gestures are narrated by Scripture and the traditions of the church, as well as by the traditions of a congregation where the gestures are performed. The authenticity of any gesture requires it to be a performance of Scripture itself, as interpreted within the context of Christ's one body. Because of each gesture's origin, gestures both have a story and embody a story; the gestures share that story with others, passing it down to the next generation of Christians.

CHAPTER THREE

Christly Gestures: Body, Mind, and Spirit

For although the best prayers are sometimes without utterance, yet when the feeling of the mind is overpowering, the tongue spontaneously breaks forth into utterance, and our other members into gesture.

John Calvin[1]

In proposing that the arena of education for Christians is the entirety of Christ's body in all its wonder and complexities, the educator explicitly assumes that the members of the body have been given the gift of being either a "foot" or a "hand," an "eye" or an "ear," a teacher or an apostle, a compassionate giver or a healer. While Paul may have been using such "body language" for the sake of "reflective realism," as Karl Barth suggests, or metaphorical imagery for discussing the nature of our relationship with one another in Christ's body as *polis,* it is nevertheless interesting in what ways the human body is itself an essential aspect of God's salvific story, for example, the bodily resurrection of Christ. Also consider 1 Corinthians 6:19-20, where Paul writes that our bodies are a temple of the Holy Spirit within us, which we have from God and not from ourselves: "For you were bought with a price; therefore glorify God in your body," and not just with mind and spirit.

1. Calvin, *Institutes,* 3.20.33, p. 897.

Furthermore, while much of our focus on educating Christians has been on the habits of the mind and heart, little has been written in terms of the systematic education of Christians in inculcating the habits of the body in the Christian life, though much of the gospel of Christ and the letters of Paul call for bodily action as well as cognitive and spiritual reflection and action. I propose to focus on the small and large gestures of Christ's body, otherwise known as Christly gestures. More specifically important for our discussion are the intricate story and "thickness" of meanings that lie behind a gesture. While gestures can be a way of expressing "body language," like the seemingly simple reflex of shaking hands or hugging another person in the passing of the peace, with the words "Peace of Christ be with you," even the simplest of these gestures is open to a wide array of interpretations.

A gesture is more than another way of saying "body language," such as a frown, a smile, shrugging shoulders, or pointing to an object; it is more than an accompaniment to a verbal cue. It is also more than symbolic representation, such as the Statue of Liberty holding high the torch of liberty.[2] Speech itself is a bodily gesture that calls on muscles to move in order to express language. Moving a body part is an act that involves neural synaptic stimulation and response, in coordination with other parts of the body and mind. For Christians it is also the awareness that the Holy Spirit is moving in our very bodily gestures.

This is to recognize what Aquinas said: our spirit and flesh, these very bones, are essential to our beings as Christians. Aquinas understood that spirit and flesh are so tight that it is impossible to define being human without the two together.[3] That is why it is more than a "body" or flesh that is being formed in gestures; one's entire being is shaped and nurtured. Similarly, John Calvin believed that the very gestures themselves were a form of communication that even God understood. Calvin says that, when we pray, we pray with the Holy Spirit and also with the mind: "The mind ought to be kindled with an ardor of thought so far as to surpass all that the tongue can express by speaking." He continues:

> As for bodily gestures customarily observed in praying, such as kneeling and uncovering the head, they are exercises whereby we try to rise to a greater reverence for God.[4]

2. Paul Connerton, *How Societies Remember* (New York: Cambridge Press, 1989), p. 81.

3. Barron, *Thomas Aquinas: Spiritual Master,* p. 144.

4. Calvin, *Institutes,* 3.20.33, p. 897.

To demonstrate to the reader the "thickness" of even the simplest gesture as an act of the body and mind, I will begin by briefly examining the history of the term "gesture" itself, the array of meanings *behind* gestures, and the anthropological perspective on the power of gesture; finally, since speaking is a major way we communicate as human beings in the church, I will highlight how speech is a gesture. In light of the popular axiom "to say something is to do something," it is obvious that speech itself is a gesture, learned in a communal setting. I am covering these approaches to show the reader not only our collective dependence on gestures in our daily lives as Christians but also how much thought, will, desire, and spirit are involved in the simplest to the most intricate bodily gestures as we strive to have the mind of Christ.

Gestures

Gesture: A Definition Considered

"Gesture" is one of those words we use a great deal, often without considering what it means; or we wrongly assume a common definition, while the opposite is very likely. According to a dictionary, a gesture is a

> manner of carrying the body; bearing, carriage, deportment; manner of placing the body; position, posture, or attitude, especially in acts of prayer or worship; in early use: the employment of bodily movements, attitudes, expressions of countenance as a means of giving effect to oratory; a movement expressive of thought or feeling.[5]

The root of "gesture" is the Latin *gestus,* which is both a posture and static way of presenting oneself as a statue frozen in time. "Gesticulation" is the dynamic or fluid way one presents oneself, as cited by Aristotle and his pupils Theophrastos, Demetrios, and Cicero in the fifties BCE; they wrote about *sermo corporis,* the "language of the body," and *eloquentia corporis,* the "eloquence of the body." Quintilian dwells on *gestus,* both posture and gesticulation, in his book *The Formation of a Public Speaker.*[6] The ancient Greek and Roman philosophers and teachers believed that gestures were an important part of speech and language, and language is nothing natural but is highly

5. *New Oxford American Dictionary* (New York: Oxford Univ. Press, 2001), p. 712.
6. Ibid., p. 38.

conventional and tied to a specific culture of the people. In other words, differences in language mark differences in and between cultures. For example, it was inappropriate during the European Renaissance for ordinary women to stand with their arms

> akimbo, while in rural Andalusia today, male domination is made known by a certain "contentious gesticulation which plays a central role in what is called the 'choreography of male sociability.'"[7]

People can recognize which region of a country or social status — otherwise known as social and economic class — other people come from based on the kind, use, or absence of certain gestures; whether the gesture is spontaneous; whether it is from daily life and common people; or whether it is a gesture of foreigners or those of a different social class.

Gestures are such a part of our daily lives that we are not aware of how basic they are or how dependent we are in using them. For example, consider that the physical gesture of smiling is one of the first things that infants learn in life. Because gestures are perceptual and praxic, by which I mean that they are learned in the practice of the gesture itself, infants use their bodies in imitation of gestures of the body they see and feel the most, usually a parent's or guardian's.[8] It is a mirrored response or reaction in which the infant receives much praise from the one seeking to coax the smile. We also try out the opposite gesture, a frown, to see what kind of response it gets.[9] And because there is not a sound necessarily associated with a smile or frown, we consider these nonverbal gestures.

How dependent are we on gestures? Gestures of body accompany our speaking for emphasis, such as pointing our fingers or nodding our heads. Writing a thank-you card to someone is a thoughtful gesture. Sometimes we refer to gestures in political talk, for example, citing the necessity of going "beyond a gesture"; or when two parties are at war, and one of them offers a hint of reconciliation, we may hear that it is "merely a token gesture." The implication is that the gesture is not important, that the question is, "When are you going to get to the serious stuff?" "Gesture" is very much a part of our common English vocabulary.

7. Keith Thomas, in Jan Bremmer and Herman Roodenburg, eds., *A Cultural History of Gesture* (Ithaca, NY: Cornell Univ. Press, 1991), p. 8.

8. Jean Berges and Irene Lezine, *The Imitation of Gestures* (London: Spastics Society Medical Education and Information Unit in Association with William Heinemann Medical Books, Ltd., 1965), p. 2.

9. Ibid., p. 4.

In this section I propose a broader understanding of gestures because there is no simple definition that operates across all cultural contexts throughout time; that is, our understanding of gesture is context-dependent. A gesture is itself a language, and language is not natural but is highly cultivated within a culture. Differences in gestured-language mark differences in culture; as Wittgenstein says, "If one were trying to understand an expressive gesture in a ceremony . . . I should need to analyze the ceremony [itself]."[10]

In arguing that the specific context in which a gesture is practiced is important, as is the methodology by which a gesture is identified and taught, I first turn to the modern discipline of cultural anthropology, where gestures have been thoroughly investigated.

Gesture: Anthropological Considerations

Cultural anthropologists study language and gesture patterns of societies to gain clues about how people live with each other. Anthony Cohen writes that it is in a community that one learns how to be in social relationships with others, that one acquires "culture" by using the unique symbols and particular gestures that equip a person to relate socially. The community is created and re-created by the gestures people use in social interactions.

Many cultural anthropologists have argued that all gestures have two primary functions as communication. One is as an expressive or referential form of communication: the hand, arm, or head may refer to an object by pointing to it; or the movement of the body may make a pictorial representation, such as holding out one's hand to indicate the size of the fish that got away. Another use of gesture is in a notational mode of communication: the physical gesture accompanies speech.[11] For example, it was said that one could turn the television's sound off or cover one's ears while watching a newsreel of New York's Mayor Fiorella LaGuardia and still know from his gestures alone whether he was speaking English, Italian, or Yiddish.[12] Gestures that emphasize verbal discourse are culturally constructed.[13] John Austin calls such notational gestures "accompaniments" of the verbal utterance:

10. Ludwig Wittgenstein, *Remarks on the Philosophy of Psychology,* Vol. I (Chicago: Univ. of Chicago Press, 1980), No. 34, p. 9e.

11. Jean-Claude Schmitt, in Jan Bremmer and Herman Roodenburg, eds., p. 64.

12. Oliver Sacks, *The Man Who Mistook His Wife for a Hat* (New York: Simon & Schuster, 1985), pp. 80-84.

13. This categorization is constructed by David Efron and cited by Connerton, *How Societies Remember,* p. 81.

"Gestures (winks, pointing, shrugging, frowns, etc.) or . . . ceremonial nonverbal actions . . . may sometimes serve without the utterance of any words and their importance is very obvious."[14] Some "performative utterances" are nonverbal or manual gestures. Donald Evans writes that bowing, saluting, and shaking hands with other people have a performative force. And such performative utterances can be deeds, as is the "I promise" of a business contract or the "I do" of a marriage covenant. All verbal utterances have a performative force as an institutional act.[15]

Gestures as Referential Language

Cultural anthropologists point out that a culture is reflected, represented, and re-created by particular symbols and signs when we perform certain gestures. For example, Walter Ong says that a gesture is a far more difficult and complicated form of communication than speech because it involves many muscular activities and often the entire body. He cites the Statue of Liberty as an American icon whose gestures are frozen in time: there is meaning behind the upraised arm holding the torch of freedom. That statue is frozen in a gesture that has a structure of meaning: "Give me your tired, your poor, your huddled masses, yearning to breathe free."[16]

The obverse of this is equally true: when the gesture is not performed, the culture is forgotten. For example, a young potter in his twenties in a re-created eighteenth-century village in Pennsylvania spoke of his craft with excitement but also a note of sadness. The last master potter who had worked and lived in this village — before it was resurrected in this twentieth-century re-creation — had died in the 1940s; lost with him was a repertoire of gestures necessary for producing certain clay pots that reflected this village's ethos. One could only guess how the potters would ply their craft from reading books about making pots; but the art of the gesture was lost to the ages.

Bruce Kapferer writes that in the representative gesture we can see how a culture is both particularizing and universalizing. On the one hand, culture in its particularity locates individuals in a specific, mundane ordering of everyday life. Desmond Morris, like other anthropologists, would argue that there are no universal gestures because "gestures vary from culture to cul-

14. Austin, *How to Do Things with Words* (Cambridge: Harvard Univ. Press, 1975), p. 76.

15. Evans, *The Logic of Self-Involvement* (London: SCM, 1963), p. 3.

16. Walter Ong, *The Presence of the Word* (Minneapolis: Univ. of Minnesota Press, 1981), p. 94.

ture."[17] Kapferer says that in the expressions revealed on our faces and in the organization of our body gestures we experience relationships with other people: "We are acting in relation to others who share a history and a set of common experiences and understandings of experience."[18] Or consider Clifford Geertz's example: there is a time when a wink is a wink, but sometimes a wink is a twitch.

> But contracting your eyelids on purpose when there exists a public code in which so doing counts as a conspiratorial signal *is* winking. That's all there is to it: a speck of behavior, a fleck of culture, and — voila — a gesture![19]

What it means to give the eye a glance in a certain way, to move the torso in another way, or to pull a chair out for someone to sit on depends on people having an understanding of the function of the gestures and on their response to them.[20] "Every gesture within a given social group or community stands for a particular act or response, demanding an answer from another to whom it was addressed."[21]

Consider the phenomenon of holding a fan as a method of communication between women and men during the American Civil War, when direct eye contact was frowned on. There was even a book that defined the rich meanings behind the fifty ways to hold a fan. For a woman to carry a fan in her left hand meant that she wanted to meet a man; but if it was in her right hand, it meant that the man was appearing too willing to woo.[22]

On the other hand, many anthropologists would argue that they know the wink to be a gesture because of a foundational, universal set of culturally constituted constructs among all people who can call certain expressions of the body "gestures." Such universality enables us to find out how we are viewed by those from another culture, since gestures are something we all have in common. Since we all use them, gestures are universal; but their meaning is particular to each culture.[23]

17. Desmond Morris, Peter Collett, Peter Marsch, Marie O'Shaughnessy, *Gestures: Their Origin and Distribution* (New York: Stein and Day, 1979), p. xvii.

18. Bruce Kapferer, "Performance and the Structuring of Meaning and Experience," in Edward Bruner and Victor Turner, eds., *Anthropology of Experience* (Chicago: University of Chicago Press), p. 189.

19. Clifford Geertz, *Interpretation of Cultures* (New York: Basic Books, 1973), p. 6.

20. Ibid., p. 44.

21. Ibid., p. 47.

22. Bruce Smith, "Hearts and fans are aflutter in Civil War re-enactments," *News and Observer,* Raleigh, North Carolina, Nov. 18, 1995, 9a.

23. Kapferer, p. 189.

The performances of a culture's gestures not only reflect or re-create but are a pattern for how we live with one another that can be understood only within a culture that practices such performances. For example, while the patterned "waggle dance" of bees may look like dancing to Jerome Robbins, zoologically speaking, it isn't considered "dancing" by the bees.[24] To Turner, cultural performances are not simply reflectors or expressions of culture but actually are

> active agents of change, representing the eye by which culture sees itself and the drawing board on which creative actors sketch out what they believe to be a more apt design for living. Cultural forms are reflexive, not just reflective.[25]

In this case, "reflexive" means an action that is highly contrived and artificial, of culture and not of nature, a deliberate and voluntary work of a person, such as an artist.[26] For example, when a parent kisses the place where a child has been hurt, it has an almost magical quality to it. The kissing gesture is the magic spark of great change, of almost instantaneous healing.Turner believes that human beings are a self-performing animal in the basic stuff of everyday social life, in which there has to be a structural relationship between the cognitive, affective, and conative (or wisdom) processes of lived experiences. Performances, like rituals, are never open-ended; but they are indeed "declarations of form against indeterminacy, which is always in the background of ritual."[27]

Kapferer, Geertz, and Turner are considered "structuralists" in their understanding of culture. They believe there is a text, a complex of signs that reveal a deeper structural interrelationship in how we communicate with each other. There is also the enactment of the text itself in the gesture that creates a culture. They are as interested in the text as they are in the ways it communicates to and is experienced by an audience.[28] But the very naming of such a theory as "structuralist" implies that it is somehow natural to all cultures and is itself a cultural construction. Again, the claim that a certain set of gestures have a specific grammar is based on the assumption that there are universal rules of performance that constitute an innate structure, and we obey these

24. Victor Turner, *The Anthropology of Performance* (Baltimore: PAJ, 1988), pp. 8, 10.

25. Ibid., p. 24.

26. Ibid., p. 24.

27. Ibid., p. 44.

28. This is similar to the viewpoint of Paul Ricoeur; Kapferer, p. 192.

rules to make ourselves understood. Stanley Fish notes that it is impossible to ignore the rules while remaining in community.[29]

Gregory Bateson proposes that we develop a whole different repertoire of gestures that serve a certain function that verbal language is unable to perform:

> It seems that the discourse of non-verbal communication is precisely concerned with matters of relationship — love, hate, respect, fear, dependency . . . they underline and amplify the message of language by stressing the emotional, non-rational elements.[30]

Consider how humor and deceit use gestures — without verbal or written language. The gesture as joke can be seen in many sight gags, for example in the "Keystone cops" silent movies, with their well-timed pratfalls, or in the hilarious antics of the "Three Stooges," with their gestures of hand, nose, mouth, foot, torso, and so on. One classic sight gag is the cream-pie throw: one person gets hit in the face with a pie; he then uses his fingers to wipe the cream off his eyes, then his nose, and finally his mouth — while he gets ready to throw another pie at the culprit who just hit him. That person ducks as the pie is being thrown, and an unsuspecting third party walking into the scene gets a pie full in the face.[31]

There are also gestures of intentional deceit that, when practiced often enough, become habit. Understanding a gesture as deceitful again depends on the context, the people, and the story in which it is being purposely practiced for personal gain. Because there is a story in the performance of a gesture, this question emerges: Can one separate the story from what is being enacted? The structuralist answer is negative: when one performs something to communicate with others, there is a unity of the cultural story and its enactment that cannot be reduced to one or the other. The story is embodied in the gesture.

29. Stanley Fish, *Is There a Text in This Class?* (Cambridge: Harvard Univ. Press, 1980), p. 244.

30. See Fritz Graf, "Gestures and conventions: the gestures of Roman actors and orators," in Bremmer and Roodenburg, p. 41.

31. In Peter DeVries's *Blood of the Lamb* (New York: Penguin Books, 1982), Don Wanderhope's daughter, Carol, has a friend, Omar, who understands something of the ritual of the pie-throwing event in American humor: "Ritual. You see, it isn't a fight in the sense of something in which you defend yourself, but basically like your bullfight in Spain . . . it's a ceremony. Every way the face is wiped off is stylized. . . . First slowly the eyes are dug out with tips of the fingers, then the fingers freed with a flip, then the rest of the face is wiped down strictly according to established rules . . . ." (p. 192).

Performance of the story in gestures is key to remembering whose we are as a people.[32] However, there are many interpretations of a story, and they largely depend on a community and its larger story, which narrates and embodies the gesture. Some gestures are ambiguous simply because no one understands the gestures' origin in a culture's story. For example, if a person taps his or her forehead with a forefinger, it means that the person referred to is either "crazy" or "intelligent," depending on the context in which it is used. "A simple hand action stands for — symbolizes — an abstract quality — craziness or intelligence."[33] This only becomes more confusing when gestures cross-pollinate. For example, some Japanese will greet their own countrymen with a handshake rather than with a bow, which is their traditional form of greeting.

Da Vinci's painting *The Last Supper* shows the number of ways we can interpret gestures: we can either see Jesus sitting among a group of scared disciples, or we can see the viewers for whom Da Vinci was painting. Leo Steinberg writes that there are several functions simply in Jesus' hands: his arms are lower than those of the disciples because he is resigned to his coming death; the shrinking shoulders serve to triangulate the body's shape, which foreshadows his designating of the traitor in the story, for Jesus is gesturing toward Judas, with his left hand extended to the viewer-as-guest. Steinberg writes that the gestures of the body are important because "the impetus to this painting, as in all art work, is not a word, but a gesture. . . . gesture is causal."[34]

There is always a story that narrates or choreographs our gestures. Like any other language, it has a beginning, a middle, and an end. For example, in 1993, during the Mideast peace summit between Israel and the Palestinian Liberation Organization (PLO) in Washington, D.C., when President Clinton, Yitzak Rabin, and Yassir Arafat came to the podium to sign the document, there was a tense moment when Arafat reached out to shake the hand of his "enemy," Rabin. For a moment, Rabin hesitated and did not offer his hand. After a few brief seconds, and with a shrug of his shoulders, Rabin completed the gesture by shaking Arafat's hand, thus moving the Mideast peace process one step further toward reality.[35]

32. Kapferer, p. 202.

33. Ibid., p. xxi.

34. Leo Steinberg, "The Seven Functions of the Hands of Christ," in Diane Apostolos-Cappadona, ed., *Art, Creativity, and the Sacred* (New York: Crossroad Pub. Co., 1984), pp. 37-63.

35. *Time* magazine, in the issue published soon after the assassination of Prime Minister Rabin, featured a statement about this handshake between Rabin and Arafat as more than a "token" gesture.

Each gesture has its own story. Jan Bremmer and Herman Roodenburg have mapped out the use of gesture throughout history in various cultures, focusing primarily on European history.[36] It was most important to know the proper gestures in certain cultural contexts, especially in the Middle Ages throughout Europe. For example, the handshake, or the slapping of hands to seal a deal, still popular in the Netherlands, is a tradition that dates back to the sixteenth century: one could not hold a firearm when shaking or slapping hands together.[37] It was believed that the human body touching another in a handshake reflected the values of the body politic, the large social body, thus touching on matters of hierarchy, equality, and relationship.

Cultural anthropologists tell us that gestures are more than simple reflexive acts of the body, easily categorized as "body language." Rather, gestures show how entwined and united body and mind are in a visual, kinesthetic, sensory-thick, and intellectually rich way as we live in and communicate with the world and with God. Mary Douglas emphasizes this power of gestures, saying that our very bodies are symbols of social relationships, and that control of the body differs according to the degree of the group pressure of a specific culture or larger body politic.[38] In the following chapters on Christly gestures, I will show how gestures are a part of the larger church body politic in which we live, which has a way of making decisions, defining membership, and carrying out certain duties in the name of Christ.

I have noted that a gesture is a form of communication among people, be it referential or notational. Yet there is a long tradition of pedagogical instruction in gesture as speech itself, with the belief that "external bodily behavior manifests the inner life of the soul,"[39] where what a person says or does outwardly is a manifestation of his or her inner life. It is fair to say that a gesture is itself an embodiment of the Spirit who resides within Christians: "Be doers of the word, and not merely hearers who deceive themselves" (James 1:22). We are able and desirous to be doers of the Word of God because the Holy Spirit lives in our hearts. Speech as gesture among Christians also reveals the fusion of body, mind, and spirit.

36. Herman Roodenburg, "The Hand of Friendship," in *A Cultural History of Gesture,* pp. 174, 178.

37. Keith Thomas, in *A Cultural History of Gesture,* p. 4.

38. Yoder, *Body Politics,* p. viii.

39. Thomas, p. 8.

Speech as Gesture

Wittgenstein says that people use gestures all the time in order to represent something or to make a point. Learning depends not only on the use of language but on gesture as language as well. To understand the gesture or speech, one needs to understand the context in which a word is spoken. "Speech and gestures are closely related," says Wittgenstein.[40] Hauerwas says that words-as-gestures cannot be separated from the context in which they are enacted as speech:

> For example, the Apostles' Creed is not simply a statement of faith that can stand independent of the context in which we affirm it. We must learn to say it in the context of worship if we are to understand how it works to rule our belief and school our faith. The Creed is not some deposit or sum of the story: rather it is a series of reminders about how best to tell the story that we find enacted through the entire liturgy.[41]

Poets, philosophers, and theologians who are "wordsmiths" have made the connection between language, mind, and gestures. Richard Blackmur says that speech itself does not simply describe or communicate existing situations but can create a new situation.[42] This is because language, written or spoken, is made up of words and communicated by gestures. Words are made up of motion, and gesture is

> made of the language beneath, beyond, or alongside the language of words. When the language of words fails, we resort to the language of gesture. The language of words most succeeds when it becomes gesture in its words.[43]

Blackmur continues:

> The highest use of language can't be made without incorporating some such quality of gesture in it. How without it could the novelist make the dialogue ring? We can't master language purposefully without remastering gesture in it. Gesture in language is the dramatic play of inward and imaged

40. Wittgenstein, *Remarks on the Philosophy of Psychology,* Vol. I, Nos. 34, 284, 635.

41. Stanley Hauerwas, "Gesture of a Truthful Story," *Theology Today,* Vol. 42, No. 2 (July 1985), p. 186.

42. This comment is found in Phillip Pfatteicher, *School of the Church* (Valley Forge: Trinity Press International, 1995), p. 23.

43. Richard Blackmur, *Language as Gesture* (New York: Harcourt, Brace, and Co., 1952), p. 3.

meaning. It is that play of meaningfulness among words which can't be defined in the formula in the dictionary, but is defined in their use together.[44]

Let me reiterate that the obvious characteristic of language, oral or written, is that it is gesture. The speaking of a word is a gesture that, like sign language or body language, can be understood only in the context in which it is performed and received. It is a corporate act, embedded in the thick complexity of the culture in which it is first learned; for language has been used by others over many generations. Too often the spoken word and gestures are seen as two distinct ways of communicating. Are speech and gesture two separate actions, and can we ask which came first, the gesture or the language? George Herbert Mead writes about the social gesture that precedes the symbol proper and is a form of deliberate communication,[45] arguing that a gesture becomes a significant symbol, a language that signifies a certain meaning in a specific context, making a person respond or be aroused. Speech emerges out of gesture rather than gesture out of speech.[46]

In verbally communicating with others, we express ourselves with the musculature of lips, teeth, and tongue, of the whole face and torso, of the neck and shoulders — some even with legs and arms — coordinated with diaphragm muscles in breathing and swallowing. Consider also the physical work of modulating the volume and tone of voice, and the muscle control necessary to make our voices "do" what we want them to do. Without the gesture of mouth and other body parts, the spoken word is not known; no one would understand us.

Second, as the above anthropologists argue, the gesture of speech also depends on the particulars — the particular context in which the specific gestures are practiced. Christopher Fry offers an insightful defense of how, in understanding the human creature's exploration of the truth, we need a stage of some kind that announces what is going on here in this time and space. On this stage, which is culture, words and gestures matter. Don't worry about its artificiality, he says, because "we get used to it. We get broken into it so gradually we scarcely notice it." If we should shake off the contingencies of life, we would be "like the old woman who looked at the giraffe in the zoo and refused to believe a word of it."[47]

44. Ibid., p. 5.

45. George Herbert Mead, *Mind, Self and Society,* Vol. 1 (Chicago: University of Chicago Press, 1934), p. 15.

46. Ibid., p. 14.

47. Christopher Fry, "A Playwright Speaks," *Parabola,* Vol. 20, No. 3 (August 1995), p. 61.

Scott Momaday tells the story of a Kiowa Indian and his wife sitting in their tipi making fine arrows. The husband crafts the arrows and straightens them with his teeth. After a while he perceives someone moving outside the tipi and tells his wife to not be afraid but to keep talking easily as he works on the arrow. Speaking aloud the entire time, he finally says to the presence outside: "If you are a Kiowa, you will understand what I am saying, and you will speak your name." But there is no answer. So the arrowmaker points his arrow all around, and then shoots it through the side of the tipi and straight into the enemy's heart. Momaday says that this story is a

> remarkable act of the mind, a realization of words and the world that is altogether simple and direct, yet nonetheless rare and profound, and it illustrates more clearly than anything else in my own experiences, at least, something of the essential character of the imagination — and in particular of that personification which in this instance emerges from it: the man made of words.[48]

A third characteristic: while all human cultures use words that have a logic and grammar underlying them, Nicholas Wolterstorff says that language has a code to it that is grounded in a logic peculiar to human communities: "To understand the role of language in human society we have to add to the code the use of that code in actions of discourse."[49] This is the theory behind the work of John L. Austin and John Searle. Austin would argue that saying "word and deed" is repeating oneself because speaking one's word *is* a deed, an action: "The uttering of a sentence is the doing of an action, which would be described as just saying something."[50] To utter a few words in a sentence is not merely describing something but is actually doing it, language as performative utterance. In a wedding ceremony, for example, when the couple recite and pledge their vows to one another, in saying "I do" they are saying "I am indulging in it (the marriage)." According to Austin, this is a performative utterance: that is, such an utterance is the performing of an action more than the thought of just saying "I do."[51] For to say "I do" is to say "I promise," which obliges one to another person, thus

48. Scott Momaday, "The Story of the Arrowmaker," *Parabola*, Vol. 20, No. 3 (August 1995), p. 21.

49. Nicholas Wolterstorff, "Not Presence but Action: Calvin on Sacraments," *Perspectives*, Vol. 9, No. 3 (March 1994), p. 18.

50. J. L. Austin, *How to Do Things with Words* (Cambridge: Harvard University Press, 1975), p. 5.

51. Ibid., p. 6.

making a wedding a marriage, a union of a man and woman, transforming their very relationship with each other and scripting their role from two individuals into understanding each other as husband and wife. To say something is to do something. Austin makes it clear that, while some words are spoken as performatives, some speech acts are constatives. In uttering a performative, one does something; in uttering a constative, one merely says something.

A fourth characteristic: in a speech-act-as-gesture, there are always a speaker, a hearer, and the act itself, says Stanley Fish. What stands out as most important in the utterance of speech is the intention of the speaker behind what is being said and the predisposition of the hearer. A corollary to this in the area of gesture is that there are the intention of the gesturer, the one who is being gestured to, and the gesture itself. According to Wittgenstein, we are caught up in a language game

> in which words are responsible not to what is real, but to what has been laid down as real by a set of constitutive rules; the players of the game are able to agree that they mean the same thing by their words, not because they see the same things, but because they are predisposed by the fact of being in the game to see them, to pick them out.[52]

Taking part in a communicative or performative act requires a narrative setting, a group of people where the speaker and hearer must be in appropriate relationship with one another for the words to be understood.[53] Fish bases his argument on his reading of John Searle, who later took Austin's idea of speech as performative utterance and emphasized that to speak a language as a performative utterance is to indeed engage in a "highly complex rule-governed form of behavior." The speech act is a gestured performance, or in this case a performative utterance, which, when performed,

52. Fish, *Is There a Text in This Class?* pp. 198-199.

53. Fish, p. 241. Also, theologians James McClendon and James Smith write that speech acts have the following conditions that need to be met: first, the precondition of the speaker and the hearer knowing a common language; the primary condition of the speaker making a request or sentence, with the sentence as a way of making a request; the representative or descriptive condition concerning the exactness of the request; finally, the affective or psychological condition, in which the speaker wants the requested state of affairs to pass. "The representative and affective conditions make for the meaningfulness of an utterance whose primary condition is that it belongs to language, as a possible move in that language." See James McClendon and James Smith, *Understanding Religious Convictions* (Notre Dame: University of Notre Dame Press, 1975), pp. 59, 63.

uses symbols, words, and sentences according to rules agreed on by a people living together.[54]

Gesture as speech act can both be misleading and contain the possibility of being a joke, provoking something humorous. In other words, in speaking to others, people can lie as well as tell the truth. Terrence Tilley writes that expressive language is defective and most unsuccessful if what one presumes to be true is actually false. One way to understand a false speech act or performative utterance is to examine the speaker's intent.[55] Rebecca Chopp writes that "words themselves are fixed neither by their essences nor by self-referentiality, but by their context, the cultural practices in which they are used, by the interests of the person using them, and by one sign's relation to other signs."[56] What Chopp helps us understand is that we decide if a speech act is false or a lie not only if it is misspoken on the part of the speaker but also if it is not congruous with the context in which it is spoken or heard.

Speech act theory in general is important in clarifying the many ways that Christians depend on gestures. However, gestures not readily seen by the eye and thus considered invisible — such as the neuromuscular activity engaged in oral communication — are important for understanding speech act theory. The gesture of a speech act is an act of mind and body. If we understand gestures to be physical acts of the body (or nonaction strategically planned) that are performed by one's will and understood within the context of people who share such gestures in common, then a performative utterance as speech act is a gesture.

In sum, there are some key features of gestures in cultural anthropology and speech act theories that are applicable to how I deal with Christly gestures in this book. I want to continue to make gestures central to our education of Christians. For example, because the church is not like other cultures in many ways, given its origin in Christ, it does not merely have a pattern of gestures that represents a culture. The church is God's gesture to the world. Christians do not merely have practices of gestures; rather, our very beings *are* a gesture of God's doing: we exist because we are God's creative gesture, created to praise and worship him. In a larger sense, gestures are our minds, bodies, and spirits in Christ's mind, body, and spirit.

54. J. R. Searle, *An Essay on the Philosophy of Language* (Cambridge: University of Cambridge Press, 1969), p. 16.55.

55. Terrence Tilley, *The Evils of Theodicy* (Washington, DC: Georgetown University Press, 1991), p. 19.

56. Chopp in Tilley, p. 31.

CHAPTER FOUR

Christly Gestures in Christ's Body

There is a kind of universal language, consisting of expressions of the face, gestures and tone of voice, which shows whether a person means to ask for something and get it, or refuse it and have nothing to do with it.

St. Augustine[1]

Small gestures reveal larger truths.

Bill Morrison[2]

The gestures we perform today are not *sui generis*, freely composed and created as we roll along in life. The opposite is true: all gestures practiced by Christians are of the church, which is Christ's body. Many gestures are ancient in origin, gestures first performed in the early church as recorded in Scripture, such as the Eucharist (1 Cor. 11) or the singing of psalms (Col. 3); some are no longer commonly practiced among all Christians, for example, the holy kiss. Other gestures are born of the tradition of the church's heri-

1. St. Augustine, *Confessions* (New York: Penguin Books, 1979), p. 29.

2. Bill Morrison's review of Billy Bob Thornton's movie *Sling Blade*, "Poetic *Sling Blade* cuts to the Truth," *The News and Observer*, Raleigh, North Carolina, Feb. 14, 1997, p. 4.

tages, such as bowing or genuflecting before the cross of Christ, or the gesture of kneeling as an act of confession and prayer. Other gestures are shaped by a single parish's tradition, which may employ its own theologically laden gestures.

The practice of such gestures in a congregation enacts what George Lindbeck calls the

> comprehensive interpretive schemes, [which are] usually embodied in myths or narratives, and heavily ritualized, [structuring] human experience and understanding of self and world.[3]

Gestures are part of the interpretive schemes and are a communal phenomenon constituted and reconstituted by a cultural and linguistic framework that shapes the entirety of life and thought. The means by which this constitutive act occurs is through a vocabulary of discursive or linguistic symbols, together with a distinctive grammar in which this vocabulary can be meaningfully deployed.[4]

The distinctive grammar of the gestures we employ is self-evident among the Christians with whom we live. Our Christly gestures are peculiar in the sense that they can be comprehended only as something performed by Christians and may not be understood by those outside the church. Because we are Christians, we embody gestures differently than do others — and at different times than do others in our various social groupings. It is important to understand that our gestures of charity or peace, for example, learned and performed within the church, are not necessarily the gestures of charity or peace performed in other religious groups or in the secular world at large, though they may seem similar in some ways. We learn of these distinctions in the church, where we are schooled in a grammar of gestures that controls how we know God and others. Christ's body is the authoritative body that determines the gestures we must all perform for the common good of the body.

The church embodies a people who become a living place of revelation where doctrines, creeds, confessions, cosmic stories, myths, and ethical directives are formed in the congregation's gestures. Such a vocabulary of gestures in a church is well documented by students of Ruel Tyson, James Peacock, and Daniel Patterson, who observed the following in churches of the American South:

3. George Lindbeck, *Nature of Doctrine* (Philadelphia: Westminster Pub. Co., 1984), p. 32.

4. Ibid., p. 33.

> A pair of raised arms and closed eyes . . . a Bible held in the upward arm of a preacher . . . the cadences and intonations of "Praise God!" and "Thank you, Jesus" . . . moistened faces and shaking bodies . . . the cacophony of drums and stomping feet . . . and the hum of silence.[5]

Tyson, Peacock, and Patterson all argue that long before there is a denominational status or theological tradition per se, a "religion" first appears in the world in a set of gestures that are the elementary forms of its life. Prior to the condition of individual conscience or soul, before declarations of belief by a member, a religion displays itself in the language of gestures, spoken and enacted by individuals and embedded in the culture of a congregation. Gesture is not distinguished from belief and ritual; it enfolds both belief and the rituals of worship. At the moment of the believer's reflection, gestures fold into the abstractions of "belief" and "ritual."[6] In the gestures we perform as Christians among Christians, people will see, hear, touch, and be moved by the one who has faith in us — Jesus Christ.

Given the previous chapter's primary focus on the union of body and mind in gestures, I turn now to the task of finding where we may witness this broad description of Christly gestures in which the presence of the Spirit is more noticeable — in the rubrics of a church's life. Karl Barth's *Evangelical Theology* is helpful in this endeavor because he addresses the "catholic" nature of the church, emphasizing the certain continuity and unity of the theology we Protestants and Catholics share, which is "God of the Gospel," grounded in the church's practices:[7]

> Such theology intends to apprehend, to understand, and to speak of the God of the Gospel . . . . This is the God who reveals himself in the Gospel, who himself speaks to men [and women] and acts among and upon them.[8]

Barth considers the context of the church to be the place of great theological work; I will use his pattern of the theological task of the church as a key rubric or rule of habits, in which the habits of the Spirit are more obvious than the habits of body and mind in the gestures we perform.[9]

5. Ann Hawthorne, "Introduction — Method and Spirit: Studying the Diversity of Gestures in Religion," in Ruel Tyson, James Peacock, Daniel Patterson, eds., *Diversities of Gifts* (Urbana and Chicago: University of Illinois Press, 1988), p. 3.

6. Ibid., p. 13.

7. Karl Barth, *Evangelical Theology* (Grand Rapids: Wm. B. Eerdmans, 1992), p. 5.

8. Ibid., pp. 5-6.

9. A rubric here is understood to be an authoritative or established rule, tradition or custom.

Gestures Comprising Christ's Body in General

Barth writes that the Word of God, Jesus Christ,

> insists upon being enunciated by the choir of its primary witnesses. The community represents the secondary witnesses, the society of men called to believe in, and simultaneously to testify to, the Word in the world.[10]

Barth continues:

> The community is confronted and created by the Word of God. It is . . . the communion of the saints, because it is . . . the gathering of the faithful. As such it is the confederation of the witnesses who may and must speak because they believe. The community does not speak with words alone. It speaks by the very fact of its existence in the world; by its characteristic attitude to world problems; and, moreover and especially, by its silent service to all the handicapped, weak, and needy in the world. It speaks, finally, by the simple fact that it prays for the world. It does all this because this is the purpose of its summons by the Word of God.[11]

If speaking is a gesture, then it is possible that the very gesture of the church's existence is God's gesture, as God literally and figuratively spoke the church into existence in Jesus Christ, the living Word of God who dwelt among us. I've already suggested in Part I that Christ's body itself embodies a certain peculiar *polis,* with particular ways that we live among one another as members of Christ, constituted by the reality of God's reign as our common destination in life's pilgrimage. And there are certain performed gestures that are "so common to Christians that we hardly notice their significance," such as peace and compassion.[12] I will provide a fuller description of some of the gestures that we perform in common as Christians, as well as gestures that are peculiar to the different gifts and services of the body of Christ.

10. Barth, p. 37.

11. Ibid., p. 38.

12. Stanley Hauerwas, *In Good Company* (Notre Dame: University of Notre Dame Press, 1995), p. 6.

Common Gestures We Perform for the Unity of Christ's Body

It is important to underscore that we must all learn and practice *common gestures* that are central to God's story, revealing the unity of our many stories in the oneness of Christ's body. The performance of common gestures happens more than in our worship together on Sunday mornings or on holy days, though they are centrally located in worship. We need to be schooled in our understanding of the complexity of performing certain Christian gestures in every part of our lives. For example, we need to know when it is appropriate to extend the hand of Christian friendship as the church to strangers, as well as when to practice the discipline that calls for some people to be confronted for actions that undermine the trust that is essential for Christ's body.

One of the first tasks that I will highlight in this chapter concerns the need to rediscover and reclaim the centrality of the common gestures that we share as Christians. What are some of these common gestures? In light of the discussion of Christ's body in Part I, particularly Romans 12, I will use Romans 12:9-21 to show some of the gestured practices of the church that will take a lifetime to learn and practice, given that our "school" of instruction is the church in the world:

> Let love be genuine; hate what is evil, hold fast to what is good; love one another with mutual affection; outdo one another in showing honor. Do not lag in zeal, be ardent in spirit, serve the Lord. Rejoice in hope, be patient in suffering, persevere in prayer. (Rom. 12:9-12)

Gerhard Lohfink lists other imperatives in the Epistles: welcome one another (Rom. 15:7); greet one another with a holy kiss (Rom. 16:16); wait for one another (1 Cor. 11:33); have the same care for another (1 Cor. 12:25); be servants of one another (Gal. 5:13); bear one another's burdens (Gal. 6:2); comfort one another (1 Thess. 5:11). Acknowledging that this is not quite an exhaustive list, Lohfink points to the rich theme of togetherness found in this New Testament ecclesiology. It is important to Paul that one of the clear signs of being this body is that we demonstrate for all the world to see that we are responsible for one another, are accountable to one another for the common good of Christ's body.[13] However, the common good of this union is Christ, where this list becomes all the more important — and all the more peculiar to those who are outside of this redeemed community. What will come to play

13. Gerhard Lohfink, *Jesus and Community* (New York: Paulist Press, 1979), pp. 99-100.

an important part in learning these gestures is creating a self- and social-awareness of the impact these gestures have on others in Christ's body, as well as the world around us. Along with gestures of mutual reciprocity will be the process of learning which gestures to practice when, and for what purpose, in our daily lives.

Lohfink's above list includes certain gestures that every member of the Christ's body should and could perform. Father Herbert McCabe says that gestures embody some of the principal virtues that bear on our friendship with God — namely, faith, hope, and charity — and on our friendship with other people — justice, courage, self-control, and good sense. McCabe is quite clear that for every virtue there is a "settled disposition" or kind of habit, "acquired by practice," or, in our terms, "performed gestures," that we are to pursue and learn in order to cultivate the virtues of the church's culture.[14]

For example, consider faith: we are to practice and cultivate a life in which we rely more on the gift of faith, which we acquire through grace by learning to live in God. It is through faith that we desire to perform the gesture of prayer, the gesture of reflection on the mysteries revealed to us in life, the gesture of listening to and reading Scripture, and the other gestures of worship. We practice hope, a "divinely given disposition by which we respond to and cooperate with God's providence,"[15] when we engage in prayer. One does not necessarily need to move one's lips in order to pray; minimal movement of the body may also be considered prayer, depending on the context and the intent of the one praying.

How practical are the gestures for our daily life? Consider the "rules of the Christian household" in Colossians:

> Children, obey your parents in everything, for this is your acceptable duty in the Lord. Fathers, do not provoke your children, or they may lose heart. . . . Conduct yourselves wisely toward outsiders, making the most of the time. Let your speech always be gracious, seasoned with salt, so that you may know how you ought to answer everyone. (Col. 3:20-21; 4:5-6)

This passage establishes a "code of conduct" of not only what, how, and when we are to practice certain gestures among one another, but, equally important, *why* we do what we do with one another as sisters and brothers in the

14. Herbert McCabe, *The Teaching of the Catholic Church* (London: Incorporated Catholic Truth Society, 1985), p. 29.

15. Ibid., pp. 32-33.

church. The question that emerges from these Scripture passages is, How does one perform them all? The good news is that these gestures are sometimes performed for each other — in the name of another or of Christ — and sometimes they are performed by another person when we are incapable of the gesture. Why do we perform gestures for others and let them perform gestures in our name? Because we are Christ's body. We cannot learn them by ourselves, nor can we perform them by ourselves. The reason we practice these things together is that we are called to be the church. For we, the church of Christ, provide a way for the world to understand who our Creator is, for we know who our Redeemer is — the One whose gesture of creation created us. The gestures of the body of Christ keep it in motion, for this body is dynamic. Yet this is not of our own doing, for the church is bound to God's time, *kairos,* moving as it will by the impulse of God's Spirit, its gestures and movement narrated by God's story. For if the body is not moving as the body of Christ, it is either filled with great discord and dissension or prone to lethargy, if not atrophy.

Different Gestures for Different Gifts in Christ's Body

While there are certain gestures that we need to learn, know, and perform in common, there are also differing gestures for the different gifts and services of Christ's body. In Romans, Paul says that there is one body, and in this one body the many members are integrally dependent "one of another" (Rom. 12:5). Along with the common gestures that we are all called to practice as "individually members one of another," we are also called to practice more specialized or specific gestures, given the measure of the gift of grace uniquely bestowed on each of us while God was forming us: "For it was you who formed my inward parts; you knit me together in my mother's womb. I praise you, for I am fearfully and wonderfully made" (Psalm 139:13-14).

Consider the various "gifts" (Romans) of God's grace for different functions within the body that Paul writes about throughout Romans:

> Prophecy, in proportion to faith; ministry, in ministering; the teacher, in teaching; the exhorter, in exhortation; the giver, in generosity; the leader, in diligence; the compassionate, in cheerfulness.

In 1 Corinthians 12:4-11 and Ephesians 4:11-13, there are similar lists of varieties of gifts. These gifts and services of God are to be manifest in the Christian community, most likely through an accompanying gesture that "makes good" on the promises of God as articulated in Paul's letters.[16] Amid gestures that we practice in common, we are also to practice gestures that reveal — in their performance — our place and function in the "building up the body of Christ," as we and the saints before us have been so equipped in the work of Christ's ministry (Eph. 4:12).

To explain this in greater detail: first, it is important for us to comprehend that not all the members have the same role or function in this body, but each has a different gift in the body, "according to the grace given to us" (Rom. 12:4, 6). I propose that we start taking this list of gifts of the Spirit more seriously in the church in general, understanding both what and how we are educating, and always with an eye on why we educate: to build up Christ. Here is the "both/and" of Christ's body: we are both to learn the gestures that, in general, build up the body of Christ, ensuring the hope in the oneness of the common good, so that we all live together in the "more excellent way"; and secondly, we are to learn the various individual gestures that are specific to the activity and service that each person has been created and called by the Holy Spirit to perform for the good of the body. There are specific gestures of those who teach, exhort, or minister; those who are called to be apostles; the healers; those who are given the gift of wisdom; the ones endowed with the gift of knowledge — each one has gestures that are specific to the gift of God's grace given to him or her.

Second, we must not forget the importance of the discernment process in discovering what gifts we have been given by God. Discernment is needed to help a person understand the source of a call, the direction of the call, and its content — and to respond appropriately. It is also needed to awaken one

16. Marjorie Procter-Smith, in her book *In Her Own Rite* (Nashville: Abingdon Press, 1990), says that there are some "liturgical actions and gestures [that] have more in common with gestures and symbols of dominance than of intimacy or equality." Procter-Smith wants to "create gestures of mutuality that can still serve the public, formal requirements of liturgical activity." Procter-Smith believes that "theologically the church has asserted that all members of the Body of Christ are equal. Thus we may begin by proposing the elimination of gestures and symbols that do not admit of this equality, or that cannot be made reciprocal" (pp. 82-83).

The problem with Procter-Smith's interpretation of the texts on the body of Christ is that there is no support for equality as understood in the American society today. The Apostle Paul makes it clear that in *this* body there is going to be a certain inequality, or God's rules will abide, which will create controversy in the world as it is, as "the members of the body that seem to be weaker are indispensable." Or is it precisely "those members we think less honorable we clothe with greater honor"? Therefore, is it not possible that those who may seem, according to the world's view, to be weaker are the ones who are indispensable, making those who think they are indispensable, dispensable?

who is "deaf" or "blind" or not capable of receiving God's call without the aid of others.[17] Having discerned these gifts along with the gestures we practice together as the one body of Christ, we need to categorize gestures into those that are particular to the gifts received from the Holy Spirit and those that are practiced corporately in the worship of God.

Third, in Acts 14:27, when Barnabas and Paul returned to Antioch, they "called the church together and related all that God had done with them, and how he had opened a door of faith for the Gentiles." The gestures of the individual members are to be learned among those who have also been given other gifts of grace. Each of us must learn, mature, and deepen in our appreciation of the gift, realizing the subtle and not-so-subtle ways we are to conform to practicing the gestures that embody the gifts we have received. We will always need to be in the company of others who are needing to be taught. It is the responsibility of the elders who know, perform, and embody the gestures to teach the young in passing on the tradition. And such practice will move from the simple and basic to the more involved and complex.

Fourth, instruction in the uniqueness of the gesture will need to be conducted among other members and their grace-filled and grace-inspired gestures. For, in the words of Paul, "If all were a single member, where would the body be?" (1 Cor. 12:19). It is in the "messiness," the often chaotic smugness, of church that we begin to get a glimmer of how our gifts and accompanying gestures fit into the mysterious oneness of the Christian body.

Gestures in Worship

Ernst Gombrich observes that the ritualized gestures of prayer, greeting, mourning at funeral rites, teaching, and triumph are among the first to be represented in art, for they capture a people in worship.[18] Barth hoped that ministers of the word and sacrament would understand that what is at stake in the life of the Christian community as we gather together in worship is the "quest for truth . . . [which] comes from the Word of God that founds the community and its faith."[19] It is in our worship together that we read Scripture, witness to the Word of God, articulate the dogmas, creeds, and confessions — which give us resistance to temptation — and practice the habits of

17. Suzanne G. Farnham, Joseph P. Gill, Taylor McLean, Susan Ward, eds., *Listening Hearts,* revised edition (Harrisburg: Morehouse Press, 1991), p. 23.

18. Gombrich, *The Essential Gombrich* (London: Phaidon Press, 1996), p. 117.

19. Barth, pp. 38-39.

prayer. Barth would argue that theology is not a separate task from the worshiping community of God: rather, theology is made incarnate among Christians worshiping together: "Theology is a service in and for the community and springs from the tradition of the community."[20]

The traditions of Christ's community are most brilliantly enacted in our times of worshiping together as God's people. In a metaphorical sense, we understand that a window has been opened by God's work and Word.[21] As we engage in the act of worshiping God, we may be most aware of the rituals that not only instruct us in the gestures of the Christian faith but also sustain us in the practice of the faith-filled gestures. It is interesting that, in many of the definitions of the term "ritual," the word "gesture" is often part of the definition. For example: "Ritual is the symbolic use of bodily movement and gesture in a social situation to express and articulate meaning."[22] Or this definition: "A ritual is non-discursive gestural language, institutionalized for regular occasions, to state sentiments and mystiques that a group values and needs."[23]

For the church, liturgy is understood as the work and praise of God's people. God exercises freely in our humanity through the humanity and divinity of the risen Christ. Jean Corbon says that it is through incarnation to crucifixion and resurrection that liturgy becomes for us the way of knowing and being in the incorruptible body of life.[24] Liturgy involves the ritual performance of the people of God in the "business" of the church.[25] Each Christian denomination has its own description, bound in its storied practices, of the purpose of worship.[26] For example, Presbyterians believe that

> worship is at the very heart of the church's life. All that the church is and does is rooted in its worship. The community of faith, gathered in response

20. Ibid., p. 44.

21. Ibid., p. 161.

22. Robert Bocock, *Ritual in Industrial Society: A Sociological Analysis of Ritualism in Modern England* (London: Allen & Unwin, 1974), p. 37.

23. Orrin Klapp, *A Collective Search for Identity* (New York: Holt, Rinehart & Winston, 1969), p. 121.

24. Jean Corbon, *The Wellspring of Worship* (Mahwah, NJ: Paulist Press, 1988), p. 39.

25. Hauerwas, *In Good Company*, p. 248.

26. In his book *Where Two or Three Are Gathered* (Cleveland: Pilgrim Press, 1995), Harmon Smith writes that Christian worship "plainly ought to be, and can be, a *purposeful* action. And it *is* purposeful when it is true and faithful to itself, when it acknowledges the holiness of God, when it hears God's word, offers prayer, and celebrates the sacraments" (p. 135).

> to God's call, is formed in its worship. Worship is the principal influence that shapes our faith, and is the most visible way we express the faith.[27]

Central to worship is the faith that the presence of Christ, who is the source of life, has empowered the church to serve God in the world. The church at worship employs gestures that embody the traditions and theologically laden rituals of God's people. Worship is the place of education in the gestures of Christ's body. Kathleen Norris observes:

> In liturgy we act out something that has been handed down to us, and in making it our own we are also responding to the *mysterium tremendum.* Taking the playful aspects of liturgy into account, we need also to recognize the utterly serious attitudes and intentions of those involved, and the serious effect it has on them. For the monk the play of liturgy is a means of conversion, a way of life. In its deeper satisfactions it confers an abiding sense of peace. . . . Liturgy must be a daily affair, a chore. They need to act it out, making the circle, singing and saying and hearing the words again and again, as a child asks to hear a beloved story many times over.[28]

Worship is that place and moment in which we among others in gestures of prayer praise God, where we are caught up in a "hot house," a "laboratory of experimentation," of gestures being learned and practiced knowingly or unknowingly. Watching my children and other children worship, I have seen them mimic our adult gestures of prayer and singing and try out new gestures along with the congregation. Slowly but surely, they are getting the knack of our Christly gestures. Furthermore, liturgy is a means of teaching and learning the performance of Christly gestures. Phillip Pfatteicher says that liturgical language and gesture creates a new situation:

> Liturgy is composed of conjunctions of signs and sounds, words and actions, that function as avenues of divine service — of both God's service to us, and our service to God. Liturgical language therefore consists of sensible and sensuous words and signs together, for the words, especially the words of liturgy, are active, performative words, which do not simply describe or communicate existing situations but which create new situations.[29]

27. *Book of Common Worship* (Louisville: Westminster/John Knox Press, 1993), p. 1.
28. Kathleen Norris, *Dakota* (New York: Ticknor and Fields, 1993), p. 216.
29. Phillip Pfatteicher, *The School of the Church* (Valley Forge: Trinity Press International, 1995), p. 24.

A gesture does not need to be accompanied by words: it is itself a statement. In liturgy, gestures speak a powerful language to those who have eyes to see, such as the simple movement of bowing before the cross or altar in a Roman Catholic or Episcopal church as an expression of prayer for consecration by the Holy Spirit. Those who witness the gesture "should be able to read in it the meaning of the sign. The faithful should see the inner sense of the outward sign, without which the actions would be a waste of time and energy."[30] Even the gathering of congregants in worship is the foremost example of a gesture of Christian community, as "we gather from diverse places to perform our liturgy with water, a book, bread, and wine."[31]

Pfatteicher says that anything less than the active practice of gesture in worship risks taking away the vitality of the spoken word as speech act. He is wary of congregations who depend too much on printed texts, "for the practice of liturgy, the living experience of performative speech acts, is deadened through excessive dependence on printed texts."[32]

Hauerwas proposes that worship and Christian social ethics are both gestures:

> Nothing in life is more important than gestures, as gestures embody as well as sustain the valuable and significant. Through gestures we create and form our worlds. Through gestures we make contact with one another and share common tasks. Through gestures we communicate and learn from each other the limits of the world.[33]

Through the liturgy of the church Christians engage in a social action that takes our contorted lives, our misconceived perceptions of the Christian life, our crooked walk of individualistic narcissism, and realigns us so that we may hear, see, and be moved by the story of God. The liturgy of the church calls forth a practice of gestures that are not of self but are of God's people as we gather together in prayer, confessing our sins to God and one another, singing praises to God for the gift of redemption, hearing the Word of God proclaimed and explicated, seeing the sacramental gestures enacted, and receiving the blessings of the Almighty as we are sent into the world to love and serve the Lord.[34]

30. Ibid., p. 26.

31. Ibid.

32. Ibid.

33. Stanley Hauerwas, *Christian Existence Today* (Durham, NC: Labyrinth Press, 1988), p. 107.

34. *Book of Common Worship,* p. 78.

Every Protestant denomination, the nondenominational churches, the Roman Catholic Church, the Greek and Eastern Orthodox Churches, and intentional Christian communities — each one has its own liturgical order of worship, and each presents for us the unique differences among the Christian denominations. For example, American Presbyterians follow an order of worship that makes the preaching moment central, while Episcopalians, Roman Catholics, and Greek and Eastern Orthodox communities practice the Eucharist weekly, if not daily, as a central sacrament in their worship. In some churches, including Pentecostal and other charismatic bodies, more obvious external bodily gestures are performed corporately as part of the worshiping life, whereas the churches of the Reformed, Anabaptist, and Quaker traditions have fewer physical corporate motions. In practicing the externals of liturgical words, signs, and gestures, we begin to shape the substance of true liturgical spirituality. According to Goethe,

> In every new situation we must start all over again like children, cultivate a passionate interest in things and events, and begin by taking delight in externals, until we have the good fortune to grasp the substance.[35]

Balthasar Fischer focuses on some of the gestures that are central to the worshiping life of parishes following the Roman liturgy. Fischer, like Goethe, believed that it is by the practice of the signs, words, and gestures that we may have the good fortune to grasp the substance of Christian life, which is grace, a gift from God (John 6:44).[36] One gesture Fischer describes is what it means to be sealed with the sign of the cross, dating back to the third century and made by mothers on their children's foreheads, which means, "You were baptized, my child. May he to whom you have belonged since then continue to protect you."[37] When the priest opens a communicant's hands from a fist during prayer, this "old gesture of prayer" is a sermon in itself as we extend our empty hands to God, "dependent on him who fills my empty hands with his gifts."[38] When receiving the body of Christ, with left hand on right hand, we are practicing a gesture that has been done for over sixteen hundred years:

> They were to form a kind of throne with their hands and to receive the heavenly king on it: the right hand is the base of the throne, and the left

35. Quoted in Balthasar Fischer, *Signs, Words and Gestures* (New York: Pueblo Pub. Co., 1979), Introduction.

36. Ibid., p. xii.

37. Ibid., p. 2.

38. Ibid., p. 27.

> forms the seat. . . . It is as though the eucharistic minister had told you: "Look! Your king is coming to you!" and you answered: "Yes, and I build a throne for him with my hands, a little altar of my own."[39]

The liturgical practices themselves usually take place within a building, a physical structure called a "sanctuary," which is itself a loving gesture of God's people in praise of Jesus Christ. For example, a bad church spire is weighed down and bulky, while a good one aspires to be almost weightless, springing forth like an arrow into the sky to the Most High.[40] Many of the Gothic cathedrals throughout Europe were constructed as the people's gesture of honor, of thanksgiving and adoration to God for his tender mercies to the people in the villages, towns, and cities. These cathedrals and chapels were gestures of the faith of God's people, with the elaborate stonework statuary of the kings, queens, prophets, judges, and the Holy Family surrounding the outside of the cathedrals and adorning the inside of this sacred space. The soaring buttresses, the lofty towers, the mighty doors, the cruciform floorplan pattern of the sanctuary itself, the jewel-like placement of stained glass windows — all embraced Scripture's narrative. Even the angry and threatening figures of the gargoyles that gape out over the edges of the boundaries of the church protect all who dwell inside from the evil outside and are gestures of God's people. Many scholars have called these cathedrals, from Cologne, Germany, to Lincoln Cathedral in England, the gospel carved in stone.[41]

As we the people worship in buildings of brick, stone, wood, clay or mud, and glass, our God-initiated movement within worship is often led by the physical patterns or habits of gestures that guide our worship. Such gestures of worship locate us and help us know our place within worship; they awaken us to the almost unnatural act of praising someone other than ourselves. In the churning cacophony of Christ-modeled gestures, some ancient and some not so ancient, intricately scripted by God's story and practiced repeatedly by Christians, we are inspired to the very marrow of our bones by the Holy Spirit with the divine knowledge of what it means to be God's people.

39. Ibid., p. 76.

40. Blackmur, *Language as Gesture,* p. 7.

41. For a great illustration of the people's works with these cathedrals, read David Macaulay, *Cathedral* (Boston: Houghton Mifflin Company, 1973).

Gestures as the Prayers of God's People

Karl Barth says: "The first and basic act of theological work is prayer . . . where theology is concerned, the rule *'Ora et labora!'* is valid under all circumstances — pray and work. Work must be that sort of act that has the manner and meaning of a prayer in all its dimensions, relationships and movements."[42]

Prayer as a dimension of work and of relationship with God and his people is a gesture we must be taught and must practice, for it is a practice learned within the context of God's people. Hauerwas says:

> If one wants to learn to pray, one had better know how to bend the body. Learning the gesture and posture of prayer is inseparable from learning to pray. Indeed, gestures are prayers.[43]

Consider the use of hands in prayer. Romano Guardini says of praying with hands flat together:

> It speaks of firm control, of overmastering homage. It is a humble, well-ordered telling of our own mind, and an attentive, ready hearing of God's word . . . we must not make of it an idle artistic play; but it must speak for us, so that in very truth the body may say to God what the soul means.[44]

For an example of prayer as gesture, consider Susan Rhymer's story of a family trip to the various Catholic missions outposts in California. Her tall father always had to duck his head to get through low doorways. Tired of always having to do this, he asked the guide why the doorways were so low. The guide responded that it was because the Catholic missionaries wanted to be sure that those who were coming to their homes or chapels would always have to assume the position or gesture of prayer, which they would not have done unless they were forced to bow. The hope of the Catholic missionaries and priests was that the simple gesture of forced prayer would soften the hearts of the enemies.

Or consider the prayer habit of children around the dinner table. Rushing around to get food on the table for dinner, I would sit down and quickly want to start eating, only to be stopped by one of my young children,

42. Barth, *Evangelical Theology,* p. 160.

43. Hauerwas, "Gestures of a Truthful Story," in *Christian Existence Today,* pp. 106-107.

44. Romano Guardini, *Sacred Signs* (London: Sheed & Ward, 1930), p. 8.

who would announce with alarm, "We forgot to pray!" We would drop our utensils, hold hands, and commence with a prayer, softly giggling at being told by the youngest member of the family that we had forgotten a right and good gesture of thankful prayer. Prayer opens us up toward heaven and God's work and word. Prayer makes sure that the realm of theology, as Barth says, is "no larger and better than the realm of human questions and answers, human inquiry, thought, and speech."[45]

Gestures in Service and Mission in the Body of Christ

At the end of the Parable of the Great Banquet (Luke 14:15-24), the servant is sent out by the host to go and compel people to come to the banquet feast. The fascinating thing about this parable is that the servant — who, we understand, is Jesus — is sent out into the world, for there is still room at the table. What does this story have to do with us and the gestures of service today? To begin with, we the redemptive body of Christ have been sent out into the world to witness to each generation, to tell people the good news of God's invitation to the banquet, the kingdom of God. And this telling, which is usually delineated as being accomplished in word and deed, is really all gesture.

Barth was clear about the duties of the Christian community. Because we serve the Word of God through our projects and institutions, what Christ's community does or does not do or say is important; for we must remember in word and deed that we have been called to proclaim God's Word to the world.[46]

More importantly, God has a bias toward the poor. Any acts of compassion toward those who are suffering, of healing and comforting the wounded, and of rejoicing with those in celebration are gestures that make an indelible mark on us. Such marks are a combination of a practice and a sign, or what Michel de Certeau regards as a "crossing point between the language of society and the enunciation of faith . . . surmounting the rupture between the two."[47] The mark can be a gesture or a miracle, a sanctuary or a charismatic priest, or a devotional relic. The gesture as a mark helps focus religious expression on a particular action in which everything is concentrated on the practice itself.

45. Barth, *Evangelical Theology*, p. 161.

46. Ibid., pp. 191-192.

47. Michel de Certeau, *The Writing of History* (New York: Columbia University Press, 1988), p. 162.

Finally, what are some of the gestures that we practice as servants of Christ? Consider the "charge" given by the minister at the end of the worship service:

> Go out into the world in peace; have courage; hold on to what is good; return no one evil for evil; strengthen the fainthearted; support the weak, and help the suffering; honor all people; love and serve the Lord, rejoicing in the power of the Holy Spirit.[48]

Each one of the lines in this charge is a Christian community practice; it calls forth a certain gesture that, as it is performed, becomes a distinctive habit marking us as Christians in this world. As in all the other parts of worship, our bodies, minds, and spirits become habituated to a certain posture and to responding in a certain way to the circumstance before us. For example, going out into the world "in peace" means performing a certain gesture of peace. As Hauerwas says repeatedly, "We practice the peace of Christ which is different than the peace understood in the world." Courage is a virtue learned in the performance of courageous gestures. Holding on to what is good involves both knowing what is good according to the gospel of God and practicing that gesture. "Return no one evil for evil" is clearly a distinctive Christian practice of specific gestures in a world that more often "returns evil for evil." In the end, "to honor all people" and "love and serve the Lord, rejoicing in the power of the Holy Spirit," are habits that must be performed over time amid the pattern of gestures that boldly remind Christians whose we are: Christ's body.[49] In performing gestures that are outlined and articulated in the "Charge," we give flesh to the story of the gospel of God not only in the church but also among the peoples of a disbelieving world. Clearly, we need to hear and see the words of Scripture made visible in the Christian community every week, as we learn and perform the faith-filled, grace-lined gestures that are becoming the habits of our lives. In exercising the gestures of faith over a period of time, in various settings and among different people, we will become more astute about knowing which gestures to perform when, and perhaps witness the unleashing of the Holy Spirit in the world through the power of the simplest but most meaningful gestures. It will often be the simplest gesture, well rehearsed, that may embolden us to be the body of Christ when we feel most insecure about our actions.

48. *Book of Common Worship,* p. 78.

49. See L. Gregory Jones, *Embodying Forgiveness* (Grand Rapids: Wm. B. Eerdmans Pub. Co., 1995), p. 163.

CHAPTER FIVE

Christly Gestures: Performing Scripture

> *I often ask myself what makes a story work, and what makes it hold up as a story, and I have decided that it is probably some action, some gesture of a character that is unlike any other in the story, one which indicates where the real heart of the story lies.*
>
> Flannery O'Connor[1]

What makes Flannery O'Connor's stories "work" is probably what makes God's story work as well: there is often a word or wordless gesture by one character — often a physically, spiritually, or morally hideous one, a weak character who is undeniably human — whose very gesture is the mystical breaking in of God's light of grace on the darkness surrounding our fallen condition. O'Connor writes that at times even the devil is the performer of such a grace-filled gesture, thereby undoing his own work in his own backyard. Like O'Connor's stories, Holy Scripture itself is a resplendent account of particular fallible and unremarkable people performing certain gestures at just the right moment, revealing God's great sense of cosmic timing in human history. Consider the stories of David the sheepherder; Moses' quiet birth and adoption by the enemy; Sarah's miraculous bearing of Isaac; the strong bond of friendship

1. Flannery O'Connor, *Mystery and Manners* (New York: Farrar, Straus, and Giroux, Inc., 1991), p. 111.

of Ruth and Naomi; Jeremiah, the young boy; Joseph, Mary's husband-to-be; and Paul, who used to be Saul, to name just a few.

In the gestures of these lives, our forebears display the truth that God chose — and continues to choose — the most unlikely characters to be the living embodiment of grace upon grace. This is made possible when our very lives are swept up into a greater involvement in gestures of Christ's body — from the simplest to the most complex. Likewise, God gives us the gift of Scripture, the story of God in human history, to be the authoritative script that speaks to us today, with the aid of the working, praying, thoughtful, and interpretive community of Christ's body among us. With human hearts and minds engaged in becoming more like Christ, and the inward working of God's Spirit, our lives are choreographed — with the motion of legs and arms, feet and hands, as well as our tongues — to enact the salvation story in our daily lives. This sentiment is captured beautifully in these words of St. Teresa of Avila:

> Christ has no body now but yours,
> no hands but yours,
> no feet but yours.
> Yours are the eyes through which
> Christ's compassion must look out on the world.
> Yours are the feet with which
> He is to go about doing good.
> Yours are the hands with which
> He is to bless us now.[2]

In this section I will focus on the way Scripture and the spoken creeds and written confessions of the church continually create, guide, and nurture the gestures we perform, all inscribing the way we are to live with one another and God in the performance of gestures. In a sense, gestures in the church not only have a story but are the story gesturally performed. Take the example of the game of baseball. Ron Shelton says that baseball is like a stage in the same way that soundstages in Hollywood re-created the nineteenth-century American West: it is a world of rules and lines; there are parameters for certain gestures on the baseball field that all players understand and accept. Outside of the context of a baseball field, however, the gestures mean little if anything.[3]

2. Quoted in Ronald Rolheiser, *The Holy Longing* (New York: Doubleday, 2000), p. 73.

3. Steve Rea, "Ron Shelton: Covering the bases with Ty Cobb," *News and Observer*, Raleigh, NC, January 22, 1995, p. 9G.

As a church, we too exist in a "world of rules and lines and games." Specific habits or the performance of certain gestures is narrated by a script — the Holy Bible — which not only forms but continually re-forms our malleable bodies, minds, and spirits in the image of the body of Christ. Scripture, as interpreted within the community of faith, is communicated by thoughtful study of its original languages, shaped by the rituals that find their root there, and highlighted by the various circumstances of life today. What kinds of current issues shape our reading? While the words might be the same, our interpretations of the texts change as God sometimes works outside the church to call us to a new reading of Scripture, for example, concerning our attitudes on slavery or the role of women in the church, or the kind of family we are called to be in the household of God, to name but a few issues.

Christ's Body Narrates the Gestures

I have mentioned above that the Christian context in which the gestures are learned and performed is itself constituted and shaped by the larger narrative — the gospel — which in turn shapes us. In reproducing the story that first constituted the church, we are shaping stories for the future as the community is embodied in the gesture-bound rituals marking the boundaries and determining our gathering in Christ's name. The Christian performance of gestures is always an interpretive act in itself, consisting in the performance of a text that, according to Nicholas Lash, bears

> witness to one whose words and deeds, discourse and suffering, "rendered" the truth of God in human history. The performance of the New Testament enacts the conviction that these texts are most appropriately read as the story of Jesus, the story of everyone else, and the story of God.[4]

The gospel narrates our lives, gives us a pattern for our human actions, and teaches us how to live with one another in the context of the new covenant established by the sharing of Christ's blood for our lives. Lash says that what Jesus and his disciples "said [and did] and suffered," is what we as his disciples in our time and place have "said and done and suffered" in his name. In our using of the words as "Holy Scripture," it is not the script itself that is "holy" but the people, the community, the body of Christ who perform the script.[5]

4. Nicholas Lash, *Theology on the Way to Emmaus* (London: SCM Press, 1990), p. 37.
5. Ibid., p. 42.

In this section I will focus on how the large and small gestures we perform are guided, given their *modus operandi*, and made comprehensible in the greater context of the Christian story we have inherited. More precisely, what guides our practice of gestures as Christ's body is more than the story of Jesus' ministry; that story is given gravitas because of the Holy Spirit. Through Jesus' story, God's Spirit infuses, inspires, and guides our performance of gestures within the body of Christ. Furthermore, in practicing Christly gestures we communicate Jesus' story by embodying or enfleshing it; in turn, we are embodied into its ongoing narrative. It is no longer "I" alone telling the story but the ecclesial "we" of Christ's body who, in telling the story, are being absorbed into it. Christ's Spirit is made known in the narrated gestures that serve the church as we are guided by his story in giving purpose to our prayers in silence (i.e., *lectio divina);* it is enfleshed in the food we take to the hungry; is performed in our Christian community's practices of confession and forgiveness "in the name of Jesus Christ"; is given weight and substance in the celebration of baptism, the Eucharist, and the holy and ordinary days in the year.[6]

To better understand the relationship of story or narrative to our physical gesture, I propose that the storyteller who is gesturing Jesus' story is none other than the body of Christ at large — this is not the work of a lone individual. For when one member of Christ's body engages in the gesture of Christ's story, one does so *as* Christ's story. Second, in the gesture as Christ's body, we perform the story in the knowledge of the text itself, remembering the people who first lived it, the past communities who beheld it, and inspiring today's community where we interpret it and live it. Finally, in the practice of the gesture that is narrated by and embodied in Christ's story, we see that our character is formed by the storied gestures of God's people.

The Body of Christ as the Storyteller

If Christ is the embodiment of the story of God's love for the world, then isn't the body of Christ — in its wholeness — both the teller of the story of God's love and the ongoing, unfolding narrative of God's love for the world? The gestures we practice as Christ's body embody God's story, giving it a certain

6. I want to make clear in this book, as I have in my other writings, that "story" is to be understood or interpreted as broadly as possible. It is too often constricted among members of the academy to be something that is either read or heard. This too often allows people to make the text "disembodied," free from authorship or membership of a human body, free from cultural moorings.

kind of flesh and blood, muscle and sinew, that involve a movement of mind, body, and spirit in the world today. The implication is that, when the body of Christ tells the story of God, it may be heard either in the small voice of a child in the name of the church or in the action of an entire congregation when it, for example, calls for the shutdown of the School of the Americas in Fort Benning, Georgia.

In reflecting on the body of Christ as storyteller, let us first look at the connection between story and storyteller by using Gerard Loughlin's argument. Loughlin argues that the church tells its story by first comprehending that it is the story of Christ incarnate, and then by embodying Christ's story in the human circumstances of everyday life.[7] The gestures of Christ's people help us understand that people, not texts, can mean things. Scripture is alive in the gestures performed by a community.

Second, the story itself, which I will call "the text," can mean something only when it is used in context for some purpose, lived in some way among other people.[8] The relationship between a word and what it means is comprehended only within a community in which it is used and hence understood.[9] The story of Christ forms, sustains, and reconstitutes Christ's body and our gestures, making the story more than a mere "text." Again, as Loughlin points out, texts by themselves mean nothing; only texts-as-being-lived by women and men mean something. As Christ is constituted by and constitutive of God's story, the church becomes Christ Incarnate, telling and retelling God's story.

Third, the uniqueness of the storyteller in this case is that it is the entire body of Christ telling the story of God's love. When most people hear "storyteller," they think of a written text or an individual who tells stories with his or her voice — as if it were a solo voice in monologue. In the case of Christ's body, it is the entire body itself that tells the story as it lives the gospel through its many ongoing Christly gestures. Arthur Frank argues that Christ's body is a communicative body that practices storytelling of sacrifice for the good of the other:

7. Gerard Loughlin, *Telling God's Story* (New York: Cambridge University Press, 1996), p. 84.

8. Ibid., p. 137. Loughlin's point is important here, for it is clear that such a statement implies a historical-critical approach not shared by the present author toward interpreting Scripture. No text is free of cultural interpretation: there are no "tools" per se for interpreting texts free of cultural interpretation; and there is no way of reading a text apart from something called "culture." All reading of any text is a cultural interpretation.

9. Stanley Fish, *Is There a Text in This Class?* p. 32.

> The communicative body . . . is the traveler whom the Good Samaritan found robbed and beaten by the roadside. The communicative body also defines itself through the chaotic body (the wounded body) . . . [it] sees itself in the chaotic body, and finds inescapable the gesture of offering itself to that body.[10]

Our capacity and knowledge to act for the good of others, reaching out as a way of being, is a result of the gift of Jesus Christ.[11] Jesus sacrificed his body for the sake of our salvation, bearing witness to God's love for us all by the wounds on his body. It is amazing that the story of Jesus is made ever fresh in each new circumstance in which we embody the gospel in our gestures. Jesus is both the narrator of God's story and is himself God's story, and we are the hearers, the ones who receive and incarnate Jesus' story into the story we live.[12]

The Christian Story Determines the Performed Gestures

In the gestured performance of Scripture, we can comprehend the logic of our gestures as the gestures of Christ's body only because of the Christian community's explicit code of conduct, found in the creeds and confessions of the church, in which we not only profess what we believe as God's people but make explicit the good we have in common.[13] Gestures narrated by Scripture, the traditions, and the creeds are now gestures that make it possible for us to discern the good of the Christian community.

Let us investigate this in further detail. First, as Barry Hoffmaster suggests, the crucial test of a story might be the sort of person it shapes. Scripture's narrative teaches us about being human, discovering what is the good we share, what is virtuous. In the Christian story we discover what kind of

10. Arthur Frank, *The Wounded Storyteller* (Chicago: University of Chicago Press, 1996), p. 104. Frank goes on to say that for most people this gesture of offering care requires limits, for even the Good Samaritan went on about his business, paying the innkeeper to care for the injured man. Still, it was a gift of the communicative body.

11. See Therese Lysaught, "Sharing Christ's Passion: A Critique of the Role of Suffering in the Discourse of Biomedical Ethics from the Perspective of the Sick"(Ph.D. diss., Duke University, 1992).

12. James McClendon, Jr., *Systematic Theology: Doctrine* (Nashville: Abingdon, 1994), p. 40.

13. I am using "code of conduct" in the way that Karla Holloway argues that there is an ethical conduct that cultures have that "either implicitly or explicitly traces the architecture of ethnic identity." See Karla Holloway, *Code of Conduct* (New Brunswick: Rutgers University Press, 1995), p. 6.

people we are becoming in Christ because of God's story. In the gestures of telling and retelling this story, we are creating and re-creating our character.[14] We are thus bound in the church's traditions and its creeds and confessions, sustaining the practice of the very gestures first engendered by God's story. In retelling, we acquire a more mature comprehension of the story, capable of discerning the ways of Christ in more complex circumstances among members of this community.

Second, the reason we tell and retell stories is not only what we learn in the story's content but what we become as listeners to and receivers of the story. For example, in Proverbs we read that the way of learning wisdom is in both the words uttered and the life lived: "I have taught you the way of wisdom; I have led you in the paths of uprightness. When you walk, your step will not be hampered; and if you run, you will not stumble. Keep hold of instruction; do not let go; guard her, for she is your life" (Prov. 4:11-13). Not only is the student learning and absorbing the wisdom, but the one doing the telling — the one walking the path of righteousness — has become reengaged in the story, remembering the ways of the wise.

Third, one's very character is being formed and nurtured by the gestures narrated by Scripture. Hauerwas shows that our character — as well as the character of the community we live in — is acquired, continually formed, and sustained by our having certain intentions and convictions with every gesture we perform. Our character is initially composed and reconstituted by the gestured stories of Christ's community and its accompanying gestures. We are constituted not by our own story per se but by a thick composition of the many different stories and the accompanying roles we play in a culture, the stories that we shape in other people's lives, and those that shape and determine our lives.[15] We are more than one story; we are created by the many stories of life. Furthermore, at times our own stories may be primary, while at other times they may be secondary, serving to support other stories in our daily lives. And each one of us has multiple stories — as parents, children, teachers, ministers, consumers, runners, and partners simultaneously.

Finally, when it comes to learning and remembering the stories that determine what gestures we practice, repetition is a good thing. Repetition can create a rut, which is sometimes seen as a tired routine; on the other hand, to quote Wallace Stegner, "ruts are a sign [that] work is being done."[16] The gesture of repeating the well-told and well-performed story in a community can

14. Frank, p. 165.

15. Ibid., p. 132.

16. Wallace Stegner, *Crossing to Safety* (New York: Penguin Books, 1987), p. 150.

itself be the medium by which one becomes the story. And as we listen to and receive other people's stories, their stories become part of our story.

Another dynamic takes place in our repeating the story of God that changes us and our understanding of Scripture. Michael Casey says that in the West we have become accustomed to a "lineal logic: we begin at A and progress to Z."[17] Casey proposes that repetition is not necessarily bad and may be a great good, for in each repetition of a prayer prayed, a book read, and a song sung, something new may strike us. Casey even suggests slowing down in our reading — which is a gesture — because it is likely that we will catch sight of something unexpected. Casey closes with a beautiful example: repetition is like repainting a wall in a house; each coat overlaps the last and results in a smooth finish. Repetition of gestures is similar: the more we repeat them, the more polished they are.[18]

Or consider the practice of *lectio divina,* a form of praying and meditating on Scripture in which we recite Scripture often during the days, weeks, and months of the year. A change in our consciousness occurs when we practice *lectio divina* that is marked by two characteristics, according to Casey. First, a recession from ordinary "sensate and intellectual awareness" takes place; second, there is a sense of being possessed by the "reality and mystery of God." In *lectio divina* we learn to live in the grace of God: Christ "becomes the doer of our actions; in contemplation we become the subject of Christ's prayer."[19]

So every time we read a verse of Scripture, a varying level of penetration of the Word of God into our lives takes place. One could say that we absorb Scripture into our lives as we are likewise absorbed into the ongoing story of God's love for the world. Casey understands the nature of the repetitive motion of reading Scripture by way of *lectio divina:*

> The repetitive character of *lectio divina* means that we pass through the same territory several times during life. Each time we will find ourselves aware of different aspects of what we are reading. As our perspective changes with experience, we will become more perceptive of the deeper meanings of the text that were previously hidden from us. This means that there is always more richness waiting to be uncovered in the Bible. It also means that as we read, we need to be patient and humble if we do not immediately attain grand insights.[20]

17. Casey, *Sacred Readings,* p. 24.
18. Ibid., p. 25.
19. Ibid., p. 39.
20. Ibid., p. 47.

One reason for repeating passages of Scripture is that they become part of us, says Paul Wilkes:

> A rabbi I once wrote about taught me that Jews constantly recite the psalms in order to make the words become a part of them, instantly available for application in life's circumstances.[21]

And when we are too weak to understand what we are reading, or vexed about how Scripture teaches us certain gestures, the Spirit comes to our aid. Casey says that our reading of Scripture is not unaided: "The Spirit is as active in the reading of the Bible as in its writing, because fundamentally the two activities are complementary facets of a single divine initiative. . . . God not only speaks but also takes steps to ensure that what is spoken is also heard."[22]

Gestures: The Embodiment of Grace

The connection between the Scripture read and the gesture we perform is made possible because of God's grace. This fusion of our mind, body, and spirit as Christ's mind, body, and spirit happens because of God's gift of grace, a truth well understood by Flannery O'Connor, with whose thoughts we began this chapter:

> I often ask myself what makes a story work, and what makes it hold up as a story, and I have decided that it is probably some action, some *gesture* of a character that is unlike any other in the story, one which indicates where the real heart of the story lies. This would have to be an action or a gesture which was both totally right and totally unexpected; it would have to be one that was both in character and beyond character; it would have to suggest both the world and eternity. The action or gesture I'm talking about would have to be on the level which has to do with the Divine life and our participation in it. It would be a gesture that transcended any neat allegory that might have been intended or any pat moral categories a reader could make. It would be a gesture which somehow made contact with mystery.[23]

Paul says in Ephesians that it is by "grace that we have been saved through faith, and this is not your own doing; it is the gift of God — not the

21. Paul Wilkes, *Beyond These Walls* (New York: Image, 2000), p. 224.
22. Casey, p. 47.
23. O'Connor, *Mystery and Manners,* p. 111.

result of works, so that no one may boast" (Eph. 2:8-9). And of faith it is written:

> Now faith is the assurance of things hoped for, the conviction of things not seen. Indeed, by faith our ancestors received approval. By faith we understand that the worlds were prepared by the word of God, so that what is seen was made from things that are not visible. (Heb. 11:1-3)

In arguing for the education of Christians as an embodiment of the story of God, located in the performance of gestures, I am not suggesting that this is a pattern of works-righteousness, a way of acquiring God's grace. Instead, we know that God's grace and faith are *manifested* in the very gestures we perform as Christians. While we cannot see faith, we know it is faith because of the gestures of God's people (Hebrews 11): from Abraham's obedience as he set out to a place he was to receive as an inheritance (Heb. 11:8) to Jesus' obedience in enduring the cross (Heb. 12:2), we know where grace and faith have been offered by God.

It is important to remember, first, that many of the gestures we practice today are a performance of Scripture itself, as interpreted, learned, and enacted within the context of a church's tradition and its story. It may be helpful to consider the key gestures from both the Old and New Testaments and in the story of the church. We perform our Christly gestures in imitation of those who preceded us in the church, and they are narrated by and also embody God's Story. Second, we understand that our community has been created by God's gesture of divine love, of divine imagination, in God's image. The church is animated, formed, and re-formed by the extraordinary Christly gestures its many members practice.

Evidence of Gestures in Scripture

An exploration of the role, function, place, and practice of gestures in the story of the church's past will remind the reader that gestures are not something new that I have introduced in a discussion of education in the church, but are something old and of God. The authentic performance of a Christly gesture must be a performance of Scripture itself, as interpreted within the context of Christ's body and the congregation's traditions. Most of the gestures that we in the church have maintained, added to, dropped, and reclaimed were first performed by our ancestors, notably the children of Israel, whose story we are wedded to and know from the Old Testament. Our gestures also follow the ministry of Jesus, our moral exemplar, and later follow Paul's ministry. These gestures not only are signs of where we have been as God's people, but also provide direction about where we are and where we are headed in the future. Finally, the story of the gesture and what it embodies brings us to our *telos,* our destiny, the peaceable kingdom of God.

Examples from the Old and New Testaments illustrate the rich weave of body movement and verbal nuance, where sacred means and ends meet and are bound together in these actions, postures, and attitudes. These, along with the church's story, provide us with an understanding of how some gestures found in the rubrics of the church came to be in the first place. Hauerwas says: "The church is but a gesture of God's on behalf of a world to create a space and time in which we might have a foretaste of the kingdom [of God]."[24]

Gestures in the Stories of the Old Testament

Annie Dillard writes of creation, God's extravagant gesture:

> [The] universe has continued to deal exclusively in extravagances, flinging intricacies and colossi down aeons of emptiness, heaping profusions on profligacies with ever-fresh vigor. The whole show has been on fire from the word go. I come down to the water to cool my eyes. But everywhere I look I see fire; that which isn't flint is tinder, and the whole world sparks and flames.[25]

We are part of something more magnificent than ourselves in God's extravagant gesture. One of the first examples of gestural activity in the context of Scripture is the creation narrative. If, as Searle and Austin argue, saying something is doing something, then nothing can be as fantastic as God's spoken gesture: "In the beginning, God created the heavens and the earth" (Gen. 1:1). Reflecting on speech act theory, Donald Evans says that God addresses men and women in an event or deed that commits God to human beings. In response to God's initiative, human beings address God in the activity of worship, committing themselves to God and expressing their reverence and awe of God through speech acts. God's people reveal their involvement in God's world through verbal and nonverbal gestural activity.[26]

24. Hauerwas, "Gesture of a Truthful Story," in *Christian Existence Today,* p. 106.
25. Annie Dillard, *Pilgrim at Tinker Creek* (New York: Harper & Row, 1974), p. 9.
26. Donald Evans, *The Logic of Self-Involvement,* p. 14.

In the two creation accounts in Genesis, both the divine use of gesture in speech as an act of doing and the human gestures of intentional formation are to be found. One of the first speech acts — in the first account — is found in Genesis 1:3: "Then God said, 'Let there be light'; and there was light." Walter Brueggemann identifies this divine speech act as a "sovereign call." It is not subject to discussion but is evocative in nature: "It hopes but it does not compel. It hopes rather than requires."[27] In the second account, God the potter molds us into creation as if we were pots. We read in Genesis 2 that the "Lord God formed man from the dust of the ground, and breathed into his nostrils the breath of life; and the man became a living being" (verses 7-8). There is no speech act per se that is creating the world by the call of the Creator; instead, God is busy planting fields and gardens, animals and food, and trees of knowledge of good and evil — all dependent on the Creator. It is all by God's gestures that earth is created, and man and woman in it.

Jacob and the Angel

There are in the Old Testament both the gesture told and the gesture performed — all part of the drama, if not the mystery, of God's people Israel. One example is the story of Jacob wrestling with the angel. Fleeing from his brother, Esau, Jacob meets an angel (Gen. 32:24-28). The power in this story is that Jacob is struggling with God, and thus God with Jacob; God is actively involved, physically touching and moving Jacob into his place in God's story. There is also the gestural speech act, or naming event, wherein Jacob, by being named "Israel," receives the commission as father of the chosen people and the special object of God's affection and protection.[28] Again, as creation came through the Creator's gesture of speaking a word, the Old Testament also witnesses to God's divine intervention, the divine gestures that continue to manifest God's response to Israel in reminding Abraham and Sarah's children that they are God's chosen people.

Proverbs

Proverbs is a book of aphorisms that echo the admonition "actions have con-

27. Walter Brueggemann, *Interpretation Bible Series: Genesis* (Atlanta: John Knox Press, 1982), p. 19.

28. Ibid., p. 34.

sequences." In other words, our actions abound with examples of wisdom and the lack thereof. The writer of Proverbs was an astute observer of life, giving satirical, often clever, sometimes sage counsel based on the gestures of people dealing with one another in life. Consider the following proverb and its wisdom based on our lives and the gestures we perform with each other:

> Those who spare the rod hate their children,
> but those who love them are diligent to discipline them. (Prov. 13:24)

And consider how instructions toward wisdom are an action, a gesture:

> Keep hold of instruction; do not let go; guard her, for she is your life. (Prov. 4:13)

Prophets

The Old Testament prophets, in letting the Israelites know what their plight would be if they failed to devote their lives to serving and worshiping God, often used practical gestures that their hearers could readily understand. It did not take a theological education to discern from the prophets' real, tangible gestures, accompanied by the gesture of speech act, that Israel would be in trouble if it did not cleave to God as the Lord of the universe. I begin with the earlier prophets, such as Samuel. There is the story in 1 Samuel of the prophets who are so engaged by God's Spirit that they are in a "prophetic frenzy," with Samuel the prophet standing in charge of them (1 Sam. 19:20). Gestures of this kind of frenzy indicated that God's Spirit was within a person:

> As you come to the town, you will meet a band of prophets coming down from the shrine with harp, tambourine, flute, and lyre playing in front of them; they will be in a prophetic frenzy. Then the spirit of the Lord will possess you, and you will be in a prophetic frenzy along with them and be turned into a different person. (1 Sam. 10:5-6)

William McNeill observes that in Israel's history there were the "literary prophets," or school of prophets, such as Isaiah and Jeremiah, who had been shaped by the earlier prophets. The earlier prophets had been shaped by the older tradition of song and dance, a gesture that gave their prophecy an imprimatur of God's Spirit. "By dancing together and thereby inducing ecstasy, small groups of men thus changed the course of human history in ways no one could have imagined at the time."[29] Concerning the later prophets and the place of gestures in their prophecies, consider Jeremiah 18:1-12. Jeremiah is at the potter's house, and God the potter is working at his wheel: "The vessel he was making of clay was spoiled in the potter's hand, and he reworked it into another vessel, and it seemed good to him" (Jer. 18:4). The vessel was Israel, and the potter makes it very clear that Israel is like clay in the potter's hand:

> At one moment I may declare concerning a nation or a kingdom, that I will pluck up and break down and destroy it, but if that nation, concerning which I have spoken, turns from its evil, I will change my mind about the disaster that I intended to bring on it." (Jer. 18:7-8)

To this day, in some traditions — Pentecostal and Holiness churches, for example — dancing and being taken by the Spirit are not foreign gestures but are a significant part of life together. They consider such physicality "biblical" because of the prophetic story.

The New Testament and Gestures

Jesus Christ

Jesus is a gesture of God's love: "For God so loved the world, that he gave his only Son" (John 3:16). Furthermore, Jesus clearly understood that symbolic acts, or what some would call gestures, matter in this life and the life to come. For Christ himself is the image of the invisible God, "the firstborn of all creation . . . and all things have been created through him and for him. He himself is before all things, and in him all things hold together" (Col. 1:15-17). Paul shows in the words of this hymn of praise that the faithful gesture of Jesus' death alone on the cross made peace between God and "all things" (Col. 1:20).

Throughout the Gospels there are the scenes of Jesus performing gestures that shape our practices in the church today. From the bounty of incredible miracle stories to proclaiming the liberating good news to the poor, from diligently and lovingly teaching his disciples how to pray to the arduous

29. William H. McNeill, *Keeping Together in Time* (Cambridge: Harvard University Press, 1995), p. 72.

task of teaching them of the importance of his death and the coming resurrection in glory — all these are gestures of Christ. There are the stories of healing the centurion's servant (Luke 7:1-10), raising the widow's son (Luke 7:11-17), curing a boy with a demon (Matt. 17:14-21), feeding the five thousand (Mark 6:30-44), and Jesus' teaching his disciples the gestures of prayer (Matt. 6:8-14). Many times these lessons of healing and teaching are given by the act of speaking to a particular condition, announcing or proclaiming the good news of faith, which itself cures, heals, and teaches those witnessing these miracles Jesus' identity as the Son of God. And sometimes a gesture of faith such as touching Jesus' hand heals people of their infirmities.

For example, consider the story of the man born blind in John 9:1-12, where Jesus says:

> "As long as I am in the world, I am the light of the world." When he had said this, he spat on the ground and made mud with the saliva and spread the mud on the man's eyes, saying to him, "Go, wash in the pool of Siloam." Then he went and washed and came back able to see.

The healing occurs in the physical touch: faith is made incarnate, is embodied, in the gesture of creating the mud that would heal the eyes of the sightless one. Interestingly enough, the Jesus portrayed in the Gospel of John uses this healing gesture with a double focus: he heals both the man's optical disability and also, implicitly, his lack of comprehension — so that now he can understand.

There are stories in which merely speaking the words that need to be spoken can heal, a true example of where speaking is *doing* something, to paraphrase Austin and Searle. The centurion, a military officer of Rome and an enemy of the Jews, comes to Jesus, asking that he speak the necessary words of faith that will heal his servant (gesture as speech): "When Jesus heard this he was amazed at him, and turning to the crowd that followed him, he said, 'I tell you, not even in Israel have I found such faith'" (Luke 7:9).

Judas Iscariot

When is a gesture devious? One interesting example of the power of gestures unspoken is the character of Judas, who said little but whose actions moved the story of Jesus' death forward with great force. This is not a discussion of whether or not Judas' actions were predestined or necessary for the drama of

Passion Week; rather, it is to testify to the power of the gesture, or more precisely, of deceitful gestures. What we know about Judas Iscariot is that he kept the common purse of the disciples. In the two accounts of his interaction with Jesus, Judas doesn't say anything; instead, his gestures move Jesus closer to his eventual death on the cross. At the Last Supper, while reclining at table with the other disciples, Jesus tells them who the betrayer will be. According to the Gospel of John, Jesus says that it is he "to whom I give this piece of bread when I have dipped it in the dish"; he then gives it to Judas, who leaves immediately to tell the Roman authorities where Jesus is going to be later in the evening. In one of the most climactic moments in the Passion narrative, Judas leads the Roman guard to Jesus, who is now at the Mount of Olives. Judas' way of identifying Jesus among the crowd of disciples is a gesture, the kiss: "He approached Jesus to kiss him; but Jesus said to him, 'Judas, is it with a kiss that you are betraying the Son of Man?'" (Luke 22:47). That was all Judas was paid to do.

The Apostles

The power of the word spoken as a gesture, a speech act, is found in the story of Ananias and Sapphira, who sold a piece of property in Acts 5:1-11. The problem wasn't that Ananias held back money from the church but that he led the apostles to believe that he was giving the church all of the proceeds from the property sale. After uncovering the lie, Peter said to him, "You did not lie to us but to God!" (Acts 5:4) Because of the truthfulness of Peter's claim, Ananias literally fell down and died; then Sapphira told the same story her husband had, and she too fell down dead.

The Holy Kiss and Other Gestures in the Epistles

One interesting gesture of the early church was the holy kiss, a gesture that is no longer part of the repertoire of most Protestant churches. For example, in Romans 16:16 we read, "Greet one another with a holy kiss," an encouragement found also in 1 Corinthians 16:20, 2 Corinthians 13:12, 1 Thessalonians 5:26, and 1 Peter 5:14. This was considered a Roman practice and therefore pagan; but Paul takes the practice and brings it into the life of the early church as a gesture of greeting among Christians. This kiss was more than just a kiss. Edward Phillips writes that this kiss was a sharing of *pneuma*, or spirit, which in effect brought about a spiritual communion among Christians. Christians kissed each other not on the cheek but on the lips, thus sharing the Holy Spirit.[30]

In Philippians, Paul writes that the very name of Jesus is to be exalted by us, for

> God also highly exalted him and gave him the name that is above every name, so that at the name of Jesus every knee should bend, in heaven and on earth and under the earth, and every tongue should confess that Jesus Christ is Lord, to the glory of God the Father. (Phil. 2:9-11)

What is striking is the combination of the gesture as speech act — the cosmic confession that Jesus Christ is to be highly exalted as the Lord of creation — and bodily gesture that at the very name of Jesus "every knee should bend." Every knee in heaven and on earth and under the earth will practice the gesture of bowing, and the voice and tongue muscle will practice the gesture of uttering the confession, "Jesus Christ is Lord, to the glory of God the Father."

Gestures and Dancing in the Early Church

It is apparent from early church records that there was great movement of gestures and dancing included in Christian worship. At the "'close of prayers, hands were raised above the head to a brief tramping or stamping dance,' signifying the hope of attaining Heaven, where by this time it was understood that departed Christian souls joined the angels in a perpetual dance around the throne of God."[31] Monastic orders also used movement in congregational worship, with singing, processionals, and later more stately forms of worship. By the late fourth century there was a more standardized chant and song, with some ritual gestures such as "crossing oneself, or bowing to the ground in prayer," which were approved by the church authorities.[32]

30. L. Edward Phillips, "The Ritual Kiss in Early Christian Worship" (unpublished diss., University of Notre Dame, April 1992), pp. 1-6.

31. McNeill, p. 75.

32. Ibid., p. 77.

Theological Perspectives on Christly Gestures

Throughout the church's story, theologians have written much about gestures. In seeking to reclaim the centrality of gestures in educating Christians, I wish to emphasize that this concept is not a fad or a new idea to try out, but it is built on theologically informed practices as old as the church itself. Therefore, I will cite various theologians who have already written on the subject of gestures in the church, starting with St. Augustine.

St. Augustine and the Gestures of the Church

One of the best places to see, hear, touch, and be moved physically by gestures is in the worship of God in the liturgy of the church. Liturgy, which literally means "the work of the people," hints at what Geoffrey Wainwright calls "worship in the Christian life as a whole. Into the liturgy the people bring their entire existence so that it may be gathered up in praise."[33] The rituals of the church are filled with the practice of gestures. John Calvin wrote that because we are flesh, we have a dull capacity and need to be led by the hand, "as tutors lead children." Quoting Augustine, Calvin says that the sacraments — these ritualistic, bodily gestures practiced in the context of worshiping God — are a "visible word" because they represent "God's promises as painted in a picture and set them before our sight, portrayed graphically and in the manner of images." The sacraments are the mirrors in which we may contemplate the riches of God's grace, "which he lavishes upon us. For by them he manifests himself to us as far as our dullness is given to perceive, and attests his good will and love toward us more expressly than by word."[34]

Augustine clearly saw that, while born with an "intelligence which you, my God, gave to me," even though he was good at "crying out and making various sounds and movements, so that my wishes should be obeyed," he could not make himself understood by everyone with whom he wished to communicate. Augustine was ever the astute observer of life, and in his own way a theoretician about language — and, more precisely, how we learn a language. In *Confessions,* in which we see Augustine learning to "grow in Christ," he observes that we learn language by being part of exchanges between people:

33. Geoffrey Wainwright, *Doxology* (New York: Oxford University Press, 1984), p. 8.
34. Calvin, *Institutes,* 4.14.6, p. 1281.

> I noticed that people would name some object and then turn towards whatever it was that they had named. I watched them and understood that the sound they made when they wanted to indicate that particular thing was the name which they gave to it, and their actions clearly showed what they meant, for there is a kind of universal language, consisting of expressions of the face and eyes, gestures and tones of voice, which can show whether a person means to ask for something and get it, or refuse it and have nothing to do with it.[35]

Wittgenstein remarks about this passage:

> Augustine describes the learning of human language as if the child came into a strange country and did not understand the language of the country; that is, as if it already had a language, only not this one. Or again: as if the child could already *think*, only not yet speak. And "think" would here mean something like "talk to itself."[36]

Indeed, there are times when the verbal language we know and freely use may not be able to completely capture what is on our mind or heart. Calvin wrote about the practice of gestures in regard to prayer: "Although the best prayers are sometimes without utterance, yet when the feeling of the mind is overpowering, the tongue spontaneously breaks forth into utterance, and our other members into gesture."[37]

John Calvin and Gestures

Calvin not only understood something about the power of gestures in word and deed, but he actually used the word "gesture" in his writings. Prior to modern speech act theory, Calvin considered the preaching of God's Word and the celebration of the sacraments as a "sign and seal" of God's presence. In the sacraments of the church we say that believers are marked by God and his people as Christians through baptism into the body of Christ and by constant participation in the Eucharist. In the reading and preaching of God's words, which are witness to God's Word, namely, Jesus Christ, it is clear that Calvin believed God's word to be itself an act, as the church exists only where God's word is proclaimed. Quoting the apostle Paul, Calvin says:

35. St. Augustine, *Confessions,* p. 29.
36. Wittgenstein, *Philosophical Investigations* (Oxford: Blackwell, 1953), p. 32.
37. Calvin, *Institutes,* 3.20.33, p. 897.

> Paul reminds us that the church was founded not upon men's judgments, not upon priesthoods, but upon the teaching of apostles and prophets (Ephesians 2:20). Nay, Jerusalem is to be distinguished from Babylon, Christ's church from Satan's cabal, by the very difference with which Christ distinguishes between them.

He also says: "He who is of God hears the words of God. The reason why you do not hear them is that you are not of God" (John 8:47).[38] Calvin truly understood God's Word as having the power to "compel all worldly power, glory, wisdom, and exaltation to yield to and obey his majesty." We are to "cleave to that doctrine [Holy Scripture] to which God has subjected all men without exception."[39] Such is the power of God's words as a gesture on the people of God. Moreover, Calvin and his followers also understood that the gestures that compose the posture of God's people at prayer or in the celebration of the Eucharist are as powerful as Scripture. Take, for example, this quotation attributed to Calvin:

> For even though the best prayers are sometimes unspoken, it often happens in practice that, when feelings of mind are aroused, unostentatiously the tongue breaks forth into speech, and the other members into gesture.[40]

Gestures are prayers, and prayers are gestures. The Eucharist involves gestures: early followers of Calvin called their eucharistic celebration a "Table Gesture." Evelyn Underhill writes that Calvin believed that, in the celebration of the "holy meat and drink of eternal life," the Spirit of God brooded over the service, and the people, after singing the *Nunc Dimittis*, acknowledged a supernatural experience. In the early Calvinist churches, during the ritual of the Eucharist, or Holy Communion, people came forward and sat or stood around a table and broke bread together, passing the bread from hand to hand, symbolizing the unity of the church in the one loaf.[41]

Interestingly enough, for Calvin the preaching of God's Word was by no means the only act or even the most significant act in the worshiping life of God's people. The sacraments of baptism and the Eucharist present the promises of God to us in Jesus Christ more clearly than does "the word, because they represent them for us as painted in a picture from life."[42] The Lord

38. Ibid., 4.2.4.
39. Ibid., 4.8.9.
40. Ibid., 3.20.33.
41. Evelyn Underhill, *Worship* (New York: Harper & Brothers, 1957), pp. 289-290.
42. Calvin, *Institutes*, 4.14.5.

here not only recalls to our memory "the abundance of his bounty, but, so to speak, gives it into our hand and arouses us to recognize it."[43] Nicholas Wolterstorff says:

> In the sermon God tells us, by way of the words of the preacher, of the promise already made in Jesus Christ. In the sacrament God doesn't so much tell us of that promise as here and now assure us that it remains in effect. Here and now telling us about a promise once made, versus here and now assuring us that it remains in effect.[44]

Wolterstorff draws our attention to Calvin's careful discrimination between whether God is present in the bread and wine per se — or in the drama of the moment. For Calvin, when the bread and wine are offered to God's people in the Eucharist, it is as a sign or symbol of reaffirmation and assurance that God has been, is, and will be active as an agent to be engaged rather than a presence to be apprehended in the ritual itself.[45] In some sense, the Eucharist is a universal, magnificent Godly gesture in which people of all ages and of all walks of life, throughout the ages, participate. It is fair to say that the Eucharist is then God's gestural gift to us, providing a sign of wheat and grape as a way of reminding us that the promise of redemption has been sealed in the life, death, and resurrection of Christ.

Finally, Calvin and Luther approved of singing as a congregation in worship, along with some restrained muscular movements that would accompany a hymn. William McNeill believed that Calvinist psalmody was an important aid in winning popular commitment to the churches of the Reformed tradition.[46]

Books on the Right Gestures in Worship

So important were the gestural practices of the Christian faith in the life of the church during the Middle Ages that Hugh of St. Victor wrote *Institutio Novitorium,* a book on the pedagogy of gestures, detailing how to learn, practice, and use certain gestures in the church.[47] Gestures *(gestus)* were defined as a movement *(motus)* of the whole body *(figuratio):* "The external expres-

43. Ibid., 4.7.37.
44. Wolterstorff, p. 19.
45. Ibid., p. 21.
46. McNeill, p. 78.
47. Ibid., p. 67.

sion of the movements of the soul had to make up a 'figure,' a symbolic image of the body in the eyes of God and man."[48] According to Hugh, there were different modes or modalities of gestures, which he classified in order to show how virtuous gestures held the middle ground "between opposing bad gestures which neutralized each other."[49] Hugh went so far as to compare the discipline of learning the various gestures of the human body with the notion of body politic. Jean-Claude Schmitt wrote that Hugh's ideas about gestures were part of the broader ethical, political, and aesthetic ideology of the twelfth-century Parisian school.[50] Erasmus wrote *De Civilitate morum puerilium* in 1530, which, like Hugh's work, specified the maxims of conduct regarding outward proprieties, such as "bodily carriage, gestures, posture, facial expression and dress, all seen as the expression of the inner person."[51]

John Wesley and Gestures

John Wesley also wrote on the correct practice of gestures, whether one is preaching or is a congregant:

> That this silent language of your face and hands may move the affections of those that see and hear you, it must be well adjusted to the subject, as well as to the passion which you desire either to express or excite.[52]

Wesley cites the importance of gestures in the context of Christian worship. He and his followers were not afraid of a certain amount of movement in worshiping God. In the early days of his attempt to reform Anglicanism, as well as up through the twentieth century in America, there were "enthusiastic meetings," both in tents outdoors and in the church, with impassioned preaching, congregational hymn-singing, reinforced by hand-clapping and rhythmic body movements. According to McNeill, "The desired and expected outcome was ecstatic visitations by the Holy Spirit for a few, and heartfelt repentance, together with healing emotional catharsis, for all."[53] Methodists are no strangers to the practice of gestures in worship.

In summary, Christians should see that the gestures we perform today

48. Ibid.
49. Ibid.
50. Ibid., p. 68.
51. Connerton, *How Societies Remember* p. 82.
52. John Wesley, "Directions Concerning Pronunciation and Gesture."
53. McNeill, p. 83.

are but the most recent manifestations of very old practices, as old as the people of God itself. When we baptize in the name of the Trinity, and break the bread, uttering the words "Do this in remembrance of me," we are continuing to practice a gesture first modeled by Jesus himself. In truth, it is Jesus in us who is revealed in the water and at table. So central were gestures to the church prior to the Enlightenment that theologians such as Augustine referred to them in their writings; and books have been written on the correct performance of gestures by Christians. This book is but the most recent discussion of a very old practice.

Performing the Gestures in Church Today

Why do we train Christians in the gestures of Christ's body? First, we do it because Jesus, who is our exemplar, calls and teaches us to imitate his gestures. Jesus' hands were kind, doing good to all by healing pain and sickness, blessing children, washing feet, and saving those who fell. In this primer, if you will, God in Christ is the curriculum of the gestures to be taught in Christ's body. Second, if Christ is the curriculum, then his body is the pedagogy. We are asking Jesus to take our hands, make them strong yet gentle and kind, and craft them — "let them work for you." This verse encapsulates what the education of Christians is: to be Christ to a world in great need. Educating happens in Christ's body.

PART III

PERFORMING CHRISTLY GESTURES

Prologue to Part III

The Apostle Paul gives us a timeless picture of the community life of members of Christ's body as if they were body parts. God has called some to be hands, others to be feet; some will be eyes, while others will be ears. In 1 Corinthians 12, we read of disagreements within the community: the foot, its feelings hurt and its self-esteem on the low end, says that it doesn't belong to the body of Christ because the hand is more important. The ear also has its nose out of joint — because it is not the eye. Paul gently takes the various "body parts" through some great harmonizing gestures by lifting up each part as invaluable to the common good within the greater whole of Christ's body. He goes so far as to admonish the more highly touted parts of the body by saying that they should give greater honor to what they might consider the less honorable parts of the body. All of these gestures are to be undergirded and infused by Christ-like love, as the body parts are to have the same care for one another: "If one member suffers, all suffer together with it; if one member is honored, all rejoice together with it" (1 Cor. 12:26).

This metaphor is timeless because such conflicts persist in the church today. Congregations are still wrestling with the fractious nature of life between those with a "holier than thou" imprint on their lives and those feeling lower, the "haves" versus the "have nots." In a group therapy session of adolescents with behavioral problems and developmental disabilities, one of the young women became furious with another one who had, in her view, stolen her boyfriend. A fight broke out, and I tried to create peace between them. After my nose caught a haymaker intended for one of the young women — clearly an accident, but it hurt nonetheless — the staff rushed in and placed the young people in restraints. After the staff had quelled the uprising physically (with four-point restraints that held each limb down until the subject could gain some composure), they said to me, "Why didn't you do something?" I told them that I *did* try to do something: I was practicing nonviolence while trying to talk the young people down from their feverish emotions. My model was "if anyone strikes you on the right cheek, turn the other also" (Matt. 5:39). In the words of Jesus, I turned the other cheek by staying calm and at peace in the middle of these hurt and angry young people — and not running away.

Where had I learned these gestures of nonviolence? Was I a pacifist? I was even surprised by my own gestures. So were the young people, especially one of the contending young women: she couldn't believe that I didn't put any of the restraints on her. She thought I was brave and compassionate; the staff thought I was foolish.

Why did I act as a pacifist? Not because it felt good to get hit in the face; normally I retreat from such violence. I performed these gestures because I believe it is what Christ would do. Sad to say, I did not learn this gesture of nonviolence in the church. Nowhere in my upbringing as a Christian did anyone instruct me in the gestures of nonviolence, let alone charity, faith, or hope. I studied Scripture references to such gestures individually and sometimes discussed them in small groups during Bible studies and large rallies. The passage from Matthew's Gospel is well known to me intellectually; but no one ever taught me to put that Gospel passage into action — to perform the gestures of peacemaking in the face of hostility. I learned that it was one thing to say "Peace, peace," with my lips, but another thing to perform the gesture with the entirety of my body. My body, mind, and spirit were engaged all at once in that demonstration of peacemaking. Furthermore, was it really I who performed the gesture? Or was it truly Christ in me? How was the body of Christ affected by such a display of a nonviolent gesture? Clearly, the lives of the young people were affected.

In Part III, I will focus on teaching the various body parts to live together as members of Christ's body. This process of instruction I call "pilgrim catechesis," because I am proposing a form of instruction that harks back to an ancient understanding of catechesis for the entire pilgrimage of our life in the body of Christ. Central to this pilgrim catechesis is the emphasis on performing Christly gestures. I propose that when we read and enact Scripture in our daily lives, it is in itself a *performance of Christly gestures.* This performance of Christly gestures is taught by a master craftsperson to a student or apprentice in the context of church life. Such instruction involves the tradition-rich life of the ritualistic rubrics in the life of the church — from worship to fellowship to service.

Finally, the context in which we learn and teach the performance of Christly gestures is the body of Christ. I am proposing that we teach and learn the gestures best by being shown them, not out of context but in the context of the body of Christ. The overarching theme throughout this section on catechetical instruction of Christly gestures is the fusion of the dialectic of enculturation with a separate program called Christian education. We are always part of a culture — the body of Christ — no matter where we might be in our lives. For there is nowhere that we can flee from God's Spirit (Psalm 139), who is forever teaching us through the life of others. Contextual education must take seriously the notion of teaching in the midst of the rush of life — along the pilgrim's way.

CHAPTER SIX

Catechesis for Christly Gestures

When will I come to the end of my pilgrimage and enter the presence of God?[1]

Liturgy of the Hours

What is the pedagogy of teaching the performance of Christly gestures? Beginning with this chapter, I will examine how we teach Christly gestures by, first, placing them within a lifelong catechetical process, with the many members of Christ's body as catechists. I refer to this process of catechesis as pilgrimage, for we continue to be taught the ways of God until we enter the kingdom of God. Second, the catechetical pilgrimage involves patterning our lives after the life of Christ himself, as it is revealed in Scripture, in the unfolding storied tradition of the church, and in the gestures we call on as we face life's issues.

Pilgrimage Catechesis

In reclaiming catechesis, I hark back to catechesis' earliest definition, which is most applicable to Christly gestures, in the Acts of the Apostles 2:42: "And they continued steadfastly in the teaching of the apostles and in the communion of

1. *Liturgy of the Hours* (Collegeville: Liturgical Press, 1987), p. 126.

the breaking of the bread and in the prayers." These and other examples of catechesis from the earliest days of the church show us the importance of instruction-as-formation in the daily rubrics of life in Christ. Catechisms have been revised in both Roman Catholic and Protestant church bodies throughout church history, reflecting subtle nuances or dramatic changes in theological thinking.[2] Amid all these changes, I believe that the primary purpose of catechesis is best expressed by Roman Catholicism today: catechesis was initially given the responsibility of the "totality of the Church's efforts to make disciples." Catechesis is meant to help people believe that Jesus "is the Son of God so that believing they might have life in his name, and to educate and instruct them in this life, thus building up the body of Christ."[3] Being educated and instructed in the ways of Christ means not only knowing about but also living the ways of Christ. To that end, catechesis is a process of continuous formation and re-formation, a pilgrimage, in the Christian faith throughout our entire lives as God's people. Daily we are shaped not only by the gestured utterance of the catechism with our mouth as we recite church doctrine or the Lord's Prayer out loud, but also as we are engaged in living and performing gestures of the Christian faith, determined daily by the structured rubrics of church life, formed by the church's story and the cycle of holy days of the Christian year.[4]

A Brief Historical Sketch of Catechism

Paul Bradshaw says that, in the early church, baptism was the actual immersion of a person in water (Rom. 6:3), preceded by a period of instruction in the Christian faith, known as catechesis. These two — baptism and catechesis — were inseparable practices of the early church. Such catechesis was necessary for many of the gentile candidates, who lacked the religious background of many Jewish converts to the Christian faith.[5] Some scholars suggest that after the baptism there was another ceremony, a "separate ritual gesture expressing the gift of the Holy Spirit, either in the form of the laying of hands on the newly baptized or by an anointing with oil," which later laid the biblical foundation for confirmation.[6] The catechetical instruction for the newly

2. As an example of such changes, note that since 1990 both the Roman Catholic Church and the Presbyterian Church (USA) have published new catechisms.

3. *Catechism of the Catholic Church* (Mahwah, NJ: Paulist Press, 1994), p. 8.

4. See Reinhard Hütter, *Suffering Divine Things: Theology as Church Practice* (Grand Rapids: Wm. B. Eerdmans Pub. Co., 2000), pp. 190-191.

5. Paul Bradshaw, *Early Christian Worship* (London: SPCK, 1996), p. 3.

6. Ibid., p. 4.

initiated is *mystagogy*, taken from the Greek verb *mueō*, meaning "to teach a doctrine," and therefore "to initiate into the mysteries" of the Christian faith.[7] As baptism is dependent on the gestures of Christ's body, so mystagogy is a gesture-bound catechesis for the newly initiated, since it literally means a

> *performance* of a sacred *action* [my emphasis], in [which] both the sacraments of initiation, of baptism and Eucharist, as well as the oral or written explanation of the mystery hidden in the scriptures and celebrated in the liturgy [of the church] are revealed.[8]

It is important to note that early initiation rituals and catechesis in the early church were modeled after Christ himself. For example, according to Matthew 28:16-20, Christ directed his followers to continue evangelizing:

> Make disciples of all nations, baptizing them in the name of the Father and of the Son and of the Holy Spirit, and teaching [catechesis] them to obey everything that I have commanded you.

Catechesis and evangelism were connected to the sacramental rite of baptism. Maxwell Johnson observes that two theological points were made in this rite of baptism: first, Christian initiation in baptism is understood as new birth through water and the Holy Spirit (John 3:5), as Jesus himself was baptized; second, Christian initiation is being united with Christ in his death, burial, and resurrection (Rom. 6:3-11).[9]

The root of catechesis is the Greek word *katēcheō*, which means "to make hear," "to re-sound again," or "echo again," which could mean "to instruct," or a "course of instructions in the Christian moral life."[10] The "cate-

7. Ibid., p. 22.

8. Enrico Mazza (Matthew J. O'Connell, trans.), *Mystagogy* (New York: Pueblo Pub. Co., 1989), p. 1.

9. Maxwell Johnson, *The Rites of Christian Initiation* (Collegeville: Liturgical Press, 1999), p. 31.

10. F. L. Cross and E. A. Livingstone, eds., *The Oxford Dictionary of the Christian Church*, 2nd edition (New York: Oxford University Press, 1978), p. 249. See also Johnson, *Rites*, p. 36. This is different from other forms of education present in the ancient world. For example, the word for education in ancient Greek is *paideia*, which shares the same root word with "play" which is *paidia*; the root word is *pais*, which is the word for child. What is interesting is that play would involve bodily gestures of some kind or another, especially among children. Plato himself saw both play and education as essential, interrelated activities throughout one's entire life. See Joseph Dunne, "To Begin in Wonder: Children and Philosophy," *Arista* (forthcoming).

chumen" was the student, and the "catechist" was the teacher. The process of induction into the church was the "catechumenate."[11] Catechesis in the early church involved the shaping of a person's character. For example, catechesis was not conducted through worksheet drills in individual workbooks but by oral instruction — a speech act — about the "principal Christian truths given to children and adults before baptism."[12]

Early practices of catechesis also depended on the correct gestures of speaking and hearing the gospel message. Bradshaw writes that repentance of one's sins, which was expressed verbally, was to accompany baptism, as was a profession of faith, such as "I believe that Jesus Christ is the Son of God."[13] The baptismal process functioned as a rite of initiation as well as an expression of the genuine conversion experience that candidates were undergoing in their lives. The early church used oral instruction — a physical gesture — because it did not have access to written resources.[14] The primary way of learning was not literary but through the senses, which involved aural and visual, touch and taste, feeling and movement as stimulation — fully an act of the body and mind.

At the same time, there were symbols and pictures referring to the church and Christian stories displayed in the catacombs of Rome and other places. This dependence on signs and symbols in church life continued clear through the medieval period and up through the Renaissance in Europe. The Christian narrative was also found in bas-relief illustrations, church architecture, stained-glass windows, sculptures, paintings, tapestries, music, in sermons, and in morality plays performed outside the cathedrals, as well as in baptism and eucharistic celebrations.[15] Because many people were illiterate, the narrative of the Christian story in art forms was instructional: the gestures of the catechist, artist, musician, priest, and storyteller mattered.

An interesting highlight of some initiatory practices of the early church, significant for the argument of this book, was the expectations of change in the life of the convert. There is evidence that the kind of person one was — one's action or gestures and therefore one's very character — mattered in the catechetical process. Bradshaw says that it is clear from early Syrian texts that

11. Bradshaw, *Early Christian Worship*, pp. 3, 13.

12. Ibid., p. 249.

13. Ibid., p. 3.

14. Obviously, there was not an assumption that the people of those ancient times could read, nor was literature freely available. Therefore, the delineation of "literate" or "illiterate" is a moot point.

15. Berard Marthaler, *The Catechism Yesterday and Today* (Collegeville: Liturgical Press, 1995), p. 11.

converts would have to express their repentance and faith before they would be allowed to hear the word of God proclaimed. Likewise, in the apostolic tradition of Hippolytus, one's conduct of life would be examined as a catechumen before one would be allowed to hear the gospel in the final stages of one's preparation for baptism. Bradshaw concludes that one's righteous actions and behaviors, displayed in the gestures of one's life, were a prerequisite of belonging in the early church,

> and that at least some believing might have been expected to come later. Indeed, it appears to have been the behaviour of Christians rather than their beliefs as such that was the principal attraction to the religion for pagans and the most effective means of evangelization.[16]

Berard Marthaler notes the same process: candidates for baptism were not only asked a series of questions, as is common in some practices of catechetical instruction today; their very lifestyle was carefully scrutinized; they memorized the creeds; and they learned the Lord's Prayer before they were baptized. The choices people made revealed to the elders of the church what kind of people were coming to Christ. Marthaler says that along with the oral instructions were rites of initiation and intensification:

> After the rites of initiation which included baptism, chrismation, and full participation in the Eucharist, the neophytes ["newly born"] reflected on the mysteries [in Latin, the "sacraments"] and heard further instructions as to what it means to be Christian. This last phase was known as mystagogy or mystagogical catechesis.[17]

Virtuous actions were considered a prerequisite for belonging to the church, where one would be taught right thinking and right believing. The sequence is as follows: (1) correct action, followed by: (2) belonging to the community, followed by: (3) correct believing. This is contrary to current practices of catechesis, in which right thinking or knowing is prior to right actions and belonging.[18] Yet the cessation of the persecution of the Christian church in

16. Paul Bradshaw, "The Gospel and the Catechumenate in the Third Century," *Journal of Theological Studies,* 50, 1 (April 1999), pp. 143-152.

17. Marthaler, *The Catechism Yesterday and Today,* p. 9.

18. Bradshaw, "The Gospel and the Catechumenate in the Third Century," p. 152. As a Presbyterian theologian, let me quickly add that I believe that infants and children should be baptized, "without undue haste but without undue delay" *(Book of Order).* For as Maxwell Johnson says, "What could be more counter-cultural, more against the prevail-

the era of Constantine (the early fourth century) meant that the baptismal process became the means of conveying a profound experience to candidates in hopes of bringing about their conversion.[19]

By the fifth century, the sacramental gesture of baptism was a more common practice, with some traditional practices found in the oral instructions themselves. For example, Marthaler points out that Ambrose of Milan and St. Augustine summed up the "principles of Christian doctrine" as embodied in the baptismal creed, the Lord's Prayer, and the twofold commandment of love — all done in Latin.[20] The church was striving for some kind of homogeneity in its catechetical instruction. By the ninth century, instruction was still in the oral tradition because very few books were available; literacy was a privilege of the clergy, yet even their ability to read was limited by their lack of access to books. But by this time instruction was given in the vernacular and included the Apostles' Creed. To this day, the Roman Catholic Church's catechesis is founded on

> four pillars: the baptismal profession of faith (the Creed), the sacraments of faith, the life of faith (the Commandments), and the prayer of the believer (the Lord's prayer).[21]

By the thirteenth century, there was a growing concern about the orthodoxy of the Christian faith among Christians, along with a wave of popular piety that shaped the worldview of Christians. In response, the church placed more emphasis on the role of catechesis, with more, different, and complicated catechisms offered to the church. More books and manuals of instruction in the Christian life were introduced to the process of catechesis. This was a significant change: from primary dependence on oral instruction and

---

ing tide of modern American culture, and still more anti-Pelagian and grace filled than doing something so apparently foolish and silly as to celebrate God's salvific activity, God's choice, God's adoption of children into God's reign as it is known and celebrated in the faith community through the initiation of infants? And who, I would ask, are more displaced in today's world than children, innocent victims of poverty, violence, hunger, and crime? As the late Eugene Maly put it: 'Through infant Baptism we *initiate* a person into a faith-community long before he or she can choose whether to belong. And through infant Baptism we also celebrate a person's salvation long before he or she consciously experiences the need to be saved or can take any responsibility for turning self toward God. . . . Infant Baptism is . . . one way we have institutionalized our conviction that community is central to Christian life, to God's plan of salvation'" (pp. 379-380).

19. "The Gospel and the Catechumenate in the Third Century," p. 22.

20. Marthaler, p. 10.

21. *Catechism of the Catholic Church,* pp. 9-10.

bodily gestured practices of the church to the act of reading, a more cognitive process. Examples of books are John de Taystek's *The Lay Folks' Catechism*, written in English and published in the fourteenth century, primarily for clergy; John Wyclif's version of *Lay Folks' Catechism* and *ABC's of Simple Folk;* Erasmus's fifteenth-century *The Handbook of the Christian Soldier*, with an emphasis on personal over ecclesial devotion, and on personal morality "and the humanist program with its emphasis on learning and return to ancient sources."[22] Erasmus's *Handbook* is interesting in its emphasis on how we are to pray: a gesture and knowledge of Holy Scripture — which had always been the domain of the clergy and not of the laity — to be used by laypeople in their struggle against sin. Erasmus criticized the religious practices that consisted of "outward signs and the multiplication of devotions"; instead, he focused on the gospel and the "inward love of God and neighbor." For Erasmus, Christianity was life itself rather than a body of doctrines.[23]

With the invention of the printing press in the fifteenth century, catechetical instruction became more and more a function of a person's mind rather than the ecclesial practice of bodily gestures; the emphasis was on correct believing and thinking prior to correct action or gesture in order to join the church. One learned Scripture not only from the oral and accompanying gestures in the ecclesial community but also as an individual act of the mind. At the same time, there was an effort to reform the catechism among both Protestants and Catholics. There were now, on the one hand, "large catechisms," which were a theological source for pastors, preachers, and teachers; and, on the other hand, there were "small catechisms" for clergy, school masters, parents, and children. Children were expected to commit the smaller catechism to memory — as a cognitive act.[24] No longer did candidates have their lives and gestures examined prior to their reading and learning. By and large, catechesis was no longer a process of shaping and changing one's life; rather, it became an instruction book in which one would cognitively learn the important creeds and confessions of the church. This shift made the church less a priest's or pastor's church and more a people's church, because the laity now had access to the biblical text. But it was also a shift away from catechism as a process of initiation and intensification of one's very life in the Christian life, which involved the entirety of the community, toward catechism as a book of confessions, creeds, and prayers that

22. Marthaler, pp. 12-17.

23. Ibid., p. 17.

24. One often hears people say that they learned or memorized the catechism "by heart," though there is little or no proof that the "heart," let alone the "body," was ever necessary in such learning.

the individual was to commit to memory, with the assumption that that person was already part of the church.

This "new" practice of catechesis and the printing press were key ingredients for Martin Luther and John Calvin. In 1529, Luther published his *Deutsch Catechismus (German Catechism)* and the *Small Catechism.* Calvin wrote his *Geneva Catechism* in 1541, and the *Heidelberg Catechism* appeared in 1563; both have become important doctrinal standards for the Reformed churches. Again, I point to the emphasis on the intellectual understanding of Scripture first, which was a prerequisite to the shaping of one's behavior or actions. This is counter to the early church practice of virtuous behavior and emphasis on our gestured actions as prerequisites to joining the church, followed by believing, then understanding. Now the church — or the Reformed churches, to be exact — followed the agenda that if one mastered certain sets of knowledge cognitively, one would, as an individual, be persuaded to act aright in order to belong to the church.

Surprisingly, Calvin mourned the passing of the ancient catechetical customs of the early church:

> How I wish that we might have kept the custom which . . . existed among the ancient Christians before this misborn wraith of a sacrament came to birth . . . a catechizing, in which children or those near adolescence would give an account of their faith before the church. But the best method of catechizing would be to have a manual drafted for this exercise, containing and summarizing in simple manner most of the articles of our religion, on which the whole believers' church ought to agree without controversy. A child of ten would present himself to the church to declare his confession of faith, would be examined in each article, and answer to each; if he were ignorant of anything or insufficiently understood it, he would be taught. Thus while the church looks on as a witness, he would profess the one true and sincere faith, in which the believing folk with one mind worship the one God. . . . There would be greater agreement in faith among Christian people, and not as many would go untaught and ignorant; some would not be so rashly carried away with new and strange doctrines; in short, all would have some methodical instruction, so to speak, in Christian doctrine.[25]

Calvin went on to suggest that in the Geneva of his day the children should be brought on Sundays at midday to catechesis. In "The Order to be observed in the case of little Children," he says:

25. Calvin, *Institutes,* 4.19.13.

> A definite formulary is to be composed by which they will be instructed, and on this, with the teaching given them examined, they are to be interrogated about what has been said, to see if they have listened and remembered well.
>
> When a child has been well enough instructed to pass the Catechism, he is to recite solemnly the sum of what it contains, and also to make profession of his Christianity in the presence of the Church.
>
> Before this is done, no child is to be admitted to receive the Supper.[26]

For Calvin and his followers, learning and knowing the catechism, along with baptism, were prior and prerequisite to receiving the Lord's Supper.[27]

Meanwhile, the Roman Catholic Church's response was the Counter Reformation, in which the Roman Catholic reformers published another catechism, *The Catechism of the Council of Trent.* Rudolph Bell says that there were in this catechism both the usual list of prayers and creeds — also found in the Protestant catechisms — and the lists of sins and prohibitions. But there were also explicit instructions to pastors to teach their congregations about living life according to a certain code of moral conduct. For example, couples were taught to

> abstain from demanding payments on the conjugal debt in order to devote themselves to prayer. They should particularly avoid sexual intercourse for at least three days prior to receiving the Holy Eucharist and frequently during the fast season of Lent.[28]

With such instruction in even the intimate details of people's sexual lives, more pocket-sized books were printed to instruct both the priest and the faithful — so that the priest himself would not become aroused when listening to his parishioners' confessions.[29] The gestures of both the clergy and laity mattered.

26. Quoted in Marthaler, p. 26.

27. In many Protestant churches today, there is little uniformity of opinion or church law regarding when children are to be welcomed to the Eucharist. It is currently a decision made by each church rather than by the church as a whole, at least among Presbyterians.

28. Rudolph Bell, *How to Do It: Guides to Good Living for Renaissance Italians* (Chicago: University of Chicago Press, 1999), p. 32.

29. Bell refers to a book by Friar Bartolomeo de Medina, in which he assures priests reading his book that there is "no sin if the man of God accidentally ejaculates while hearing a particularly libidinous confession or poring over relevant materials for noble purposes" (Bell, p. 195).

With the creation and development of Sunday school in the 1780s, there has been less a focus on any kind of catechesis per se, and more Sunday school and seminary instruction in theology, interpreting the Bible, and the history of the church. Sunday school made instruction in and performance of the Christian faith more an act of the mind, as the individual strove to accumulate and memorize certain sets of knowledge (e.g., the creeds, confessions, and prayers of the church), while it left unaddressed one's acts of body and spirit in Christ's body.[30]

Modern Practices of Catechetical Instruction

In the early days of the church, the emphasis in catechetical instruction was on virtuous actions or gestures followed by belonging and believing. I have shown the chronological shift in the church in which correct believing or thinking is prior to belonging or correct actions. In today's church, catechesis is no longer considered a lifelong, deepening process; it is reduced to a short pamphlet formula to be recited, memorized, and perhaps discussed in a small group (e.g., the new catechism of the Presbyterian Church USA), or it is produced as a book (e.g., the Roman Catholic Church). The Presbyterian Church's new catechism gives the narrative of God's people in the Old Testament and the New Testament, interspersed with the confessions and creeds, plus a section on the sacraments and the great ends of the church; little is said about ways of living the Christian life.[31]

Furthermore, it is assumed that no one takes part in a process of catechesis for his or her entire life. Methodologically, catechesis is reduced to a kind of short course, called "catechetical instruction," in which one learns a body of doctrines from a workbook, some activities are suggested, and questions for small-group discussions are proposed — all conducted within about fifty minutes. This takes place weekly for a short period of time — anywhere from a month to a year — often as just one more programmatic feature of a church's already crowded schedule of programs. Young adults may read and

30. As an example, a cash award is given by the Presbyterian Church (USA) for the rote memorization of the Shorter Westminster Catechism by those candidates for ministry in the Presbyterian Church's seminaries. No questions are asked or judgments rendered concerning the candidate's character; nor is there any follow-up to see how memorization of the Shorter Catechism influences his or her actions or conduct as a minister of the word and sacrament in the Presbyterian Church.

31. Again, the two latest forms of catechism to date have come from the Roman Catholic Church and the Presbyterian Church (USA).

memorize the catechism of their denomination during their confirmation instruction period, which is part of the rite of initiation into church life. Others learn a particular church's catechism during the new members' class when they join a church. Some churches may use a formal lecture style, question-answer recitation, and critical-reflective activities — often in a self-contained classroom with other children or adults of the same age (a more homogeneous setting). In either format, the problem with catechism in the church today is that it is seen as a form of "giving" or "echoing back" a set of answers to formula questions; these are usually memorized at a certain age and, unfortunately, forgotten soon after one leaves the course of instruction.[32] There is no follow-up on right living and belonging, which is an ecclesial act of body, spirit, and mind.

John Westerhoff says that in this kind of learning process, in which one first receives the knowledge and review skills needed and then goes on to live a "responsible life as a member of the body of Christ," there is little evidence of such connection in the current catechetical instructions.[33] Because the practice of the catechism is not reinforced outside the "educational moment," or called on again in the life of a church during worship, congregational meetings, educational programs, or theological discussions, the catechism is lost. Similarly, because baptism can occur either when one is an infant or as an adult, the ancient catechetical practices are no longer a prerequisite for the performance of this initiatory sacrament. Nor is catechesis a prerequisite for participating in the Eucharist in many Protestant churches.[34] Indeed, it is more than likely that, especially in some Protestant churches, catechism class is a Sunday elective at best, and absent at worst.[35]

32. Laura Lewis, Austin Presbyterian Theological Seminary Luncheon, 209th General Assumbly Meeting, Syracuse, NY, June 19, 1997.

33. John Westerhoff and Caroline Hughes, *On the Threshold of God's Future* (New York: Harper & Row, Pub. Inc., 1986), p. 126.

34. I am fully aware that Protestant denominations such as the Presbyterian Church (USA) and the United Methodist Church would like to make it mandatory that a parishioner be baptized *before* receiving the elements of the Eucharist. However, the United Methodist Church, for example, has an "open table" polity, in which one who is not baptized is invited to come to the table of the Eucharist. And instead of "catechism," some Presbyterian and Methodist churches have children participate in what is called "worship preparation courses" prior to partaking of Holy Communion. However, there is little evidence that anyone knows who may or may not partake in the Eucharist in either denomination.

35. For example, while the Presbyterian Church (USA) has had various catechisms in its history, including a new one in the 1990s, few Presbyterians have participated in learning any of them. Some Protestant churches, such as the United Methodist Church, have no such catechism.

Herein lies the problem: catechesis no longer necessarily takes up or shapes one's entire life in Christ's body. The careful, intricate practices of the ancient church's catechesis have been lost to the church today. And something more critical was lost when we forgot the performance of catechesis of the early church: the formation of our bodies, our very being and character, by the continual shaping of certain gestures that nurture body, mind, and spirit in the context of Christ's body. That formation meant that Christians could be the kind of people who would not only hear but comprehend, with the entirety of their being, the mystery of the Good News of the gospel.

In the following section, I propose a catechesis-as-patterning of the performance of Christly gestures. I am reclaiming some ancient catechetical practices and focuses, in which we begin the catechetical process with correct practices — or correct performance of gestures. Such formation should not occur once or twice in a person's lifetime but should be continual, beginning with one's baptism, along with a yearly examination of one's life according to the creeds, confessions, and prayers of the church. Through continual formation and nurture, as well as participation in the ritualistic life of Christ's body, we will be drawn deeper into the real yet mysterious practices of God's people.

Pilgrimage as Catechesis

What I am proposing is a pilgrimage catechesis, one that would have have what Westerhoff proposes as a formal process of instruction that is separated from the informal moments of learning what it is to be in Christ.[36] Westerhoff would define the current catechetical approach as "intentional activities by which a community of Christian faith makes God's saving work known, conscious, living, and active in the lives of persons and the community."[37] The other primary activity of formation is the community's ritual or ceremonial life — those "repetitive, symbolic gestures expressive of the community's story."[38] Whereas this kind of formation represents "intentional, relational, experiential activities within the life of a story-formed community that shape

36. A similar move is made in theological education, in which there is the more discursive or didactic practice of education, usually with teacher/lecturer imparting knowledge, topic by topic, in a decent and orderly fashion. The student is to learn while seated in his or her seat, presumably actively taking notes. This practice is often contrasted with "community building" or "character creating" formation, in which the student learns in a more experiential manner.

37. Westerhoff and Hughes, p. 126.

38. Ibid., p. 126.

our perceptions, consciousness, and character," it blends in the other kind of learning — "informal" and "unintentional" learning that also occurs in many spontaneous moments but is known as formation or catechesis only when we become conscious of it.

The idea of *pilgrimage* in catechesis comes in part from the ancient Christian and Jewish practice of pilgrimage as a growing transformational event. It also comes from the work of Reinhard Hütter, who suggests a two-tiered catechetical process in attempting to reclaim some kind of catechetical instruction in the church. First, there would be an initiatory catechesis, followed by a "peregrinational" catechesis.[39] The initiatory catechesis is for either old or young people, but it has the key feature that the catechumen is learning "new, unfamiliar configurations of language and activities, at the end of which he or she has acquired a certain competency in language and action."[40] Peregrinational catechesis, meaning a way of learning that is a continual actualization of baptismal recollections, maintains "the praxis of faith amid the most varied contexts of life and interpreting these life situations within the context of the praxis of faith itself."[41]

Westerhoff and Hütter provide some very helpful ways of thinking about catechism that I would like to build on. By pilgrimage catechesis I mean the following: on a Christian pilgrimage, one is a member of a community of pilgrims in which we learn and teach others the intricate relationship that embraces us in being known by God in Christ. It is a journey onward with others, in friendship, in which we both belong and learn to live aright as we move toward something better and more beautiful. On Christian pilgrimage, God is our path, Christ our companion, and the Spirit infuses us with grace.[42] Pilgrimage catechesis emphasizes that, first, being in the church is itself a catechesis because the church is constantly forming and nurturing us in God's love; as pilgrimage is an act of a Christian community, so catechesis is

39. Reinhard Hütter, *Suffering Divine Things,* pp. 190-193. "Peregrinate" means "to be on a journey": thus "peregrinational catechesis" implies that one is on a journey of some kind.

40. Hütter suggests that this catechetical learning "among both young and adult candidates for baptism will assume the form of baptismal instruction ultimately leading to the praise of God's salvific actions in the confession of faith" (p. 190). This runs counter to the practices of infant baptism in the Roman Catholic Church, as well as Reformed Protestant churches, such as the Presbyterian Church (USA), and even Hütter's Lutheran tradition.

41. Ibid., p. 191.

42. I will say more about pilgrimage in connection with catechesis throughout the next three chapters, borrowing much of it from my manuscript-in-progress "Leaving Development and Beginning Pilgrimage."

an act of Christian community. Second, catechetical formation, like pilgrimage, is a lifelong vocation. Third, we are always rooted and grounded in God's grace through faith, thus knowing God's charity and God's kingdom as our collective *telos.*

Catechesis is the church's effort to make disciples, instructing and integrating throughout a person's life the gestures of body, mind, and spirit that are embedded in and integral to the gestured practices of Christ's body, mind, and spirit. As such it is concerned with the correct instruction and performance of Christly gestures that embody the virtues of the church and are necessary for the "excellence" of living as the one body of Christ.[43] Catechesis needs to be comprehended as the totality of the church's efforts to make disciples: "To help people comprehend the faith in believing that Jesus is the Son of God so that believing they might have life in his name, and to educate and instruct them in this life, thus building up the body of Christ."[44] To live in such a way is right living for Christians.[45]

Calvin was quite clear that the entire church needs to be involved in shaping us to "profess the one true and sincere faith, in which the believing folk with one mind worship the one true God." It is the body of Christ that is constantly attending to the growth and change of all its members, invigorated by the gift of grace through faith.[46] One cannot comprehend what it is to be a member of Christ's body as an isolated individual, just as one cannot be on pilgrimage alone. It is in the gestured practices of Christ's body that we receive unity and purpose, as the Christian narrative is enacted by the members of Christ's body who have come before us and those who will come after us — that we begin to comprehend the real divine mystery, which is God.

As Christ's body in the world today, the catechist writ large will struggle against sin and will celebrate God's gift of grace. In other words, as the catechist writ large, the church is to enact the virtue of constancy and perseverance as well as show us the ways of faith and hope performed in the ever-expanding, often tedious, instruction in the intricate ways of Christ. The

43. Father William Harmless writes something similar about the Roman Catholic's Church's RCIA process. Catechism is an apprenticeship, which is to be more than mere schooling. It is supposed to do more than instruct in dogmas and precepts. Rather, it is to instill a profound sense of the mystery of salvation; it is to give students experience in the different ways of prayer; it is to implant in their hearts the morality of the New Testament; and it is to place them in the context of a liturgical setting. See William Harmless, *Augustine and the Catechumenate* (Collegeville: Liturgical Press, 1995), pp. 4-5.

44. *Catechism of the Catholic Church* (Mahwah, NJ: Paulist Press, 1994), p. 8.

45. Warren, p. 46.

46. Calvin, *Institutes,* 4.19.13.

church needs to make it clear that there are both correct performances of gestures and also harmful performances of gestures that are detrimental to the body as a whole. Michael Warren says that the

> goal . . . in the early catechumenate . . . [is] its gradual correction of lifestyle, completed only when the [catechumen is] able to walk as a follower of Jesus among the followers of Jesus.[47]

So too with pilgrimage: as pilgrims we live a life in motion as Christ's body, constantly learning "while on the road" and confronting the way we live our lives in the light of how others live their lives. Second, such instructions in the ways of Christ, like pilgrimage itself, will take the entirety of one's life. Catechesis is lifelong instruction in the essential gestures of Christ's body; by that I mean that, as members one of another, we need to learn and practice certain gestures that bring coherence to our own comprehension of the changing flow of life in the body of Christ. It is also important to uphold and build up other members of Christ's body by learning the many gestured practices that embody the greater posture of the body toward the worship of and service to God. As Henri Nouwen reminds us, community is the fruit of our capacity to make the interests of others more important than our own (Phil. 2:4): "The question . . . is not 'How can we make community?' but 'How can we develop and nurture giving hearts?'"[48]

As pilgrims depend on the charity and hospitality of others, beneath this catechetical practice is the necessity of doing catechesis in a spirit of Christian charity, a discipline that is the key to good catechetical instruction and needs to be performed from a gesture of gratitude for the love we first received from God in the person of Jesus Christ. But we don't learn these gestures as a new plan of "works righteousness" or a semi-Pelagian exercise; we learn and perform these gestures out of the deep gratitude for the gift of God's grace, of which we are the debtors.

Considering the early church's description of "catechesis" as "to make hear" or "to instruct" one in the moral life, which involves gesture, I propose that pilgrimage catechesis is the patterning of Christly gestures through right instruction of faithful discipline along the pilgrim's way. The goal is to pattern our bodies, minds, and spirits after Christ's body, mind, and spirit.

47. Warren, p. 46.

48. Henri Nouwen, *Bread for the Journey* (San Francisco: HarperCollins, 1997), p. 23.

Pilgrimage Catechesis-as-Patterning in the Ways of Christ

There is a reference to "patterning" in Titus 2:1-2, 6-8, concerning teaching "sound doctrine." In this passage Paul admonishes the church to teach what is consistent with sound doctrine:

> Tell the older men to be temperate, serious, prudent, and sound in faith, in love, and in endurance. . . . Likewise, urge the younger men to be self-controlled. Show yourself in all respects a *pattern* of good works, and in your teaching show integrity, gravity, and sound speech that cannot be censured; then any opponent will be put to shame, having nothing evil to say of us.

Paul makes it clear that, in instructing the younger members of Christ's body, he did not see right living as involving the body and sound doctrine involving the mind. Right living and sound doctrine are not two separate entities but are united, as are the mind, body, and spirit of Christ's followers. Right living is the embodiment of sound doctrine, and sound doctrine is based on the lives of people infused with the Holy Spirit, who aspire toward right living.

Bonhoeffer argues persuasively about patterning in regard to being "in Christ," and thus being "like Christ." Bonhoeffer says that we have been transformed into the image of Christ and thus are destined to be like him:

> He is the only "pattern" we must follow. And because he really lives his life in us, we too can "walk even as he walked" (1 John 2:6), and "do as he has done" (John 13:15) and "love as he has loved" (Eph. 5:2; John 13:34; 15:12), "forgive as he forgave" (Col. 3:13), "have this mind, which was also in Christ Jesus" (Phil. 2:5), and therefore we are able to follow the example he has left us (1 Peter 2:21), lay down our lives for the brethren as he did (1 John 3:16). It is only because he became like us that we can become like him. It is only because we are identified with him that we can become like him. By being transformed into his image, we are enabled to model our lives on his. Now at last deeds are performed and life is lived in single-minded discipleship in the image of Christ and his words find unquestioning obedience.[49]

For Bonhoeffer, the "pattern of (all) good works" is Jesus Christ. Catechesis is concerned with the work of patterning the many members and the

49. Dietrich Bonhoeffer, *Cost of Discipleship*, p. 344.

gestures they practice into the pre-existing oneness of Christ's body. It is the communal structure of the church that serves Christ's Spirit, who "vivifies it by way of building up the body," according to Paul Minear.[50]

To begin constructing what the patterning of Christian gestures as catechetical instruction might look like in the church, we can use a corollary example from special education. There is the practice of patterning with young children who exhibit autistic-like behavior that is designed to improve malfunctioning nervous control by means of constant feedback from muscular activity imposed by an outside source or induced by other muscles.[51] Often it takes a team of people to reconfigure, or "re-wire," the child's muscles and nervous system. This patterning is called "neuromuscular reflex therapy": it involves promoting motor development through constant repetition of the primitive patterns of movement. It is known to require both a significant time commitment and a large group of caregivers, since each person, along with a team of caregivers, works on just one body part.[52] Teaching a child with a disability to crawl on legs and hands may involve a patterning team of four or five people, one at each limb and one at the head, who, for a long period, practice "range of motion" exercises moving the arms, legs, and head in the motion of a frontward crawl. They repeat this often throughout the day, seven days a week, for many days. Consistency matters. Getting a child to a kneeling posture is a long and gradual process — and can be arduous as well. There are indications that this kind of patterning is extremely effective among some children with neuromuscular disorders.

What we as Christians can draw from this example is that patterning is more than an isolated individual's act of the body; rather, it is an act of a community working in unity with hands, minds, and spirits with the one being patterned. Furthermore, patterning begins by breaking down one harmful practice in order to reconstruct a new practice. It begins with one-to-one relationships, and it calls on the model of imitation — from simple to more complex practices to habitual movements first learned in a community of people.

When my daughter was six years old, she would jump into the water, splash a great deal, and actually move around in the water. We declared her a "natural swimmer," that is, until we took her for her first swimming lesson.

50. Paul Minear in Hauerwas, *In Good Company* (Notre Dame: University of Notre Dame Press, 1995), p. 23.

51. See *Merriam Webster's Collegiate Dictionary*, 10th edition (Springfield, MA: Merriam-Webster, Inc., 1993), p. 853.

52. Sharon Raver, *Strategies for Teaching At-Risk and Handicapped Infants and Toddlers: A Transdisciplinary Approach* (New York: Merrill, 1991), p. 56.

Instead of placing her a grade or two above the other "beginners," the instructor held her back with the other beginners. Why? Because Adrianne had learned to churn in the water but not necessarily to swim. Day by day, the instructor broke Adrianne of her habits of a "natural style" of swimming and taught her the "unnatural" habits, which in the long run made it easier for her to swim. Soon Adrianne took what was new and unnatural and, through repetition, made it natural. The pilgrimage-patterning catechesis I am describing here is similar to the work of physical/occupational therapists or swim instructors. Catechetical instruction involves touching each other physically, and thus in mind and spirit reaching out to shake hands with the peace of Christ or to utter with our lips the words of the Lord's Prayer.

The process of patterning gestures will be awkward and difficult at times. It will begin with teaching a person to move his limbs while telling him the great reason for moving his body. For example, if one were to teach a child — or reteach an adult — the gesture of sharing, one might begin by putting an object that someone else desires in the hand of the one to be instructed. In a one-to-one instruction one may talk to the person about the reason she may not want to share, or about the benefits of sharing. With a young child, it may take putting one's hand over the hand of the child and guiding the action. As one grows older, the instruction in the gesture can be accompanied by a gospel account of sharing from what one has, demonstrating the connection between the gospel and one's actions. The next action would be to take this gesture of sharing into the home and learn to work on the impulse to share when the opportunity avails itself. The one practicing this sharing gesture might report to the master craftsperson or the community the opportunity that he or she had to share during that week. Having successfully worked on gestures of sharing, the person may continue to grow by finding more opportunities to share while learning about other virtue-bound gestures of the body of Christ.

The process of patterning into Christ will be awkward, difficult, and perhaps divisive at times, for in becoming members of Christ's body, we are required to take on ourselves a practice by which we learn that our bodies and lives are not our own, but Christ's. Such patterning demands a lifetime of practice, not by ourselves but among members of the church, with its many disciplines, gifts, and services. Though we would hope to escape the inner conflicts and weaknesses of life, like Paul, we struggle with not doing the good, which we want to do, but instead doing the evil that we don't want to do (Rom. 7:20). But Paul knows that the gift of God's grace in Christ is sufficient, "for power is made perfect in weakness" (2 Cor. 12:9).

Yoder calls the Christian community's posture against an inflated individualism a "revolutionary subordination," or a radical submissiveness. To give up what the world construes to be one's "rights," or the "ownership" of one's life, and to understand it in the context of the body of Christ, may seem to some to be quite radical. Christians are called to willingly submit to the will of Christ's mind, body, and spirit, that is, the church.[53] For Christ, the author of our salvific narrative, has saved us from ourselves and swept us into eternity, which is God, demonstrating such a will when he prayed in Gethsemane before his death, "My Father, if it is possible, let this cup pass from me; yet not what I want but what you want" (Matt. 26:39). One of the implications of this stand of radical submissiveness is that if my mind, body, and spirit are not mine alone, they are now the shared responsibility of the larger body of believers, of whom I am a part and to whom I am related and accountable. In the radical submissiveness of baptism, in which we recognize the dying of and to self, we rise with the risen Lord of creation.

Another way to consider this good that is shared among the members of Christ's body is as follows: in patterning Christian gestures we are instructing students to practice the gestures wisely, or as an embodiment of what Aristotle understood as *phronēsis,* roughly translated as "practical wisdom" or "wisdom in action."[54] Or, as Reinhard Hütter says, theological *phronēsis* is the "theological power of judgment" that makes possible our capacity to make use of theological knowledge in making theological decisions.[55] In learning and practicing the Christian gestures of the church, we are embodying: (1) the knowledge of the gesture and its practice in the narrative of the larger Christian community; (2) the judgment of which gestures to exercise — and how and when; (3) the way, the touch, the matter of "taste" or "style" in how one applies which gestures. It is through experience, the act of performing the gesture, that *phronēsis* is not only best "explained" but is "bred in the bones," part of the very marrow of Christ's body.

Friendship is a thick and complex, ever-changing and patterned, gesture that is forever being learned, unlearned, and relearned in Christian community. Because of our friendship with God, and through our friendship with other people, we are called to comprehend that the gestures practiced as

53. John Howard Yoder, *The Politics of Jesus* (Grand Rapids: Eerdmans Pub. Co., 1972), p. 190. I realize that Yoder was applying this term of "revolutionary subordination" to the posture of the church with regard to its place in the world. But it seems quite apparent that the world has constructed a worldview that leads us to perceive our mind, body, and spirit as something we have control over, while the opposite is true.

54. Aristotle, *Nichomachean Ethics (NE)* (Indianapolis: Bobbs-Merrill Educational Publishing, 1985), p. 312.

55. Hütter, p. 34.

Christian community further the cause of the kingdom of God, where we acquire Godly justice, courage, self-control, and good sense.[56]

One question remains: What is the greater good of Christ's body? In 1 Corinthians 12:31, Paul poses the rhetorical question concerning which gift of the Spirit is most precious for the body of Christ. We are left with this answer about the "greater gifts": "And I will show you a still more excellent way." With that Paul explores the gift of *agapē* love: it is a kind of love that is learned and understood as if it were a craft that is to be practiced, quite different from our sympathetic musings. This love-as-gesture is a love that is patient, kind, not envious or boastful or arrogant or rude (1 Cor. 13:4). We first learn and know such love for the good of the Christian community. To say that 1 Corinthians 12 and 1 Corinthians 13 fit together like "hand in a glove" is to put it mildly.[57] It is important to note that by creating and re-creating gestures of Christ, such as the gesture of charity, we are given the means to understand better what is the *telos* of our being in the church. Through the moral truths of the Christian community, our very characters — our will and judgment to know and do what is right before God — are being formed, as we practice these gestures within a congregation. I am arguing not for works-righteousness but that Christian gestures are but the means necessary in learning how we embody the "more excellent way" of living in Christian community — that is, love. Daniel Erlander puts it eloquently:

> Never does our status before God depend on how we feel, having the right experience, being free of doubts, what we accomplish, our success or our position (or the gestures we perform per se). We are Christians because God surprised us. Coming in water, God washed us and grafted us into Christ.[58]

The many patterns of Christly gestures are best taught along the pilgrimage; they are taught in the dynamic give-and-take life of a church as they are personally performed — monthly, weekly, daily, even by the minute — with flexibility to change in the context of the church season. The logic of teaching this way is similar to that of other learning contexts, each with its own language, rituals, and practices. If we teach baseball, we do so on the baseball diamond before, during, and after a baseball game; if piano, then we teach using a keyboard, both in performance and the practice room; if art,

56. McCabe, pp. 29-31.

57. See discussion in Chapter 2 on *agapē.*

58. Erlander in Maxwell Johnson, *The Rites of Christian Initiation,* p. 378.

with plenty of paint, canvas, brushes, and colors, building up to an exhibition; if dance, then in a dance studio with bar and mirror, leading to a recital. If we teach Christ, we do so in Christ's body.

In catechesis-as-patterning, the bodily gestures of our life are patterned after the life of Christ. Our being is both formed and nurtured simultaneously; our character is being shaped in the community of God's people and by the choices we make in performing certain gestures over other gestures that we could have made. Since our character is not a fixed or pre-existing thing, but something we have the responsibility of shaping in our living context, the gestures we perform daily as Christ's people mark us. That is why the ancient Greeks call character "that which is engraved." In proposing that education in Christ's body is the formation and nurturing of certain gestures, I am saying that it is about the forming of one's very being and character.

CHAPTER SEVEN

Performing Christly Gestures

What's the point of knowing good if you don't keep trying to become a good person?

Robert Coles[1]

How do we know what gestures to perform? What is our motivation in performing certain gestures? Alasdair MacIntyre's response to these questions is simple yet daunting: we must learn from others who already possess the moral education that we lack.[2] It is the same with performing gestures in Christ's body: we must learn from others who already possess the wisdom and charity that come from performing such gestures. Circumstances change; people's characters never stay the same. Intentions have passions; life is fluid and dynamic. Aquinas says that "things never happen the same way twice, and we don't even fully know ourselves, so how can we always know what is the best thing to do?"[3]

MacIntyre explains the unpredictableness of life this way:

> [In human affairs] I cannot predict my own future actions so far as these depend upon decisions as yet unmade by me — under the descriptions

1. Robert Coles, "A Disparity between Character and Intellect," *Duke Dialogue,* October 20, 1995, p. 7.

2. Alasdair MacIntyre, *Whose Justice? Which Rationality?,* p. 113.

3. Aquinas, *Summa Theologicae,* 29.109.9.

> which characterize the alternatives defining the decision. . . . If life is to be meaningful for us to be in possession of ourselves and not merely to be the creations of other people's projects, intentions and desires . . . this requires unpredictability.[4]

Life seems immune to any kind of generalization. As soon as we begin to formulate some kind of generalization about a given human action, claiming "we can predict," there is always a counter-example that trumps the plausibility of our prediction. Mary Midgley observes that there are no systematic or scientific rules here; we're always moving into new and uncharted territory.[5] The same is true of gestures: it is impossible to predict what gestures we will need, and when. We need to use our best judgment, or discernment, and this is not merely an intellectual game. Rather, these judgments involve our whole being and the entirety of Christian community, which help direct us through a whole forest of choices to make. MacIntyre says: "Practical understanding of goods, virtues, rules and relationships . . . is presupposed by our commitments . . . which we share with many of those same others."[6] We rely on the lessons we have learned from our own past of practicing certain gestures in similar circumstances, or having heard of others' experiences in the richness of the storied Christian community in which we live.

Character and the Performance of Gestures

I am interested in how the movement of a performed gesture can be the cause of an entire action for the greater good of Christ's body. It is important to understand, when someone performs a Christly gesture, that he or she is a certain kind of person, that his or her gestures are judged good by others. For Aristotle and Aquinas, the kind of people we are is bound up with the capacity we have to give reason for our actions, to be able to say, "I performed this gesture in this way because . . . ." This means that we can conceive of a "best" way, or at least a "good" that we share in common, in the action, and we can deliberately plan to attain it by performing certain gestures that embody a theological virtue.[7]

4. MacIntyre, *After Virtue,* p. 104.

5. Mary Midgley, *Can't We Make Moral Judgments?* (New York, NY: St. Martin's Press, 1991), p. 22.

6. MacIntyre, *Dependent Rational Animals* (Peru, IL: Carus Pub. Co., 1999), p. 156.

7. Ibid., p. 92.

Stanley Hauerwas and Charles Pinches say that character is produced by actions that embody certain virtues.[8] People of certain moral character are people of virtue: they have the skills — the repertoire of certain virtue-laden gestures — to keep them steady through the good and bad times of their lives.[9] But endurance is not an end in itself; rather, it produces a person of a certain kind of character. Character names the continuity of our lives — of what God is doing for us, and often in spite of us. Character arises out of our enduring suffering and what we recognize in those times as the narratives that live through us, making us more than we ever could have hoped. This is possible because Christ arose from the dead.

Here is the crux of the matter: the challenge for Christians is to understand and put into action Christly gestures, which we desire to perform because of our character. Since we strive to be persons of certain character with certain virtues, we can stand and march with our feet for truth over racism, and with charity we can stare hatred in the face. To be people who perform such gestures means that we have first observed others, then imitated and learned from their examples the complex gestures narrated by the numerous confusing and overlapping stories. We learn from others the power of gestures of truthfulness in a society that demands complicity. To literally and figuratively stand up and speak out for the truth, all of which is gesture, is possible only if we are people of character whose lives are shaped and nurtured by the virtues, both infused and theological. As MacIntyre reminds us, we are interested in raising children and others who do not act to please others but to achieve what is best for others as well as for self.[10]

Hauerwas says that Christian character is formed not only by experience but by one's intentional association with the church that embodies the language, rituals, and moral practices — or Christly gestures. We become certain kinds of Christians not necessarily by deducing certain actions from general rules or descriptions but performing gestures in accordance with our beliefs and practices, obligations and responsibilities, which are woven tightly into the fabric of the church.[11]

One caveat: the sanctification of our character is not a result of our own works, but, as John Saward reminds us, it is the

8. Stanley Hauerwas and Charles Pinches, *Christians Among the Virtues* (Notre Dame: University of Notre Dame Press, 1997), p. 12.

9. Ibid., pp. 124-135.

10. MacIntyre, *Dependent Rational Animals,* p. 84.

11. Stanley Hauerwas, *Character and the Christian Life* (San Antonio: Trinity University Press, 1975), p. 210.

> beautifying work of the risen Lord [which] starts in this life in the sanctification of men and reaches its fulfillment in the life to come in their glorification. . . . The Word made flesh is the Head, and we are His members; His victory over death is, therefore, ours too.[12]

Phronēsis and Christly Gestures

As our character and the church's character are being formed and nurtured through certain narrated gestures in particular experiences, those experiences contain certain judgments, or *phronēsis.* It is *phronēsis* — rooted in experience and not in theoretical reason alone — that fosters virtuous character and its fruit, virtuous living. Repeated performances, shaped and held by memory, give us experience, shaping us to be a certain kind of people.

Phronēsis, or practical rationality or wisdom, determines how we know when to perform which gesture, and why.[13] *Phronēsis* is a way of knowing that is difficult to "pin down," according to Hans Gadamer, because

> one is never sufficiently at a distance from *[phronēsis]* to simply be able to use it. *[Phronēsis]* gives someone a peculiarly intimate kind of self-knowledge without making it transparent. *[Phronēsis]* breaks out of an instrumentalist way of knowing, and therefore it can't be understood in categories of means and ends.[14]

Phronēsis

What is *phronēsis,* and why is it integral to this discussion on performing Christly gestures? Aristotle says that *phronēsis* is practical wisdom, a disposition for the good rather than for correct action.[15] *Phronēsis* is difficult to de-

12. See John Saward, *The Beauty of Holiness and the Holiness of Beauty* (San Francisco: Ignatius Press, 1996), pp. 64-65. Saward also quotes St. Augustine, who explains to his catechumens: "We also believe in the resurrection of the body that has first come out of Christ, so that the Body also may hope for what has already been done for the Head. The Head of the Church is Christ: the Church is the Body of Christ. Our Head is risen and has ascended into Heaven. Where the Head is, there also the members will be."

13. MacIntyre, *Dependent Rational Animals,* p. 5.

14. I found this reference to Hans Gadamer in Joseph Dunne, *Back to the Rough Grounds* (Notre Dame: Univ. of Notre Dame Press, 1993), p. 126.

15. MacIntyre, *Whose Justice?* pp. 97-98.

fine because it is not an abstract ideal involving a higher faculty of judgment but is an action or mode of knowledge that remains open to experience and action, and because action is an ineluctable movement that a person can never step out of.[16] Indeed, *phronēsis* is known retrospectively rather than prospectively. *Phronēsis* is unlike pure science or pure art, for in science or art the purpose of the activity is found in the act itself and in the completion of that act. Instead, *phronēsis* is the virtue that is the capacity of seeing, of knowing, of deliberating what is good for ourselves and good for those with whom we live and share life together. Knowing and seeing the good, *phronēsis* is the virtue that directs our actions or gestures toward living for the good of all.[17]

How do we know what is the good? MacIntyre says that *phronēsis* is the capacity to apply certain truths about what is good for such and such kind of person, or for people as such, and to do the good generally and in certain particular kinds of situations to both oneself and others.[18] *Phronēsis* — practical reasoning — gives rise to practical action — or praxis — which is learned in relationship with others.[19]

I want to outline briefly the ways in which *phronēsis* (Aristotle) and *prudentia* (Aquinas) are instrumental in the performance of virtue-laden gestures. While we have a large, varied repertoire of gestures to choose from in living our daily lives as Christians, the key is to know when to perform the gesture, how to perform it, and always to what purpose. John Howard Yoder says that if Jesus is Lord, obedience to his rule cannot be dysfunctional. Principled, virtuous behavior generally cannot be imprudent. "*Phronēsis,* if Christian, must always be suspect — to be expected to be at some point subversive," says Yoder.[20] A Christian *phronēsis* makes it possible for us to make the right kinds of judgments about which virtue-bound gesture to enact for the good of the body of Christ.[21]

MacIntyre says that in this *polis,* there is an interdependence of practical intelligence or rationality (*phronēsis*), which shapes the virtues of character. In order for *phronēsis* to be practiced, there is the presupposition that the society in which we live already has an understanding of what is the good that all members share in common. Likewise, the practice of virtue, and being virtuous people, is required if there is to be a right choice of actions; and

16. Aristotle, *NE,* 1140a25-1141b20.

17. Aristotle, *NE,* 1140a-1140b.

18. MacIntyre, *Whose Justice?* pp. 113-115.

19. MacIntyre, *Dependent Rational Animals,* p. 74.

20. John Howard Yoder, *The Priestly Kingdom* (Notre Dame: University of Notre Dame Press, 1984), pp. 17, 37-40.

21. Hütter, p. 34.

phronēsis ushers in and guides right action. Any *polis,* including Christ's body, needs both the specific virtues *and phronēsis.* They are inseparable, for without both we would become as if we were wild animals.[22]

Phronēsis, then, involves the act of deliberating well.[23] In the investigative excellence of deliberation we learn to assess what is conducive to a result that reinforces the common good.[24]

Phronēsis is an intellectual virtue itself, and it is united with all other virtues as well. Aristotle says that it is impossible to be good in the

> full sense of the word without practical wisdom or to be a man of practical wisdom without moral excellence or virtue. For while a virtue might determine the end or the goal of what we are trying to do together, it is *phronēsis* — practical wisdom — which makes us do what is conducive to that end which is laid out by the practice of the virtue.[25]

While *phronēsis* makes possible the practice of other virtues, it is important to remember that it is an intellectual virtue whose exercise is internally motivated for the desire of the good we have in common. It is a desire for the fulfillment of the virtue itself that determines what we will do in each changing circumstance of life. *Phronēsis* is not a knowledge of ethical ideas per se, but it is a resourcefulness of mind that responds uniquely to the situation in which these ideas are to be realized. For example, to know what is just — a moral virtue — requires more than knowledge and practice of what exactly is a just action. This kind of knowledge would be more theoretical. *Phronēsis* as intellectual virtue causes the purposes of life to be right. Seeing what is to be done in order to achieve the good requires a cognition, which needs an infusion of moral virtues for right practice.[26]

Phronēsis is a virtue bound up with experience. We know *phronēsis* only through directly experiencing *phronēsis* in action. Dunne writes that there is a two-way relationship between experiences and *phronēsis.* On the one hand, *phronēsis* is able to be maintained in experience, grounded in a connectedness or concern with particulars that characterize *phronēsis* and experience. On the other hand, in experience the universals of the context in which we live reach to include a reference to the particulars in life and the first causes in life.[27] As is

22. MacIntyre, *Whose Justice?* pp. 126, 351.
23. Aristotle, *NE,* 1140a25-1141b20.
24. Aristotle, *NE,* 1142b30.
25. Aristotle, *NE,* 1144b30; 1145a5.
26. Dunne, pp. 271-272.
27. Dunne, p. 293.

true with any other acquired virtue, we learn these virtues through narrated experiences. The experience of *phronēsis* needs to be narrated by the community members who understand its performance; without such a narrative, we will most likely not understand *phronēsis,* for we will not know what we're looking for in the first place.

Phronēsis is known inductively rather than deductively, taught from and in the experience rather than outside of the experience, to be applied later to an experience. *Phronēsis's* gestures remain unpredictable, open-ended, and frequently irreversible. *Phronēsis* is noninstrumental, meaning there are no instruments or computer software program by which one learns to perform it. *Phronēsis* is not a completed state of knowledge, one that can be made into a set of behavioral objectives for easy classroom instruction. Nor is this virtue able to be reduced to one or two quick pointers learned in weekend seminars. *Phronēsis* does not ascend to a level of abstraction or generality that leaves experience behind. Rather, like any other virtue, there is an openness in the experience of *phronēsis,* in which one is continually involved in a learning process.

It is in the immediacy of the moment of life experiences that we are taught *phronēsis.* There are no "teaching moments" set aside in which one can say, "that is education." Instead, all of life, in every gesture performed, is a teaching moment, as *phronēsis* is best learned in the thickness, the unpredictable, flexible, and improvisational aspects of life.

Yoder reminds us that *phronēsis* demands that we make certain actions that are illuminated by the general faith commitments of those with whom we live. Yoder goes so far as to suggest that it is not possible, in the strictest sense, to discuss the place of *phronēsis* without a context in which to discuss and live it. It is in the context in which we live that we know *phronēsis.*[28]

Praxis

If *phronēsis* is concerned with human affairs and with matters about which deliberation is possible, then *praxis,* or — in the Aristotelian use of the term — a practical action, is informed with practical interest. Aristotle says that what separates us from animals is *praxis:*

> Now, there are three elements in the soul which control action and truth: sense perception, intelligence [*nous*] and desire. Of these sense perception

28. Yoder, *Priestly Kingdom,* p. 17.

> does not initiate any action. We can see this from the fact that animals have sense perception but have no share in action [moral action or praxis]. . . . Therefore, since moral virtue is a characteristic involving choice, and since choice is a deliberate desire, it follows that, if the choice is to be good, the reasoning must be true and the desire correct; that is, reasoning must affirm what desire pursues. This then is the kind of thought and the kind of truth that is practical and concerned with action [praxis].[29]

For the ancient Greeks, who were concerned about the life of the *polis*, *praxis* was key in order that free citizens not only cooperate with one another but that they attain the goal of a happy life together *(eudaimonia)*.[30] Furthermore, Grundy writes that *phronēsis* itself has its own action — outcome in a form of *praxis.* Grundy explains that *phronēsis* and *praxis* are dependent on one another, as *praxis* follows *phronēsis.* Grundy supports this claim by citing Aristotle's *Nichomachean Ethics:*

> Choice is the starting point of action: it is the source of motion but not the end for the sake of which we act. The starting point of choice, however, is desire and reasoning directed toward some end. That is why there cannot be choice either without intelligence and thought or without some moral characteristic; for good and bad action in human conduct are not possible without thought and character. Now thought alone moves nothing; only thought which is directed to some end and concerned with action can do so. . . . Therefore, choice is either intelligence motivated by desire or desire operating through thought, and it is as a combination of these two that man is a starting point of action.[31]

Praxis is dependent on both *poiēsis* — doing-action — and *phronēsis* — practical rationality; for *praxis* is the action resulting from such reasoning, keeping in mind at all times the good of all. Like *phronēsis,* praxis assumes a just society or one in which the good is known. In the case of the church, the *polis* that is good and just is the body of Christ.[32]

In sum, what kind of persons we are as Christians does matter in the decision of which Christly gesture we will execute or perform, when we will perform it, and for what purpose we are performing it. Yet the gestures we per-

29. Aristotle, *NE,* 1139a15-25.

30. Hütter, p. 35; Shirley Grundy, *Curriculum: Product or Praxis?* (New York: Falmer Press, 1987), p. 181.

31. Aristotle, *NE,* 1139a30-35.

32. Grundy, p. 183.

form have a double action. In one movement, the gesture we choose to perform as members of Christ's body, given the circumstances facing us, may be understood as a reflection or an effect of our character, since the Christly gesture itself is an embodied virtue. Yet our beings are being re-formed by the very experience of performing the Christly gesture, as are those who are directly affected by the performance of the Christly gestures.

Performing Christly Gestures

The focus of learning Christly gestures — what we do that reveals our moral character — is the performing of those gestures. Emphasizing the performance aspect of gestures may challenge or confuse conventional ways of educating in the church, because when many hear the word "performance," they automatically think of the "performing arts" in the theater, or preaching as performance. According to Philip Auslander, thinking of performance as theater is an idea deeply ingrained in modern Western society; the theater haunts all understandings of performance, whether in an actual theater or simply among a group of actors and an audience, with a script and a director, perhaps a musician, maybe even a dancer.[33] Yet while "performance" is usually related to the creative arts in our modern world, I argue that that is only one way of understanding performance.

"Performance," like "community" and "gesture," is a context-dependent term. Here I am interested in the performance of gestures as a social or communicative act in which the use of our bodies, including our voices, is central to the way we live as Christians in Christ's body.[34] Second, I will outline the way I use "performance" theologically. Third, I will describe a methodology of teaching, learning, and performing the Christian faith through the performance of Christly gestures.

The word "performance" comes from two sources: the middle-English *perfouren* and the French *parfournir* (*par* means "thoroughly," and *fournir* means "to furnish"). Performance is a process of bringing something, such as a message, to a complete action or accomplishment. In this regard, perfor-

33. Philip Auslander, *From Acting to Performance* (New York City: Routledge, 1997), pp. 3, 4. I understand that there are many forms of performance that can fit under this broad descriptive definition — from a guitarist playing in a subway station to a striptease dancer.

34. Reinhard Hütter experiments with a presentative-communicative aspect of learning the Christian faith by being drawn into the core church practices. See *Suffering Divine Things*, p. 190.

mance is a combination of *poiēsis* and *mimēsis,* though the performance is learned through the repetitive act of imitating someone else's actions.[35]

However, our understanding of performance also depends on the cultural location and the common narratives for determining what is being performed, who is performing, or for whom it is being performed. It also depends on whether the performance is something aesthetically gratuitous or bound by certain rituals, and the purposes of the rituals — whether in a play, one of the creative arts, or a sporting event. Other times, the focus is solely on the performer himself or herself. What is considered a "competent" performance in music, speech, dance, or church depends on the traditions of the communities in which the performance is given.[36] Consider the following examples.

Theater is an investigation, a judgment, about the daily small social dramas of everyday occurrences.[37] It is "twice-behaved behavior," neither free nor easy; there are constraints of time, place, and people. Richard Schechner says that a theatrical performance is a kind of "restored behavior," whether rehearsed or previously known, learned by osmosis since childhood, or revealed in the performance by the master performers. A theatrical performance presumes that a gesture has already been performed in everyday life before being brought to the stage.[38]

Similarly, Victor Turner says that "theater" comes into existence when there is a separation between performer and audience.[39] Such a separation allows an audience and the actors to see the world of ordinary existence in dramatically new ways.

People derive their understanding of performance from the theater because it is a common entertainment venue for a wide cross section of people in many cultures; it communicates ideas with the three-dimensionality of the performer appearing before our very eyes. People are drawn by the visual na-

35. Victor Turner, *From Ritual to Theatre* (New York: Performing Arts Journal Publications, 1982), p. 103.

36. It is important to distinguish "performance" from "practice" as defined by Alasdair MacIntyre in *After Virtue:* "Any coherent and complex form of socially established cooperative human activity through which goods internal to that form of activity are realized in the course of trying to achieve those standards of excellence which are appropriate to, and partially definitive of, that form of activity, with the result that human powers to achieve excellence, and human conceptions of the ends and goods involved, are systematically extended" (Notre Dame: University of Notre Dame Press, 1984), p. 187.

37. Richard Schechner in Victor Turner, *From Ritual to Theatre,* p. 112.

38. Schechner in *Between Theater and Anthropology* (Philadelphia: University of Pennsylvania Press, 1985), p. 118.

39. Turner, *From Ritual to Theatre,* p. 112.

ture of the theater, and they are especially engaged by performances whose themes resonate with daily life's joys and struggles. Turner says that spectators' interest in the performance lies not necessarily in the novelty of a story told but how well the playwright deals with the issues of life.[40] According to Erving Goffman, all performances are socialized, molded and modified to fit the understanding and expectations of the society — the audience — in which they are presented.[41]

Furthermore, as Hans Urs von Balthasar observes, existence has a deep need to see itself mirrored:

> And this makes theatre a legitimate instrument in pursuit of self-knowledge and elucidation of Being — an instrument that points beyond itself. As mirror, it enables us to attain ultimate theological understanding of self.[42]

While performing Christly gestures in daily life may not constitute moments of great theater — for many gestures are small and subtle rather than grand — nevertheless gestures are grist for theater. If theater is made up of "twice-performed behaviors," how helpful would it be in churches if we could reflect on our gestures both before and after they are enacted? We understand the importance of gestures only when they are reproduced, or as von Balthasar says, are provided a mirror in the theater.[43]

Improvisational Theater and Gestures

Sam Wells proposes that improvising is an offer that an actor makes when delivering a line that is unscripted yet within his or her character and the context of the play. Once he or she makes such an offer, the other actors may either accept the improvisation or block it. In accepting and playing off the initial actor's move, the responding actor shares the space with him or her, which re-

40. Ibid.

41. Erving Goffman, *The Presentation of Self in Everyday Life* (Edinburgh: Univ. of Edinburgh, Monograph #2, 1956), p. 22.

42. Hans Urs von Balthasar, *Theo-Drama, Vol. 1* (San Francisco: Ignatius Press, 1988), p. 117.

43. For example, consider the movie made from the novel *Primary Colors*. In the opening of the movie, the President is busy shaking hands and holding arms along a line of people who have come to see and be seen with the President. Meanwhile, one of his aides is telling another character the meaning behind each handshake, suggesting that the way the President shakes a hand or holds an elbow with his other hand reveals what he wants from each person whose hand touches his.

quires imaginative creativity. But blocking the first actor's improvisation is subtly aggressive and undermines him or her. The good improviser accepts all offers and perceives no end to the story; such story continuation requires a disciplined imagination and creativity. Keeping the story going suggests that we understand that the story is not just our story; rather, we are the kind of people who have the courage to keep the story going, even when it looks dangerous or when it threatens to reveal uncomfortable parts of ourselves.[44]

Christly gestures of daily life are like the performances of improvisational theater. From the moment we awake to when we go to bed, in the ways we respond to neighbors, friends, family members, strangers, or God, we perform gestures that are at best improvisational. We Christians have the basic "story line" of the gospel, and the gestures we choose to perform in the improvisational theater of Christ's body are hewn to circumstances.

Performance in Music

Frances Young understands music as culturally conditioned in its conventions, harmonies, and rhythms; all are characteristic of a particular place and historical period. The Romantic music of nineteenth-century Germany is quite different from traditional Balinese gongs. Musical performances are also culturally conditioned: those who perform and those who hear the performance determine what is good. What was true about the theater is also largely true in musical performance: playing an instrument — or using one's voice to sing — can take place in a living room, in a rehearsal practice room of a university's music building, in a subway station, or on a concert stage. As a pianist, I am aware of the importance of gestures when I play the piano. Learning to play the piano begins with the body, but it is more than mere body movements or physical flexing; rather, playing the piano is an act of body, mind, spirit. Depending on the composition I am performing, I approach the piano keyboard differently with my body: I play a Bach prelude with feet away from all the pedals, holding down keys with certain fingers while other fingers dance in an attack pose, ready to create a staccato effect. This is different, for example, from playing the adagio movement of a Beethoven sonata: there I lean into the piano with my entire body, burying my fingers in the keys, using the pedals liberally for mood and affect.

44. Sam Wells, *How the Church Performs Jesus' Story: Improvising on the Theological Ethics of Stanley Hauerwas* (University of Durham, UK: unpublished dissertation, 1995), p. 205.

There is also the performance of musically listening to and understanding what one hears. Listening to the combinations of sounds in music requires knowing something about the conventional meanings of agreed-on musical elements. The audience matters in performance, and listening itself is a performance — because music is culturally determined.[45] A musical performance is an experience of discourse among composer, musicians, and audience.[46]

A good performance requires a certain skill that is acquired over a long period of time, through commitment and disciplined practice, including many rehearsals and recitals. Young says that tradition is indispensable for a classical performance; while a creative artist will bring something fresh and inspiring to every performance, a completely novel approach would not necessarily be a good rendering of a classical work.[47] For example, a classically trained pianist's goal is to give a performance of a composition that is in keeping with the intent of the composer. That's why the pianist carefully studies all the markings of rhythm and tempo in the score, the fortes and pianissimos in certain sections — as well as historical facts about the composition and composer. Playing a baroque, classical, romantic, or modern composition, the pianist may come upon a passage containing a measure or two of improvisation — a trill here or there — in keeping with the style of the composition.[48] These opportunities for improvisation allow the performer to display technical skills and brilliance within the given score, though they must still fit within the unity of the whole composition. The musician becomes the bridge between the classic work and the audience.[49]

It is also important to know what Christly gestures one can use improvisationally. As in piano performance, there is room for improvisation in the performance of Christly gestures, even though they are learned and rehearsed. A performer learns to discern which improvisational style to practice by imitating the improvisational style of those who have mastered the art of improvising — within his or her musical talent and within the composition's style. There is nothing freeing about improvisation that is outside the bounds of the composition; rather, the exhilaration comes in performing the

45. Simon Frith, *Performing Rites* (Cambridge: Harvard University Press, 1998), pp. 109, 204.

46. Frith, p. 204. Philip Auslander, quoting Auguston Boal, writes about being a "spect-actor," a single entity that subsumes both functions within a single body of spectator *and* actor (Auslander, *From Acting to Performance*, p. 101).

47. Francis Young, *Virtuoso Theology* (Cleveland: Pilgrim Press, 1990), pp. 23-45, 105.

48. Ibid., p. 161.

49. Ibid., p. 161.

piece as the composer intended it to be played, even with an improvisation that the composer might have used.[50]

Performance and Dance

Dance is a performing or performance art in which the performer's body is central, similar to the performance art of Christly gestures. Just as one cannot remove the gesturer from the gesture, one cannot remove the dancer from the dance. The dancer and the dance also communicate different "languages" or cultures via the movement of the body.[51] It is intriguing that what is considered "dance" is also context-dependent: dance depends on a group of people, their time, and their physical location. I believe that dance can provide a powerful way of understanding gesture and the pedagogy of gestures. In dance, just as in Christly gestures, the body is the expressive medium in which mind, body, and spirit are one; a dancer must think about his or her next step, and it too is willed by the Spirit of God. Dance is willed movement, chosen for both aesthetic and functional reasons; it incorporates means and ends as the dancer draws attention to herself or himself in the act of ceding control of movement to music's rhythm and sound.[52]

There are two kinds of dance or choreography. The first, representational dance, is about metaphor and analogy: the dancer's intention is to translate life's events into body movements on a stage, while it is the audience's role to find the allegorical significance in those movements. Some dances, such as the narrative-driven ballet *The Nutcracker Suite,* can be decoded quite easily by the audience. In the second kind, ideological dance, the dancers' purpose is radical: they seek to change the world through a certain kind of representation.[53] But this dance is more than social commentary on world events; instead, the dance itself becomes something on which a social commentary is made.[54]

50. It is important to remember that improvisation in a Mozart piano composition is radically different from the saxophonist's improvisation in a Duke Ellington composition for orchestra.

51. Merce Cunningham, quoted in Auslander, p. 74.

52. Frith, pp. 218-220.

53. Auslander, pp. 74-90.

54. Auslander, p. 79. This was true with the Arnie Zane–Bill Jones Dance Company's 1990s dance performance in which the faces of those who are dying, especially of AIDS, were flashed on a background screen while dancers were in front of the screens dancing. There was much debate about the profundity — or sacrilege — of the dance itself.

Both styles of dance are important to performing Christly gestures, because it is the performing body of the dancer and the gesturer that is doubly encoded: it is defined by the code of whether a particular performance itself is good or poor.[55] But it is encoded or inscribed by the audience's social discourse as well, that is, what the dance ought to be saying or doing. To that end, the dance and the dancer are in dialogue with the audience as well as with the choreographer and composer. Similarly, the one performing the gesture is in a kind of discussion not only with those who first taught him the gesture but also with those to whom he is gesturing, as well as with Christ's Spirit.

Among all the creative art forms of performance, what is not clear is how the very character of the one performing influences the performance itself. Aristotle notes that it is by playing the harp that one becomes either a good or bad harpist — just as with builders and all the other craftspersons.[56]

Performance Considered Theologically

Christ's body is not a static body but a living, performing body. Turner says that religion, like art, continues to "live" insofar as it is performed, that is, insofar as its rituals are the ongoing concerns of the community: "If you wish to spay a religion, remove its rituals, its generative or regenerative process."[57] In writing about the performance of the Eucharist, von Balthasar draws a comparison between the theater and the Eucharist by observing that theater is itself a self-actualizing analogy between creation and redemption: "The water of the Jordan washes [us] clean, the earth offers wheat and vines, air fashions the words of one creation, and fire is the event itself." Theater, like the Eucharist, keeps us aware of the fluidity of meanings in creation in general, and in the Eucharist in particular.[58] In other words, performance-as-creative-art and performance-as-theological-task have some similarities. However, there are also important ways in which they are different from one another. First, we worship a performing God. Fodor and Hauerwas say that Christian faith is a performance because Christians worship a God who is pure act — an eternally performing God.[59] "God is a performing God who has invited us to join

55. Here I would add that the character of the dancer and gesturer also matters.

56. Aristotle, *NE,* 1103b7-9.

57. Turner, *From Ritual to Theatre,* p. 86.

58. Von Balthasar, *Theo-Drama, Vol. 1* (San Francisco: Ignatius Press, 1988), p. 117.

59. James Fodor and Stanley Hauerwas, "Performing the Faith: The Peaceable Rhetoric of God's Church" (unpublished manuscript), p. 2.

in the very performance which is God's life. . . . [It is] the eternally performing God, who creates *and* redeems" the world. Fodor and Hauerwas understand that Christ is God's most defining performance, and through him we who are Christians become holy performers.[60]

Von Balthasar says that this performing God is not distant but always involved in the world, which means that there is always a "divine-human dramatic tension," that is, the mystery of our life in God. This revelation of truth can be made only in connection with the unveiling of God's radical initiative on the world's behalf in the Christ event.[61]

This leads to the second characteristic: because we are created in the image of the eternally performing God, we are created as human beings to perform. Cultural anthropologists draw the same conclusion: to be human is to perform. As *homo performans,* says Turner, we understand ourselves better through our acting in daily life; we also know ourselves by observing others.[62] In simple conversations, in telling a joke, in relaying a story using hand gestures, in crying, in squinting, in playing games with one another and playing certain roles in society, and in listening to and watching others, we are engaged in a performance. Turner says that the basic stuff of life is performance, the presentation of ourselves in everyday life circumstances.[63] We use performance to express an impulse either to be serious or to entertain; to collect meanings or to pass the time; to display symbolic behavior in the act of being oneself with others.[64]

Performing Christly gestures is a godly performance because we perform the gestures in God and with God's Spirit working through us. No human action can be described as independent of God, as a self-initiating, self-generating movement: "Rather, we act only insofar as we share in the divine life, for we exist solely within God's reality," according to Fodor and Hauerwas. To perform the Christian faith is to work in the grain of God's grace.[65] It is important to highlight the centrality of Christ in performance and the divine-human dramatic tension. Christ far outstrips or out-narrates this dramatic polarity between God and human beings because he is the epitome of all holiness, the only figure of consequence. Similarly, Christ's "performance" always eclipses our performance of gestures in life, thereby taking

60. Ibid., pp. 9, 10.

61. Von Balthasar, *Theo-Drama, Vol. 1,* p. 129.

62. Victor Turner, *The Anthropology of Performance* (New York: Performing Arts Journal Pub., 1988), p. 81.

63. Ibid.

64. Schechner, in Turner, *From Ritual to Theatre,* p. 103.

65. My paraphrase of Fodor and Hauerwas, p. 27.

us up into his gesture. There is no divine-human dramatic tension in the risen Christ, for God emptied himself so he can use the world according to his purposes, not ours. God's action of giving us Christ comes from above us as well as from outside us. Von Balthasar says that God does not necessarily do something for us; rather, God is and does everything.[66]

> For in Christ all the fullness of God was pleased to dwell, and through him God was pleased to reconcile to himself all things, whether on earth or in heaven, by making peace through the blood of his cross. (Col. 1:19-20)

In Romans 5:12, 15, 18, Paul also captures the drama of the gospel with God's performance in the gift of the risen Christ to liberate us from the ways of Adam:

> Therefore, just as sin came into the world through one man, and death came through sin, and so death spread to all because all have sinned . . . (and) if many died through the one man's trespass, much more surely have the grace of God and the free gift in the grace of the one man, Jesus Christ, abounded for the many. . . . Therefore just as one man's trespass led to condemnation for all, so one man's act of righteousness leads to justification and life for all.

The Incarnation — God with us in the flesh in Christ — is the opposite of all disguises or masks; in Christ, God is completely and utterly himself.[67] It isn't a question of whether or not "God is in the audience," or whether "God is the stage of life." God is all and in all, and God's people are called and given the task of following Christ, which consists not only in doing some right things but in fundamentally surrendering everything to the God who gave us his Son.[68]

Just as Christ is God's performance, so too the church as Christ's body is God's performance as the people of God. More specifically, the church as Christ's body is a performing body. Sam Wells says that the church-as-performing-body is an "improvising community" since we are not necessarily always in control of the church's agenda. Rather, God is in control and is the agenda of the church,[69] because our vocation is to perform the good news of

66. Von Balthasar, p. 33.
67. Ibid., p. 52.
68. Ibid., p. 33.
69. Sam Wells, p. 203.

God's redeeming love in Christ, as Fodor and Hauerwas remind us.[70] In turn, the church-as-good-improviser accepts all offers and perceives no end to the story unless there has been a thorough reincorporation.[71]

Finally, the church's performance of gestures is not just a means to an end but is always eschatological. While there is a practical/technical dimension to all performances of gestures, we perform the gestures often as a means toward a certain end, which is the good of Christ's body and the glory of God's kingdom. Again, Fodor and Hauerwas:

> Because the Christian story has already ended victoriously, and definitively in Jesus, the church is free to bear witness to that ending. The church is the prolongation of Christ's body on earth and in that sense the proleptic presence of the eschaton.[72]

The eschatological purpose of the church-as-performer is manifest when we celebrate the Eucharist. Turner says that the Eucharist was a drama with a scriptural script long before it gave rise to medieval passion plays. The interest for the parishioner-as-spectator lay not in the novelty of the story but in seeing how the priest-as-dramatist had chosen to treat the well-known story in the context of the day's events.[73] Nicholas Lash echoes Turner's observation in describing the Eucharist as the best interpretative performance that is in the whole of the Christian life. Praise, confession, and petition enact the meaning they embody: the story is told so that Christ's story may be performed after the participants depart in peace.[74]

In conclusion, to live daily as church is a performance: the presentation of oneself in everyday life. Life is a collage of dramas in which we cope with significant others, constancy and freedom, finding ourselves endlessly scripted but seeking to act gracefully and freely, working the script in a new way:

> Drama teaches us that we need other characters to play with and against; the biblical drama teaches us that God is a "genuinely other character who takes a decisive role in the drama," and that we are "others" to God.[75]

70. Fodor and Hauerwas, p. 25.
71. Wells, p. 219.
72. Fodor and Hauerwas, p. 20.
73. Turner, *From Ritual to Theatre,* p. 103.
74. Nicholas Lash, *Theology on the Way to Emmaus,* pp. 37-46.
75. Turner, *The Anthropology of Performance,* p. 81.

A Performance Pedagogy of Christly Gestures

In reviewing the ways in which other disciplines and fields understand performance, I wish to turn the reader's attention to pedagogy — the method of teaching gestures to others, recognizing the coherent yet thick and complex forms of gesturing as intentional physical actions that embody the virtues themselves. The performance is complex because there are many intricate parts to any performance and to the gestures themselves, which are dynamic and continually shifting. On the one hand, there are issues regarding the intentionality of the gesturer as well as the one receiving the performed gesture, and the coordination of body, mind, and spirit in the performance itself. The flexibility of performing gestures needs to be done without rejecting the institutional constraints, the historical dimension, or the competing theological claims of the church. On the other hand, God is active in the performance of the gesture; the gesture mediates the virtue infused by God and teaches the person performing the gesture the embodiment of a theological virtue, for example, charity. Yet our performance of Christly gestures is itself a gift to us from God in that our will and desire, intellect and physical capacity to move our bodies according to the ways of Christ, infused by the Holy Spirit, draw us closer to God. By performing a Christ-like gesture of a theological virtue such as charity, we become charitable as Christ himself is charitable to us. The very gesture, then, is a theological interpretative action that shapes our character and the character of Christ's body.

Some important characteristics of a performance pedagogy of Christly gestures are drawn from theological, educational, and cultural anthropological sources.[76] Anthropologists also see the idea of performance-in-the-everyday as quite distinct from performance-as-theater. After all, the roots of all performances are not in the creative arts but in the performance of ordinary daily life, which is pregnant with social dramas from which theater draws its subjects and its scripts. When we act in the ordinariness of life, we act out of certain "frames of reference," out of relationships established with others in Christ.[77]

76. Turner calls the anthropology or ethnography of performance, "ethnodramaturg," as dramaturgy is the art or technique of dramatic composition and theatrical presentation. Ethnodramaturg is observing the pattern of performance technique or dramatic composition in our daily life. See Turner, *From Ritual to Theatre,* p. 100.

77. Ibid., p. 122.

Performance Pedagogy of Gestures: Body, Mind, and Spirit

The entirety of our being is involved in the actual doing of the gospel narrative. It is body in Schechner's theatrical sense of a performance text placed in the body of the performer through a training whose bases are integral parts of the performance text itself. Once it becomes a habit of the performer's body, the performance text is manifest during performances and passed on to other performers.[78] All performances involve the human body as the site of knowledge. Each of us, before we have a name, is a body. And language itself is an act of the body and mind, whether we express ourselves verbally or use our hands in sign language.[79] Marked by discourse and as a place of the communication, the body is not a "value-neutral site."[80] Instead, our performances are in a specific "field of cultural codes."[81] For example, a handshake can express a greeting, agreement to a contract, or the passing of the peace of Christ — depending on the narrative underlying the gesture. Our flesh is folded, our bones move, and our muscles are stretched as we exercise the movement of certain gestures. After repeated movements, it is as if our very bodies know the gestures; we receive comfort from repeating the known.[82] In time, certain gestures will take on our individual characteristics or style as we move, walk, shake hands, genuflect in our own inimitable fashion.

Our "bodies" themselves have a memory, says Jean Stewart:

> How long is the body's memory? If there were no cut, no bruise, no crater where they took out muscle tissue, if all the evidence could be whisked away and the line of her hip restored to its old, sweet curve, would she not still carry that memory in her bones, carry it forever, the act so savage that no amount of anesthesia could have prevented her knowledge?[83]

While the mind has forgotten the loss of a limb, and thus commands the leg to walk, for example, it is not until the disabled person falls down that she or he remembers the current circumstances of disability. Along with body is spirit. Aquinas says that the only properly human actions are those that

78. Schechner, *Between Theater and Anthropology*, p. 234.

79. Auslander, p. 98.

80. Ibid., p. 102.

81. Alice Rayner, *To Act, To Do, To Perform* (Ann Arbor: University of Michigan Press, 1994), p. 32.

82. Another way of thinking about this is as if one were on "automatic pilot," performing without necessarily being conscious of what one is doing.

83. Jean Stewart, *The Body's Memory* (New York: St. Martin's Press, 1989), pp. 18, 19.

mark a person out as a person, within sight of the ultimate goal, which is God:

> A man's human actions are those lying under his control and proceeding from deliberate will. But the sort of action proceeding from a particular power (from sight, say, or hearing) is determined by how objects present themselves to that power. . . . Man's ultimate goal, then, if it is a human action, is action done at the will's command. . . . So whatever a man does he does for a goal, even the doing of his ultimate goal.[84]

That "ultimate goal" of all gestures for Christians is God, who alone can satisfy our deepest longings.[85] The Holy Spirit is active in gestured performances, which may not be known previously but are made known as we acquire the theological virtues such as charity and honesty. In turn, the performance of charitable gestures makes known to us the gift of God's grace. Flannery O'Connor writes that in the performance of charity we understand that grace has been offered, but this is not necessarily a knowledge that is consciously "thought out" but rather a discovery that is made.[86] To quote Aquinas, "The right use of grace . . . is in the loving activity of charity."[87]

Finally, there is the mind, or cognitive thought, behind all performances. We depend on the capacity to think intentionally about moving the body in performing because there is usually some kind of thoughtful intention in each performance act. Thomas Tracy says that any intentional action or gestured performance is one that is antecedent or has an intended outcome; each performance has a purpose that is determined by the performer.[88] Tracy gives the example of ringing a bell: I pull a rope to ring a bell, moving my body in certain ways to pull the rope. I may also have to perform certain volitional mental acts in order to turn my body in the appropriate ways. Though I may move in certain ways to pull the rope, I may not intend to ring the bell beyond the successful execution of a behavior.[89]

Lash says that the performance of a text is an intellectual, intentional, interpretative action that is construed as a "rendering," bearing witness to one whose words and deeds, discourse and suffering, were "rendering" the truth

84. Aquinas, *Summa Theologicae,* 16.1.1.

85. Ibid., 16.2.1.

86. Flannery O'Connor, *Mystery and Manners,* p. 118.

87. Aquinas, *ST,* 30.108.2.

88. Thomas Tracy, *God, Action and Embodiment* (Grand Rapids: Wm. B. Eerdmans, 1984), pp. 20-25.

89. Ibid., pp. 26-27.

of God in human history.[90] Such rendering-as-performance involves mind and spirit as well as body.

Cognitive, rational thought is needed to lend insight into body movements, and to name and reflect on the presence of God's Spirit. Again, it is helpful to think of "the mind" as Aquinas did: the mind is the form of our bodies; we have an *embodied* mind.[91] Robert Barron wrote of the ensouled bodies: "For God made us good — body and soul — and God thus intends that we live our lives and reach our final consummation precisely as embodied souls."[92] Another way of stating this body-mind-spirit formula is to think of gestured performances as an embodiment of the gospel. Tracy says that the human body is a pattern of organic activity that the human being does not choose or intentionally enact per se, but that permits a limited range of intentional variation in basic action. We are bodily beings because our capacity for intentional action is rooted in a basic pattern of life; the given pattern of activity at the foundation of our lives is, according to Tracy, one of organic activity.[93] Aquinas helps us understand that the kind of gesture we must practice voluntarily must advance happiness, if happiness is God. We must also discern what gesture or action blocks the road. God can move us to action, directly influencing our will, if God so desires.[94]

Performance of Gestures as Incarnational Action

Marva Dawn says that the gospel has always been incarnated: "As in Christ, so in human beings who have died to themselves and risen again to life engaged in by the power of the Holy Spirit."[95] God is, by power, everywhere and "by presence everywhere (seeing everything), and by substance everywhere (causing everything's existence)," says Aquinas.[96]

> The grace comes to mankind through the Son of God made man; grace first filled his human being and then flowed over to us. The Word was made flesh, full of grace and truth, and of his fullness we have all received, grace

90. Nicholas Lash, *Theology on the Way to Emmaus,* p. 42.
91. Aquinas, *ST,* 11.76.1.
92. Barron, *Thomas Aquinas: Spiritual Master,* p. 151.
93. Tracy, pp. 110-121.
94. Aquinas, *ST,* 17.6.1.
95. Marva Dawn, *A Royal Waste of Time* (Grand Rapids: Wm. B. Eerdmans, 1999), p. 127.
96. Aquinas, *ST,* 1.8.3.

> upon grace. Grace and truth came through Jesus Christ. It was fitting then that the grace overflowing from the Word made flesh should be channelled into us by externally perceptible means; and that this inner grace should subject flesh to spirit and bear fruit in externally perceptible behavior. So grace and external activities are related in two ways: certain external activities — sacramental actions like baptism and the eucharist instituted in the new Law — draw us to grace; and grace interiorly prompts us to other external activities. . . . Now the grace of the Holy Spirit is like an inner disposition instilled into us inclining us to right behavior, and so it makes us freely do what accords with grace and avoid what runs counter to it.[97]

We do not perform gestures to garner God's gift of grace. Rather, it is because of grace that our outward activities are prompted by the inner workings of God's Spirit, through which we are inclined to "right behavior," shaping us to be the kind of person God in Christ desires.

Performance of Gestures as Ecclesial Action

We learn to perform in the community where we live. Richard Schechner says that a performance is an activity done for and in the presence of another person or group.[98] Bertold Brecht has said that, in the gesture performed, the attitudes people adopt toward one another are of socio-historical significance, because we learn from one another all the complicated ways and reasons we perform.[99]

Consider Tracy's illustration above: the unintended result of ringing the bell may be that it brings people from all around to see the performer, or it may bring people to dinner because they thought it was the dinner bell.[100] Because we are members of Christ's body, our Christly gestures impact the other members, and we are not alone in our performances but perform the gestures on behalf of and as an extension of the church. When we perform the gesture of charity, for example, we do so as the "one body in Christ, and individually members one of another" (Rom. 12:5). Because we learn the performance of the gesture as an intentional act rooted in the Christian faith, that performance is not necessarily something novel. Rather, the gesture is part of

97. Ibid., 30.108.1.

98. Richard Schechner, *Essays on Performance Theory* (New York: Drama Book Specialists, 1977), p. 30.

99. In Auslander, p. 102.

100. Tracy, p. 29.

the social memory of a certain group of people. This is in keeping with what I believe to be the point of educating Christians in the first place: we teach something old.

Paul Connerton says that all beginning actions or gestures contain an element of recollection, or re-membering — that is, being again made a member of a community greater than ourselves. We transfer crucial commemorative ceremonies and bodily practices, formally and informally, from one generation to another simply by performing gestures. Re-membering has a personal claim as well as a cognitive claim when we reproduce certain performances of particular gestures.[101] Fodor and Hauerwas claim that true performance in the church is an act of remembrance more than creativity per se, a pseudo *creatio ex nihilo,* because the narrative being re-enacted is larger than our own and is an act that is older than we are. Furthermore, good performers of the gestures of the Christian faith — such as talented musicians, imaginative painters, or inspiring dancers — are those who give themselves to the work being performed, so it is as though they are the ones being performed rather than the ones in control of the performance itself.[102]

The Unpredictable Nature of Performed Gestures

Performing gestures is more improvisational and impromptu than strictly choreographed or patterned. We may begin with some basic moves, but there will be room for improvisation on those basic moves: think of it as "theme and variations." The permanent unpredictability of life is not the only contingency that makes our performance fluid and dynamic; being in God makes it such. For we are neither an audience seated far away from God nor solo performers on a stage before God. Rather, living our lives in Christ's body means sharing in the divine life with God in control. This is what keeps our performance improvisational. The Christian life is never the same one day to the next. When we come to trying situations where we don't have an answer in the script, we respond analogously, placing events before us in the larger, providential story of God.[103]

Fodor and Hauerwas say that the loss of control attending a Christly gesture is also an expression of remarkable loss of self-control because of a profound engagement with memory. It is a loss of self-control because we are

101. Paul Connerton, *How Societies Remember,* pp. 22-39.

102. Fodor and Hauerwas, p. 24.

103. Ibid., p. 17.

giving ourselves to God in order to be performed by God. True performance takes us out of ourselves *(ekstasis)* and into God, then returns us to ourselves as fuller, richer, more deeply changed selves. As God's people, we are an extension and improvisation of that singular performance of God's creation.[104]

The Boundaries of the Gospel

While much of our performance is improvisational, it is still set within a context that is outlined by the gospel. Actors have a script, musicians a composition, and dancers a set choreography. We have the biblical narrative, which is like a script — a determinative narrative for the daily performance of gestures. Performances depend on the narrative process: there are beginnings, middles, and ends to all performances. Bruce Kapferer writes that there is a unity of text and enactment: one cannot separate the text from the performance of the narrative itself in the gesture performed.[105]

Turner suggests that all social dramas or performances have these following stage-like sequences: (1) a breach in the everyday routine of life; (2) redressive action to the stated breach; (3) a crisis ensues, due to the incomplete redressive action; (4) crisis gives way to reconciliation; and (5) consensual recognition. Overall, then, social performances have a beginning, a middle, and a certain end.[106] Lash argues that the performance of Scripture is the life of the church, which does have limits and boundaries. Lash proposes that reading itself is always a matter of interpreting a text, putting the reading of Scripture to appropriate use. In worship there are the principal forms of discourse: praise, confession, and petition, which seek to enact the meanings

104. Ibid., pp. 24-25.

105. Bruce Kapferer, "Performance and the Structuring of Meaning and Experience," in Victor Turner and Jerome Bruner, eds., *Anthropology of Experience* (Chicago: Univ. of Illinois Press, 1986), p. 202. Kapferer takes a structuralist approach to narrative in performance. By that I mean that he assumes, along with Paul Ricoeur, that there are the text, which is a complex of signs, and the signs' structural interrelationship with one another, all bound within the performance of the text itself. Such a structure is both foundational and universal for Kapferer.

106. See Turner, *From Ritual to Theatre,* p. 92. A similar logic is located in James Loder's theory of the movement of the Holy Spirit, in which one begins learning in one context (1), spurred on to learn by a conflict (2), in which there is a long section of one's life of introspection (3), until the Holy God merges in the void, giving one insight into resolving the conflict (4), and then (5) taking one back to the context of the original problem and applying this new insight to the old problem. See James Loder, *Transforming Moment* (San Francisco: Harper and Row, 1981).

of Scripture. But in the narrative liturgy, Lash reminds us, we tell the story with the hopes of performing the texts in following Christ and not merely as something we relish or remember with nostalgia. Furthermore, Lash understands the intricacy of interpreting and performing Scripture: how we use the New Testament "as ordinary Christians, and the responsibilities of 'authoritative' interpreters, whether ecclesiastical authorities or academic experts." These authorities also put limits on the performance of Christly gestures. The other sign of caution that Christians must consider is performing the text as it was "originally meant" to be performed, which, though often a futile search, keeps both church historians and textual critics busy.

Lash shows the determinative nature of the text by adding that the performance of biblical texts ends at death:

> The stage on which we enact our performance is that wider human history in which the church exists as the "sacrament," or dramatic enactment, of history's ultimate meaning and hope. If the texts of the New Testament are to express that which Christian faith declares them capable of expressing, the quality of our *humanity* will be the criterion of the adequacy of the performance. And yet this criterion is, in the last resort, hidden from us in the mystery of God whose meaning for man we are bidden to enact.[107]

Yet Scripture in itself cannot be self-sufficient; Christians do not worship Scripture but Christ. The church, as Christ's body, is primary in our reading, interpreting, and performing the gestures of Scripture within Christ's body, which is itself constituted by the unity found in baptism and in the Eucharist. Again, God is the curriculum and the agenda of the church, and the body of Christ is its pedagogy. The performing pedagogy of Christly gestures does not simply translate a biblical text into an act, because our doing is a result of our being. The gesture reveals whose we are and is a result of what others have done for us in the first place. Henri Giroux and Patrick Shannon say that the "act of doing" as performance is inextricably bound to one's "being-in-transit," or the human being-in-motion.[108] When we perform the gesture, it is not

107. Nicholas Lash, *Theology on the Way to Emmaus*, pp. 37-46.

108. Henri Giroux and Patrick Shannon, eds., *Education and Cultural Studies: Toward a Performative Practice* (New York: Routledge, 1997), pp. 1-5. A good description of the kind of performative pedagogy that Giroux and Shannon are referring to is in an essay by Robert Miklitsch, who looks at the pedagogy of the punk culture, which is a kind of performance pedagogy. The punk pedagogy of performance is one of "confrontation and contradiction," though this is now difficult to see in American society, which has coopted "punk culture" into everyday apparel. See Giroux and Shannon, p. 257.

necessarily something we do once and then cross off our list of "things to do." Rather, it is the intent of the performer to repeatedly practice the script-narrative of the gospel until it becomes a part of life — like breathing.

The gospel story out-narrates our narrative, over-accepts us and our story, out-performs our human performances, and shows us how our lives are narrated by the gospel of God. Sam Wells says that when God builds his kingdom, God does not throw away the rawness of our lives but over-accepts us, seeing what we can be, and incorporates us into God's kingdom through the incarnation and resurrection of Jesus Christ.[109]

Frances Young says that it is in the struggle to perform Christological and sacramental theology adequately, which bears on the struggle to perform the Bible, that we will begin to exercise the wide range of dynamics we need to exploit as Christians and people of character.[110]

The Church as Improvisational Acting Company

A performance, says Frances Young, requires skill, which is acquired over a long period of time through commitment and disciplined practice.[111] By repeatedly rehearsing — and later performing — gestures of the gospel, we are changed: the very repetitive characteristic of performance makes possible the construction of certain catechesis continuities and an identity within the next generation of the Christian community.[112] Von Balthasar says that the more civilized people are, the more they are actors; they adopt the appearance of respect toward each other, of good manners, of unselfishness:

> For by playing the role, people are aroused to a full exercise of the virtues whose externals they've cultivated for a space and acquire the disposition itself. It is the question of affirming a role given to us in a religious context and of schooling ourselves to become existentially identified with the role.[113]

We become the role that we play, and those gestured virtues once external to us become internalized and habituated. Wells suggests that we are to be the

109. Wells, p. 208.

110. Frances Young, p. 105.

111. Ibid., p. 182.

112. See Phil Kenneson, "The Reappearance of the Visible Church" (Duke University, unpublished diss., 1991), p. 284.

113. Von Balthasar, p. 54.

kind of people who have the courage to keep telling God's story, even when it looks dangerous or when it threatens to reveal uncomfortable parts of our selves.[114] To keep performing the gospel, even to the point of laying down our lives for the love of our neighbor, does take a courageous performance of certain gestures. In some sense, educating Christians to perform Christly gestures is a matter of life and death — an education of one's life in the church.

The Goodness of Repeating Gestures

Once rehearsed, Christly gestures are to be repeated often throughout our daily lives. Because of God's grace, we not only are able to perform the gestures of Christian faith but we desire to do so; nevertheless, like any kind of performance, it will take a certain kind of training. Phil Kenneson says that the repetitive character of practices marks the body in a way that extends over time, constructing continuities and identities.[115] Fodor and Hauerwas put it this way: "All performances as God's people are repeat performances, at once emulating the one true performance of God — but also as an extension and variation — an improvisation of that singular performance" of Christ.[116] This "repeatability" is seen in the church's liturgy itself, which is, according to Connerton, a performing language that is restrictive in its pattern, hence predictable and repeatable. Liturgy is an ordering of speech acts that occurs when we repeat certain utterances: if there is no repetition of performance, there is no ritual. These repetitions of gestures also appear in certain set postures and moving gestures in the church. For example, to kneel in subordination before the cross of Christ is to display, through a bodily posture, one's disposition toward God: the subordination of a life in its entirety to God's will.[117]

The Character of the Performer of Gestures

Finally, the character of the performer matters. Performance-as-art and performance-as-virtue are similar: as one becomes a clarinetist by playing the clarinet, so one becomes a just person by practicing just acts. Herein lies the

114. Wells, p. 205.
115. Kenneson, p. 238.
116. Fodor and Hauerwas, p. 25.
117. Connerton, pp. 58-59.

difference between performance-as-theater and virtue: we don't know if a person performing a just act is a just person until we come to know him or her; and we need to be of a certain character to discern those who are virtuous.[118]

Performing Christly gestures not only makes a mark on the lives of others; it marks us all as Christians. Michel de Certeau says that when we engage in the practice of Christly gestures, we are marked as Christ's own. That mark can be a miracle, a sanctuary:

> A priestly or charismatic personage, a devotion, a sacramental gesture, and so forth. In every manner of its appearance, it focuses religious expression upon particular actions. Everything is concentrated on practices. A religious group experiences its cohesion through them. In them it finds its mooring and its differentiation in respect to other social units, whether religious or of other fabric.[119]

The profundity of how we are marked physically and our character is shaped by performing Christly gestures is captured in this simple confession: "If you confess with your lips that Jesus is Lord, and believe in your heart that God raised him from the dead, you will be saved."[120]

If catechesis is to be not only about changed minds but changed hearts, changed bodies, and changed lives in a Christian community that is forever changing, I am arguing that one learns in this pilgrimage a catechesis-of-patterning, the performance of Christly gestures that embody the virtues of Christian life, as one learns a craft or a performing art.[121] St. Augustine understood that there was an obsession with rule books during his time. A performer of sermons himself, he thought that "orators needed raw talent, much practice, and good models, and that great orators fulfilled rules because they were eloquent, rather than applying them that they might be so."[122] Oration is a craft — a performance art — in which there are apprentices and master craftspersons. Catechists — those who are learning the craft of the orator — should be instructed as any other performing artists are; they need to undergo the exacting discipline of rehearsals. Harmless says: "Catechesis is an art etched in the ephemeral," and the catechesis of Christly gestures is an act of Christ's body and spirit.

118. Hauerwas and Pinches, p. 24.

119. Michel de Certeau, *The Writing of History*, p. 162.

120. I prayed this often while attending morning prayers at St. John's Abbey and University Chapel in Collegeville, MN, and at St. Benedict's Monastery in St. Joseph, MN.

121. Harmless, pp. 5, 350.

122. Harmless, p. 350.

Pilgrimage catechesis of performing gestures is a craft in which we learn the good that we have in common as Christians, which is God's love. In this craft we become "imitators of God, as beloved children, and living in love, as Christ loved us and gave himself up for us" (Eph. 5:1-2).

CHAPTER EIGHT

Crafting Christly Gestures

> *Anything we produce we produce by craft, and we consider a craftsman's work specially good if it has some sort of greatness, be it in quantity or value or worthiness. . . . The really great works are those directed to the honor of God.*
>
> St. Thomas Aquinas

In this chapter I will discuss the nuts and bolts of learning the craft of performing Christly gestures, which will be a lifelong commitment to the good of Christ's body.

The Master Craftsperson

In pilgrimage catechesis, the life of the catechumen or apprentice is to be examined with a certain rigor as he or she continually grows in the understanding of the nuances of Christly gestures under the tutelage of a master teacher, or catechist.[1] No matter what our chronological age, we are always in need of master craftspersons to help us cultivate our gestures, even if we are master craftspersons ourselves.

1. The language is important here regarding instruction. Other crafts use the rhetoric of teacher-student; master-disciple; parent-child; mentor-follower. I'm not aware of one's being necessarily better than another. Jesus himself was rabbi or teacher, while he had followers whom he called his "disciples."

This is akin to Paul's understanding of the master teacher, *didaskalos*, and the student (or apprentice). The *didaskalos* was to artfully guide a disciple into perceiving God's will by living right with God.[2] One characteristic of the *didaskalos* is that she or he would be expected not only to teach the craft but to have a profound impact on the student's life in its entirety — welcoming the student into her or his own life. The master would be an expert in the knowledge of the craft and the guidance of the student's skill, passing on to the student-apprentice a judgment of what is considered "good" in the performance of a skill.[3]

John Howard Yoder notes that in a church the *didaskalos* guides not only the individual but thereby a part of a community with the language he or she uses; for language can steer the community with a power disproportionate to other kinds of leadership. In pilgrimage catechesis the master craftsperson shapes the apprentice in the very craft of performing the gospel in Christly gestures. The *didaskalos* needs to watch for the "sophomoric temptation" of purely verbal solutions to substantial problems. The *didaskalos* is like a shepherd.[4]

The rhetoric of craft is not new to catechesis. William Harmless cites Augustine's comparison of the theater of the world with the theater of the Word: "Its drama was salvation history, its script was the Scriptures, and its actors included everyone."[5] Furthermore, if catechesis is like theater, there is the drama's director or coach, who, in crafting the actors' performances, makes demands of students and exacts discipline. But it isn't only what the master teacher says that impresses Augustine; it is the very eloquence of the teacher's life that matters most — in his case, the life of Ambrose.

Or consider piano performance. My master teachers were people who taught me not only piano performance but life itself. Physical conditioning shapes and sculpts students' bodies into a specific discipline so that they can play more intricate, complicated compositions. Repetition is a fact of life in piano playing (warm-up scales can last a good hour) as the body's muscles and nerves memorize a composition. Performance is not only about the head but also the heart and body, where the very lives of composer and performer touch one another. My master teachers would open up their lives, bringing

2. Aaron Milavec, *To Empower as Jesus Did* (Lewiston, NY: Edwin Mellen, 1982), p. 83.

3. Stanley Hauerwas, *After Christendom?* (Nashville: Abingdon Press, 1993), p. 104.

4. John Howard Yoder, *The Priestly Kingdom* (Notre Dame: University of Notre Dame Press, 1984), pp. 32-33.

5. William Harmless, *Augustine and the Catechumenate* (Collegeville: Liturgical Press, 1995), p. 349.

me into their homes, regaling me with stories of Juilliard and concert tours of Japan, while introducing me to the habits of a concert pianist, educating me over dinners about the lives of Chopin, Bach, Liszt, and Copland. Discussions of mind-brain/mind-body theories abounded, as well as stories of travels to play that one exquisite piano in Russia.

Such involvement of one's life in another's life is in keeping with the way many master craftspersons teach, and this is what I am proposing for those who teach the craft of Christly gestures. One teaches with one's life in the church because of the *telos* of our instruction, Christ's body. For example, Augustine took seriously the traditional theme of the church as God's household, and what keeps this household together is God's love. One should approach catechesis with "a brother's, a father's, and a mother's love."[6] This love is so great, so infectious, that in the process of catechesis there is this unexpected effect:

> For so great is the power of sympathy, that when people are affected by us as we speak and we by them as they learn, we dwell each in the other and thus both they, as it were, speak in us what they hear, while we, in some way, learn in them what we teach.[7]

If all else fails in catechesis, it does not mean that all is lost; where neither the catechumen nor the catechist succeeds, grace does. For Augustine, writes Harmless, the outer teacher matters "far less than Christ, the inner teacher."[8]

The Apprentice in Crafting Gestures

Corresponding to the catechist is the catechumen, or apprentice, whose life is being shaped and nurtured by that master teacher. We have all been, from time to time, apprentices ourselves, no matter how old or well-schooled we are in performing Christly gestures. If catechesis is a lifelong process, then before we are ever master craftspersons, we are first and foremost apprentices. As such we are to be transformed by the very practice of the craft. Hauerwas describes this craft-learning process as terribly undemocratic since the stu-

6. Alasdair MacIntyre makes a similar point in suggesting the many ways parents teach their children to be independent practical reasoners, showing children good reason to act other than as one's urgent feelings would dictate. See MacIntyre, *Dependent Rational Animals*, p. 69.

7. Quoted in Harmless, p. 136.

8. Ibid., p. 357.

dent has no voice in his or her earliest formation. The master craftsperson assumes that apprentices know little about the craft; it is the master's responsibility to teach.[9]

In performing Christly gestures, the apprentice is to be baptized literally and figuratively into the traditions and secrets of the craft. The student will eat, sleep, dream about, lie down beside, talk to, walk with — even fight against and contemplate ways of undermining — the master craftsperson. There is a good chance the apprentice may not even like the master craftsperson at first; but this may be considered a joy, because one is *called* to learn the craft with the master in the first place.[10] One traditionally chooses the craft as one's vocation, one's gift and service in the body, and in that there is much joy.

In the Roman Catholic Church the catechumen is in a kind of apprenticeship in Christian living for the entirety of his or her life. The instructions for the Catholic Rite for the Christian Initiation of Adults (RCIA) assume that there are master Christians with whom catechumens can become apprentices in the complex art of living the gospel:

> One learns how to fast, pray, repent, celebrate, and serve the good of one's neighbors less by being lectured on these matters than by close association with people who do these things with regular ease and flair.[11]

The apprentice is to learn how to practice the church's

> rich, pluriform traditions; it also insists that they propose a practicable ethics, that they catalyze interior explorations, guide prayer, and discern spirits; that they nurture apostolic action and embody a virtue worth imitating.[12]

How does the apprentice learn the gestured virtues that are worth imitating? Augustine wrote that "the life of the speaker has greater weight in determining whether he is obediently heard than any grandness of eloquence." Teachers and those baptized are to live lives that may be imitated.[13] This matters if we consider that one practices being a teacher of the catechism with one's whole life as a deep resource; there is no methodology that is separate

9. Hauerwas, *After Christendom?* pp. 102-105.

10. Ibid., p. 107.

11. Harmless, citing Aidan Kavanagh, p. 10.

12. Ibid., p. 17. Sad to say, I am not aware of a Protestant catechism that, at least in print, holds the same kind of rigor for its initiates.

13. Ibid., p. 179.

from who "I" am or what "I" believe as a person. If we hark back to the generations of teachers who teach this way, we will finally return not only to the disciples but to Jesus himself, the one true teacher from whom all of us continue to learn. Furthermore, the goal of the master craftsperson is to instruct apprentices well enough in the gestures so that they become catechists to a new generation of apprentices. In doing so, the teacher leaves an imprint of his or her life on the next apprentice's life, and so on.

An example of being and learning as an apprentice of gestures is Mickey Hart's story: his drumming was neither a vocation nor a hobby but was life itself. As Hart says, to know drum playing, one doesn't study *about* drumming; one simply drums, for "the real knowing is in the playing. Drums give up their true secrets to players, not to Ph.D.'s."[14] His apprenticeship to the drums began in earnest in high school; though his band director tried to dissuade him, Hart's intensity persuaded the director to let him play. Yet Hart always felt incomplete:

> An eight-year-old Minianka hanging around the drum huts in his West African village knows more about his tradition than I knew about mine. At least he knows the origin myth of his instrument; I couldn't have begun to tell you where mine came from. . . . Nobody, no drummer, no teacher, no wise parent ever took me aside and said, "Mickey, in the beginning. . . ."[15]

Through years of drumming he became part of and a beneficiary of a longer, well-crafted tradition of drummers who preceded him.

The Process of Learning to Perform the Gesture

Alasdair MacIntyre lists the following characteristics of learning a craft explicitly: first, the apprentice will need to learn what really is good to do and what only seems good in a particular circumstance; this discernment comes from his or her teachers and through continuing self-education. The apprentice learns that there are standards for any craft. Second, what is good at a particular level of training and learning has to do with what is unqualifiedly the "good" and "best" in the field. The apprentice must learn to distinguish between the kind of excellence he or she can expect of himself or her-

14. Mickey Hart, *Drumming at the Edge of Magic* (New York: Harper Collins, 1990), p. 22.

15. Ibid., p. 68.

self and the excellence that is the *telos* for both the master craftsperson and apprentice.

Third, the apprentice needs to learn in the company of other learners what about his or her craft has to be eradicated, transformed, or cultivated; there may exist certain desires that must be drawn out of the person and into the good. The master craftsperson needs to understand that the apprentice has both the capacity and need for learning how and when to perform the virtuous gestures as a member of Christ's body. Such an understanding is necessary to help one discern heresy and to craft Christians for learning how to live together as Christ's body in its totality.[16] The key to this learning is a continually open-ended dialogue or discourse between the master craftsperson and the apprentice. In teaching the performance of Christly gestures with their very lives, the master teachers will share both the great skills and the glaring shortcomings of their lives. The act of confessing to the apprentice is a performance of the virtued gesture of humility. So too is the need for the apprentice to share with the master craftsperson what is going on in his or her many-storied life. In that act of two Christians sharing their lives is the church, is Christ, as he promises that wherever two or three are gathered in his name, "I am there also."

Fourth, as one learns the craft of the gesture, one comes to understand the narrative of learning. For the apprentice, there is a beginning to the learning of the craft; in the intensification of learning there is a deepening of skill to better discern what is good versus what is of poor quality; and there is a period of passage, of leaving one's master to either come under the guidance of a new master or to become a master craftsperson who is ready to take on an apprentice. In the process of learning the craft the apprentice begins to share in the logic of the craft, which requires sharing in the contingencies of its long history, coming to understand the story of the craft as his or her own, and finding a place as a character in the unfolding story that undergirds the craft.[17]

An example of learning a craft, like a gesture, is Hart's story of drumming in Africa, told by a master drummer:

> My first instrument was a cowbell. The first rhythm I learned was what we call conconcolo, which is a very simple rhythm but difficult to hold. The first time you play with the master drummers they will usually say, "Grab

16. See Marva Dawn, *A Royal Waste of Time*, Chapter 20.

17. Alasdair MacIntyre, *Three Rival Versions of Moral Enquiry* (Notre Dame: University of Notre Dame Press, 1990), pp. 61-62.

the bell and let's hear you play conconcolo." The next time they let you play with them they will say, "Take the bell again," and only after many times like this will they let you play the shaker, and then finally the drum.

It takes years to become a master drummer. The reason for this is that you have to know not only the rhythms but the dances as well. Once you know all the parts of all the dances, then you will be given the opportunity to lead the band . . . you become the keeper of the rhythms.[18]

Authority in the Craft of Gestures

The authority of the master craftsperson is important in the apprentice's life, for the good of both the apprentice and Christ's body. Authority and obedience are crucial in a catechesis of crafting people in Christly gestures. The *Rule* says: "The first step of humility is unhesitating obedience, which comes naturally to those who cherish Christ above all."[19] The authority of the master craftsperson in relationship to the craft itself is mysteriously complex; it is almost impossible to write down rules that would govern the master craftsperson. The master knows how to go further in the craft, using what he or she has learned to link the past and the future, drawing the tradition and interpreting and reinterpreting it so that the craft is still directed toward the *telos* in the future.[20]

Besides teaching the craft, the master craftsperson is engaged in teaching a certain kind of "knowing," that is, passing on the method of learning to a new generation, which is a legitimate concern of the community of the craft.[21] Aaron Milavec observes that there is a time in the learning process when the apprentice has the skills that rival those of the master: he or she now understands the craft and appreciates the depth of the story well enough so that it is appropriate for him or her to become a master of the craft, or to go on to another master craftsperson to further hone the craft.[22] Apprentices become beholders of the craft, embodying the craft's traditions as they practice them.[23]

In the process of learning the thick complexities of gestures, in light of the ways one's character is formed and sustained by the virtues of a given context, the key is to focus on ritual in order to rehearse and learn the gestures —

18. Hart, p. 215.
19. *Rule of St. Benedict*, Chapter 5.
20. MacIntyre, p. 65.
21. Ibid., p. 67.
22. Milavec, p. 191.
23. John Fare, quoted in MacIntyre, op. cit.

to make the once awkward gesture so practiced that it becomes an integral part of one's habitual life.

Rituals in the Craft of Christly Gestures

If it is through narrative and the traditions of a community that we are given the knowledge of which gestures we are to practice as Christ's body, then it is in the repetition of rituals that we rehearse and polish the many intricate performances of Christly gestures — because the church is a culmination of many rituals that repeat themselves. Among the many small and large rituals we live as Christians, the church is a ritual event writ large, making our lives together one large, extended ritual. Consider the ritual of the church's worship on Sunday morning, often followed by the rituals of fellowship and/or a meal.[24] The call to order of a parish committee or a session meeting begins and ends with ritualized prayers; the ritualized format of a weekly youth group; the special, unspoken rituals of the fellowship potluck on a Sunday evening — all these constitute the context necessary for the initial crafting of gestures. Kathleen Norris observes that "good liturgy can act like an icon, a window into a world in which our concepts of space, time, and even stone are pleasurably bent out of shape."[25] Christian rituals in general can be iconic windows into the world as God would see it and us, and a mirror in which we see ourselves living in the light of God's grace.[26] The obverse is most likely true as well: poor rituals can act as idols that block our godly vision of the world.

Rituals of worship are gesture-dependent because liturgy demands the use of our bodies in celebration of the entire church.[27] Liturgy, the work of God's people, is an embodiment of the Christian community's life; it involves repeated and rehearsed gestures, patterned ways in which we as Christ's followers follow his lead — from how we should pray (the Lord's Prayer) to how we should eat and drink in remembrance of him.[28] Furthermore, gestures are

24. Mass daily if Roman Catholic.

25. Kathleen Norris, *The Cloister Walk* (New York: Riverhead Books, 1996), p. 266.

26. I've come to understand recently that while the Roman Catholic Church has often seen icons as windows into the holy, the early Byzantine Church understood icons as mirrors of the soul.

27. See Colleen Griffith, "Spirituality and the Body," in Bruce Morrill, ed., *Bodies of Worship* (Collegeville: Liturgical Press, 1999), p. 82; see also Paul Colvino, "Christian Marriage," p. 109 in the same volume.

28. Michael Warren, *Faith, Culture, and the Worshiping Community* (Mahwah, NJ: Paulist Press, 1989), p. 71.

intrinsic to both the discursive and nondiscursive presentation of the church through worship to itself and to the world. Good worship depends on an understanding of the intention of the gestures we perform as Christians, and in worship we perceive the Holy Spirit as the Christ-bringer,

> in the breaking of the bread and the passing of the cup, and that will bring the Church, through the unfolding story of its story, to the promised second meeting with its Lord at the end of time.[29]

In worship we incarnate Christ, who precedes not only our actions but our beings.[30] We know Christ before we know ourselves, for we can only know ourselves as those in the body of Christ. Christ's body is evident when we engage in the liturgical posture and gestures of praise, prayer, and worship of God.

In this section I want to focus briefly on worship and other churchly rituals that embody Christly gestures.[31]

What Is Ritual? Where Is Gesture?

Among psychologists and scholars of religious communities, ritual is often considered the basic social act of human beings, reeking of meaning and depending on bodily gestures in specific, narrated contexts.[32] Be it in oral or literate traditions, every culture performs rituals, including rites of initiation, rites of intensification, and rites of passage.[33] But the kinds of ritual performed and what they mean are made particular by the many narratives that shape the ritual. Catherine Bell says that every ritual "comes fully embedded in larger discourses," such as religion, anthropology, sociology, psychology, or social psychology.[34] Christian rituals are those practices that are dynamic,

29. Gerard Loughlin, *Telling God's Story* (New York: Cambridge Univ. Press, 1996), p. 192.

30. Paul Hoon, *The Integrity of Worship* (Nashville: Abingdon Press, 1971), p. 129.

31. For more on the process of education in the ways of the church through worship, I recommend Philip Pfatteicher's *The School of the Church* and Marva Dawn's *A Royal Waste of Time.*

32. Roy Rappaport, *Ecology, Meaning and Religion* (Richmond: North Atlantic Books, 1979), p. 174; Catherine Bell, *Ritual Theory, Ritual Practice* (New York: Oxford University Press, 1992), p. 54.

33. Gwen Neville Kennedy and John Westerhoff, *Learning Through Liturgy* (New York: Crossroad, 1978).

34. Catherine Bell, *Ritual Theory, Ritual Practice* (New York: Oxford University Press, 1992), p. 13.

gesture-bound, participated in by a community of God's people, patterned by the narratives of our traditions and repetitive performances, and based on Scripture as it is proclaimed and expressed in the art of symbols, signs, and other human gestures that continually remind us that we are Christ's. The rituals we practice communicate God's story, which in turn determines the way we live: by performing the multitude of Christian rituals, we are being absorbed into the story that narrates all gesture-bound rituals.

Second, in performing the church's rituals we understand that, before we were members of a church, there were already others who practiced these ritualistic gestures in a congregation — that is, we are doing something very old. Christian rituals are never a static, solo act, stripped of time, place, people, geography, or narrative; they are dynamic, fully enmeshed in the radical hope of our life in Christ, and they give us some sense of decent orderliness when disorder pushes hard against us. The patterned, gesture-bound rituals embody the past in present practices, which then guide us to our future in God.

Third, it is intriguing that in the rituals of Christ's body we are doing more than learning new gestures; we are carrying on the tradition of our forebears, the communion of saints, to the next generation of Christians.

Rituals Order Our Lives, Directing Our Gestures to God

In 1 Corinthians 14:26-40, Paul describes what we should do in the rituals of the church when we come together to worship: "When you come together, each one has a hymn, a lesson, a revelation, a tongue, or an interpretation. Let all things be done for building up." Amid all the gifts of the Spirit, Paul calls the church not to live in disorder, "for God is a God not of disorder but of peace" (v. 33). In worship we struggle not to be a gaggle of babbling individuals, isolated from one another with nothing in common, or competing against one another to see who can worship loudest or best. Instead, our capacity and desire to worship corporately are based on our being "buried with him by baptism into death, so that, just as Christ was raised from the dead by the glory of the Father, so we too might walk in newness of life" (Rom. 6:4, 6, 8).

All churchly rituals give order and structure to our lives together. The order occurs in narrative: rituals and stories share a common starting point of corporate worship. Ritual has a beginning, a middle, and an end, just as stories do. As there is a final chapter to the story, there is a necessary end to the ritual for the participant to feel complete. Good order is important for good ritual, because, as Calvin reminds us, Christians know freedom only within order. Yet order itself is not the "end," or purpose, of Christian rituals; whether explicit or assumed, the purpose of even our mundane rituals is to bring praise to God. Worship brings order and focus to the chaos of our lives, so that we may come to refocus on the primary purpose of being a woman or man — to worship God and enjoy him forever.[35]

Rituals Shape Character as an Act of Christ's Body

The rituals of the church involve those community members who are present, those who are absent but who have already shaped certain rituals, and those who are members of the communion of saints — and all of us in Christ. As Norris learned while living in a Benedictine monastery, individuals "can't create true ceremony for themselves alone. Ceremony requires that we work with others in the humbling give-and-take of communal existence."[36]

Christian character is being shaped in all the ritualistic gestures in the life of the church.[37] Because truthful worship of God requires that we proceed in decency and good order (1 Cor. 14:40), we are reminded that God is the *telos* of our gestured rituals.[38] What does it mean to have our character changed? First, to be changed by the church's rituals is to recognize that the gestures we practice are not "mine" but "ours." Bonhoeffer says that Christ is our unity:

> "Behold, how good and how pleasant it is for brethren to dwell together in unity" — this is the Scripture's praise of life together under the Word. But now we can rightly interpret the words "in unity" and say, "for brethren to dwell together through Christ." For Jesus Christ alone is our unity. "He is our peace." Through him alone do we have access to one another, joy in one another, and fellowship with one another.[39]

35. Shorter Westminster Catechism, *Book of Confessions* (Louisville: Office of the General Assembly, 1991), 7.001.

36. Norris, *Cloister Walk,* p. 266.

37. Marva Dawn, *Reaching Out Without Dumbing Down* (Grand Rapids: Wm. B. Eerdmans, 1995), pp. 75-104.

38. Stanley Hauerwas, "Worship, Evangelism, Ethics: Eliminating the 'And'" (unpublished essay), p. 8.

39. Dietrich Bonhoeffer, *Life Together* (New York: Harper & Row Pub. Co., 1954), p. 39.

Our very being changes as we perform the gestured rituals of church life. Again, this affirms Aristotle's famous aphorism that one becomes a "just person by performing just acts," for we do so in the context of Christ.[40] And Christ is our hope as we pray, "Thy will be done, on earth as it is in heaven." The ritualistically trained gestures we practice are not of selfishness or solipsism if we perform them in Christ.

Furthermore, if our character is shaped in a Christian community's gestured rituals, the character of the community is also shaped by our participation in that community's rituals. For example, I have observed a change in many people who live in a Christian community such as l'Arche, which includes people with mental retardation. The change of heart comes when the issue is no longer what the community offers "me"; instead, Christian community and character are revealed when we begin to practice gestures of hospitality, asking about the ways we can and should serve others. In turn, the community itself changes as we pray at meetings or simply sit and enjoy each other's company after a delightful dinner.[41]

Rituals are created by the rehearsing and performing of patterned gestures that are pedagogically profound and culturally explicit. Frederick Bauerschmidt observes that Christianity is a culture with a large ensemble of contradictory beliefs, complicated and narrative-laden traditions, and well-worn practices that form a "more or less coherent matrix by which we understand the world." In the rituals of Christian life together we barely begin to comprehend the traditional and intentional unfolding and the always emerging pattern of Christly gestures.

What do the rituals teach us? First, ritualistic practices of gestures teach us that our gestures reveal the Holy Spirit's timing and order as first learned in the narrative of the gospel among the diversity of God's people. Second, the rituals teach us to recognize how our minds, bodies, and spirits are engrafted to the mind, body, and spirit of Christ. There is a sense of purposefulness and history behind the ritualistic gestures that we may have not known or been conscious of. Ritual reveals the purpose for the choreographed performance: Why do we move our hands and mouth, feet and knees, eyes and ears, and teach others the gestures that further shape us? James White says that it is precisely through actions that Christians discover God's expression of love for them. In the moments of flesh touching flesh with others, our hu-

40. I recognize that Aristotle also said that "people may perform just acts without actually being just men, as in the case of people who do what has been laid down by the laws but do so either involuntarily or through ignorance or for an ulterior motive, and not for the sake of performing just acts." See *Nichomachean Ethics,* 1144a12-15.

41. Norris, p. 363.

man gestures make incarnate the divine action, especially in the context of worship.[42]

In the rituals of Christian community we are not only told about the gestures we are to perform as Christians; more importantly, we are shown the reason behind the gestures, the timing of gestures, and their lasting implications for our life beyond the setting where ritualistic gestures were first performed.

Imitation in the Craft of Christly Gestures

Imitation is the key to learning the ritualistic performance of gestures. We learn gesture, as a form of mimetic communication, early in life — earlier than spoken language — and continue to use both gestures of hand and mouth (speech) throughout our lives. Cognitive developmental psychologists observe that one of the most profound gestures of intentionality is that of a toddler pointing at something. How is gesture-as-language learned? It is through imitation.[43] Ronald Rolheiser says that what Christ wants from us is not admiration but imitation, not like a mime on a street corner but undergoing "his presence so as to enter into a community of life and celebration with him . . . as [Christ] is a presence to be seized and acted upon."[44]

Origin of Systematic Imitation as Education of Gestures

The word "imitation," or "mimesis," is more complicated in its usage than the simple mimicry or imitation of someone's visual, outward behavior. For the ancient Greeks, knowledge was fixed to oral language: through imitation, repetition, and "formulaic expressions" one learned what one was supposed to know. The very origin of mimesis lies in oral culture, which is all about gesture.[45] Aeschylus said: "If you are shut off from our language and do not un-

42. James White, *Sacraments as God's Self-Giving* (Nashville: Abingdon Press, 1983), p. 22.

43. Frank Wilson, *The Hand* (New York: Vintage Press, 1999), pp. 49-50.

44. Ronald Rolheiser, *Holy Longing* (New York: Doubleday, 2000), p. 74.

45. Günter Gebauer and Christoph Wulf, *Mimesis: Culture, Art, Society* (Berkeley: University of California Press, 1995), p. 316. I am arguing that this is all gesture, because to hear is bodily gesture, the movement of tiny hair follicles carrying sound waves to the ear drum and stimulating nerve cells into hearing. To speak involves coordination of the musculature of lips and lungs, coordinated and determined by the mind.

derstand our reasoning, speak to us in barbarous gestures." Gestures are a language that is considered "anaphoric," one that is before oral instruction, a way of participating in life's events that includes and yet is prior to verbal ability. To assume a certain posture is a combination of interlinked gestures.[46]

In oral poetic presentations in ancient Greece, imitation was a significant ingredient. Poetry demanded a psychological and physical involvement as an audience was taken up by the rhythm of the poet's speech, which was designed to support learning. Günter Gebauer and Christoph Wulf note that in such poetic speech there was a two-sided mimetic process:

> People often describe the immediate physical effects of such an oral poetic presentation as a contagion. . . . Spoken and heard sounds, rhythm, schema, melody, bodily movements, and shared participation together form a kind of dance, comparable to an intricately choreographed gymnastic exercise.[47]

In such mimetic-poetic oral presentations the "formulaic expression, rhythm, repetition, gesture, and the relationship between the speaker and audience" were means for teaching a cultural memory.[48] Gebauer and Wulf propose that mimesis is a practical knowledge, bound to the body and to the mind; because it is known in the practice of movement, it is difficult to create a theoretical formation: "It is a product of human practice and must always be regarded as the issue of a deed, as a part of practice."[49]

Repetition of gestures is the core of the gesturer's understanding of mimesis. Gestures are known in time and space, in the rhythm and execution of movement. With this emphasis on mimetic practices in an oral culture, it is not surprising to find Aristotle's observation: "Man is the most imitative of all animals, and he learns lessons through mimicry."[50] Through examples we

46. Julia Kristeva, "Gestures: Practice of Communication," in Ted Polhemus, ed., *The Body Reader: Social Aspects of the Human Body* (New York: Pantheon Books, 1978), pp. 265-276.

47. Gebauer and Wulf, p. 47.

48. Ibid., p. 47.

49. Ibid., p. 316.

50. Pierre Bourdieu, *The Logic of Practice* (Stanford: Stanford University Press, 1990), p. 25. On a PBS special, broadcast on the PBS station in Chapel Hill, North Carolina on August 12, 1996, actor Alan Alda was filmed with a group of chimpanzees and children in a study of how well chimps imitate human actions compared to how well human children do. Alda made a production of turning over a toy rake in order to obtain a small puzzle piece. The human children imitated him on their first try; the chimps, on the other hand, failed to imitate Alda's gesture no matter how many times he showed them.

learn from one another, often beginning with family members, how to walk and talk, sit and eat, read and listen.[51]

Cultural Anthropology and Imitation of Gestures

Intentional imitating is a cornerstone of most theories of learning; it is a form of education practiced in all cultures. For example, a child in the African !Kung tribe learns the rituals of community by mimicking his or her parents' actions — from scarification, hunting kudu bucks, food gathering, and pretending to lead the ritual of the healing dance — on the heels of his or her parents. In this education there is no formal or separate schooling, nor age and grade grouping; all of life is understood to be a "school" in which one learns to be part of the !Kung community.[52]

This is in marked contrast to the current Western tradition of squirreling children away in a building called "school" for a six-hour period and telling them what they need to know — out of context, yet in a systematic form of rote learning called "education." This continues as children learn to read, in not only a sterile but undisciplined process that is intellectualized to such a degree that it need not be based in any kind of community. In this learning process the student becomes an isolated individual, separated from a community of learners, studying at a lonely desk. It is assumed that students will take what they learn in this intellectual environment and live it in their lives. But such a transfer of knowledge, from reading facts in a book to applying such knowledge to one's life, is not easy. Yet even in this educational style a student learns by imitating someone else who studies and learns in just that isolated and individualized way.

Imitation in Modern Theories of Education

Like Aristotle and the !Kung, Maria Montessori understood that there is nothing in the mind that does not first exist in the senses. For Montessori, children are great discoverers because everything in the living world is active and attractive to them. Echoing William Poteat's understanding of "mind-

51. Jean Berges and Irene Lerine, *The Imitation of Gestures* (London: Spastics Society Medical Education and Information Unit in Association with William Heinemann Medical Books, Ltd., 1965), pp. 1-3.

52. Jerome Bruner, *Theories of Instruction* (Cambridge: Harvard University Press, 1966), p. 151.

bodiliness," in which the mind and body are inextricably entwined, Montessori notes that the hands and the mind act together, making the learning experience one of doing rather than merely observing. While the child appears to have some actions we call "instinctive" at birth, such as sucking, these actions are done with our knowing. Children grab things with their hands and try to imitate the smile of the parent or guardian. All movements that evoke a response from someone else shape children's complex actions and gestures. Children acquire things from their culture at a very early age, taking knowledge of the world around them by doing certain tasks. Hands allow minds to reveal themselves, enabling children to have a whole relationship with their environment.

The older children become, the more actively they participate — enthusiastically absorbing knowledge, developing perception, and increasing in manual dexterity. The repetition of learning, of putting a small block on top of a larger block, over and over again, brings about the education of the senses. Children not only learn their colors, forms, and objects but also refine their senses through exercising attention, comparison, and judgment.[53] Imitation is such an effective way of educating in Christly gestures for young and old, rich and poor, intellectually brilliant and developmentally disabled, and across ethnic cultures, simply because imitative learning begins with the body and the senses. Pierre Bourdieu says that the body, like a living memory pad, remembers everything that happens to it. John Dewey observed that bodily experiences have everything to do with learning:

> An experience, a very humble experience, is capable of generating and carrying any amount of theory (or intellectual content), but a theory apart from an experience cannot be definitely grasped even as a theory. It tends to become a verbal formula, a set of catch words used to render thinking, or genuine theorizing, unnecessary and impossible. Because of our education we use words, thinking they are ideas, to dispose of questions, the disposal being in reality simply such an obscuring of perception as prevents us from seeing any longer the difficulty.[54]

53. Elizabeth Hainstock, *The Essential Montessori* (New York: Plume Book, 1986), pp. 65-80.

54. John Dewey, *Democracy and Education* (New York: Free Press, 1916), pp. 140, 141.

Imitation and the Moral Life of Christly Gestures

Nancy Sherman believes that we learn the virtues by imitating those who are masters of virtues. She says that imitating seems to be something human beings delight in: "Learning is the greatest pleasure. 'This is a that' is, within the mimetic mode, a classification of actual characters — through represented form."[55] We learn through a complex process of acquisition that presupposes a conscious effort to reproduce a "gesture, an utterance or an object explicitly constituted as a model."[56] Such a model is necessary in the act of patterning-as-catechesis, a model proposed by imitation; the imitator needs a pattern to imitate.[57]

Bourdieu says that it can also "take place below consciousness, expression and the reflexive distance which they presuppose." He argues that the body believes in whatever it is playing at: for example, the body weeps if it is miming grief; the body laughs if it finds something funny; the body hugs another when it is practicing the virtue of compassion. Bourdieu says that it does not represent what it performs, nor does it merely intellectualize the past; instead, it enacts the past, bringing it back to life in the present to guide future discourses. Bourdieu suggests that what is "learned by the body" is not something that one *has*, such as knowledge, which one can then brandish or abuse, but is something that one *is*. For example, the gestures learned by the body are no longer just actions, but they mark who we are.

Interestingly enough, as Bourdieu points out, this is more evident in nonliterate or preliterate cultures, such as the !Kung, the ancient Israelites, or the early church, where inherited knowledge can survive in the incorporated state of body, mind, and spirit only among people who can understand the place of the body in such imitative knowledge.[58] The virtues can be expressed only by the body, which itself is shaped by the culture in which we are members. The virtues of our character are not detached from the body, mind, and spirit — or from our social context. For the body bears it and can be reconstituted only by means of a certain kind of gymnastics that is designed to evoke it, a mimesis that implies total investment and deep emotional identification.[59] The body is constantly involved with all the knowledge it reproduces,

55. Sherman, *The Fabric of Character* (New York: Cambridge Univ. Press, 1991), p. 168.

56. Pierre Bourdieu, *The Logic of Practice* (Stanford: Stanford University Press, 1990), pp. 68, 73.

57. *Merriam-Webster's Dictionary, 10th Edition,* p. 853.

58. Bourdieu, p. 73.

59. Ibid., p. 73.

and this knowledge never has something called "objectivity," for there is no freedom from body.

This discussion of Christian gestures and virtues is fascinating because they involve the body in such a profound way as one learns the right performance of gestures through mimicking the bodily gestures of other people. Each gesture that has meaning in the church is first learned or named by the church: one's use of that gesture, as a member of the body of Christ, is a way to learn and practice the greater good of the body of Christ. Milavec understands that imitation of one's elders is tied to the gift of grace that is performed in gestures: while faith is a gift from God, it still has to be named by a congregation, and people have to be trained to comprehend the Christian faith with their minds, bodies, and spirits. Early training greatly determines how one will hear, see, taste, touch, move, and know God, "if indeed one has been trained to hear God at all."[60]

Imitation as Learning in the Bible

In teaching wisdom to God's people, Proverbs admonishes the elders of the community to teach the younger ones the ways of God. The children, those who know little of the wisdom and knowledge of the Lord, are open to all kinds of influences and are in danger of being led astray by evil. Those who hunger to know God will learn from their elders: "Hear, my child, your father's instruction, and do not reject your mother's teaching" (Prov. 1:8); or "My child, do not despise the Lord's discipline or be weary of his reproof, for the Lord reproves the one he loves, as a father the son in whom he delights (Prov. 3:11-12).

Michael Fox says that children desire to learn the wisdom of the Lord because of their upbringing.[61] Children are promised that if they do what their parents instruct them to do — a gesture — then they will learn wisdom, which will bring them both the fear of God and righteousness. Children learn wisdom through the gesture of listening to the words (and saying them) and watching the actions of their elders. Children learn by absorbing their parents' gestural utterances: not only is the gesture of the parents' spoken words a way to wisdom, but the spoken words themselves are wisdom.[62] They set before us

60. Milavec, *To Empower as Jesus Did,* p. 11.

61. Michael Fox, "Pedagogy of Proverbs 2," *Journal of Biblical Literature,* 113, 2 (1994), 234.

62. Ibid., p. 237.

an example not only of how to talk but how to move in goodness, to know wisdom. Wisdom is traditionally taught by being handed down from parents to children through oral instruction, as the people of ancient Greece did.[63]

It is not only a matter of students accepting the words orally but also "walking in the way of the good, and keeping to the paths of the just." There is a kind of knowing that embodies goodness and justice. Jesus Christ said that we learn to do what he wants us to do through mimicry:

> For I have set you an example, that you also should do as I have done to you. Very truly, I tell you, servants are not greater than their master, nor are messengers greater than the one who sent them. If you know these things, you are blessed if you do them. (John 13:15-17)

This is Jesus as teacher, as rabbi or *didaskalos*. Jesus understood well that God's kingdom was being proclaimed both by what he said in his words and by the actions of his body. He presented an example to all his disciples throughout the ages, systematically reminding them that what they are doing in his name is a performance skill learned under the direction of the Teacher himself. Jesus is teaching our bodies, minds, and spirits to be his body, mind, and spirit by imitating his earthly ministry. Discipleship, according to Bonhoeffer, "means adherence to Jesus Christ alone, and immediately."[64] Discipleship and obedience to Jesus precede knowledge of Jesus as Lord, as well as a knowledge of who we are and whose we are. The practices of the church teach us discipleship and obedience to Christ, which lead us to a right understanding of not only who Jesus is but whose we are as God's people.[65] Calvin says that knowledge is born of obedience: we do not come to a right knowledge of God by taking someone's word for it, but by actually obeying God's word. Obedience is not a substitute for knowledge but is a way to the knowledge of God. Calvin emphasized that obedience rather than cognitive knowing is the path to a knowing that is significant.[66] And we know and practice obedience by watching and imitating others being obedient in Christ's body.

Jesus set himself as an example to be imitated: he was obedient to the point of death on the cross (Phil. 2:8). The Beatitudes (Matt. 5) constitute a list of what we are to do and not to do, and why we perform gestures:

63. J. Terence Forestell, C.S.B., "Proverbs," in R. Brown, J. Fitzmyer, and R. Murphy, eds., *Jerome Biblical Commentary* (Englewood Cliffs: Prentice-Hall, 1968), p. 499.

64. Dietrich Bonhoeffer, *Cost of Discipleship* (New York: Macmillan Publishing Company, 1975), p. 136.

65. *Rule of St. Benedict,* Chapter 5.

66. See Brueggemann, *The Land* (Philadelphia: Fortress, 1977), pp. 158-159.

> You have heard that it was said, "You shall love your neighbor and hate your enemy." But I say to you, Love your enemies and pray for those who persecute you, so that you may be children of your Father in heaven; for he makes his sun rise on the evil and on the good, and sends rain on the righteous and on the unrighteous. (Matt. 5:43-45)

Jesus not only told his followers what they are to do with their enemies; he also gave them a model when he prayed for his tormentors in his agony of death: "Father, forgive them."

St. Paul reminds us that in the Eucharist we eat bread and drink wine in remembrance of Jesus: "For as often as you eat this bread and drink the cup, you proclaim the Lord's death until he comes" (1 Cor. 11:26). As long as we perform the numerous gestures of the Eucharist, we remember the risen Christ until he comes again in glory. Paul learned this ritual from Jesus: "I received from the Lord what I also handed on to you" (1 Cor. 11:23). Jesus Christ's disciples continue to live and imitatively perform in his way of instruction, showing others both what to do and what not to do — since the body of Christ actually matters. Paul continually holds himself and his companions up as role models of the Christian faith, telling the various churches to imitate — *mimeisthai* — his example: "I appeal to you, then, be imitators of me" (1 Cor. 4:16); "Brothers and sisters, join in imitating me, and observe those who live according to the example you have in us" (Phil. 3:17).

Bonhoeffer says that being imitators of God is the highest calling of Christ's followers:

> The disciple looks solely at his Master. But when a man follows Jesus Christ and bears the image of the incarnate, crucified and risen Lord, when he has become the image of God, we may at last say that he has been called to be the "imitator of God." The follower of Jesus is the imitator of God.[67]

The Habit of Christly Gestures

In imitating Christ, as in learning anything new, we must acknowledge that our first moves are usually the most awkward. But after continuing rehearsal and practice, we soon find ourselves becoming more comfortable with some of the Christly gestures, and after years of performing them, there comes a time when we notice that once-awkward gestures are now habits — "holy

67. Bonhoeffer, *Cost of Discipleship,* p. 344.

habits." Aquinas says that habits are acquired dispositions that form us "all the way down," at the level of the body, the will, and the intellect — shaping our entire being. Furthermore, according to Joel Shuman, habits are prerequisites to living well in the body of Christ:

> Because we are complex creatures who are continually acting and being acted upon by a multitude of forces, habits require for their development the consistent repetition of very specific habituating acts that form our bodies in particular ways; without these acts, Aquinas seems to say, we cannot hope to develop the dispositions requisite to living well.
>
> Habits are . . . not valuable in themselves, but because they dispose [us] toward particular valuable ends. *Virtues* are the name given to habits that dispose the agent toward good ends.[68]

Eventually we will perform Christly gestures so often that they will become habits, not because they are valuable in themselves but because they frame our lives to make us open to doing God's will. Nancy Sherman discusses the making of virtuous character through the habituation of the "non-rational part of the soul" — being trained early in life by certain habits.[69] The hope is that, if we perform Christly gestures well and often enough, they will become habitual, as if it were "natural" for us to love God with our whole being.

Pierre Bourdieu notes that habits are a product of a habitat, the community in which we live, and they are also a "product of history." The narrative structure of the habit means that habit itself embodies a story already told and lived. Again, we are but the most recent beneficiaries of learning something quite old.[70] John Dewey further clarifies the complex patterns of habits by noting that a habit is not the same as a routine. For Dewey, a routine is an arrest of growth; however, an active habit involves or fosters growth through thought, invention, and initiation. By practicing certain habits, we have the capacity to adjust and readjust our lives in order to meet new circumstances; this gives us a sense of control amid circumstances over which we seem to have little control.[71]

The craft of gestures is not contained like a seed in some kind of original inspiration, nor is it dependent on something called "spontaneity." Instead, there is a dialectic between the intent of the artist or musician and his

68. Joel Shuman, *Body of Compassion* (New York: Westview, 1999), pp. 158-159.
69. Sherman, p. 162.
70. Bourdieu, *The Logic of Practice*, p. 54.
71. Dewey, *Democracy and Education*, p. 53.

or her habit-trained, gesture-bound skills. According to Bourdieu, being habituated into the basics of one's art or craft, like every other art of inventing, is what makes it possible to produce an infinite number of gesture-bound practices that are "relatively unpredictable — due to the corresponding situations — but also limited in diversity."[72]

Learning Habits of Christly Gestures

Dewey understood that a habit is not an autonomic nervous system reaction, which would make it essentially biologically determined; it is not simply of the body with no thought involved, just as no gesture is pure bodily act. A habit entails a person's practice of gestures undergoing a modification as the habit connects physical gesture and critical reflection. Knowledge is important in the practice of habits because we need to know which habits to practice — and when and how — in the diverse experiences of our lives.[73]

The performance of gestures takes place primarily in response to the requirements expected of us in highly concrete, increasingly complex, and practical situations. One of the by-products of habit-formed virtues is a sense of pleasure that only stimulates further growth and further practice.[74] In learning to sail on the sea, for example, we cannot replicate every possible situation to dispel a fear of drowning. While we can provide similar dry-land experiences in preparing someone for rough waters, we cannot predict how a novice will react to high seas except that he or she will use the habits learned on dry land to cope with the real thing. Similarly, while we cannot replicate precise examples of exercising specific virtues for every circumstance, we can instruct people about them while on "dry, flat ground." However, we cannot know when, where, or how certain virtues will come to the test and thus demand that they be practiced for specific occasions. It is only "out there" — in the very nexus of Christian community life, where people disagree with one another and are lost on the way toward reconciliation — that we are called on to practice patience and friendship in challenging one another for the good of the body of Christ.

72. Bourdieu, p. 55.

73. Dewey, p. 340.

74. Sherman, pp. 178-179, 191.

A Habitation for the Habitus of Christly Gestures

Belden Lane says that talk about God cannot be easily separated from a discussion of place.[75] A structure such as a house or sanctuary, or a landscape such as a meadow or a desert place, plays a central role in shaping how we imagine God or Christ's body. He says that meaningful participation in any environment or structure requires us to learn "gestures of approach," which he describes as disciplines of interpretation that enable us to enter such places: geography is simply a visible form of theology.[76] If theology is rooted in the life of the church, then the very atmosphere of a habitat can have an effect on all the ideas of a people, including their art, literature, and theology.[77]

I propose that our habit-of-being, shaped by our habits of Christly gestures, depends on and is shaped by the habitation in which we rehearse and perform those gestures. As Lane reminds us, meaningful participation in an environment such as a church requires us to learn certain "gestures of approach." By performing the correct gestures of approach, we can participate more fully — with a correct interpretation of the space that would be missing without a proper approach. Performing Christly gestures-as-habits aright matters in entering the habitation where we continue to learn and are sustained by Christly gestures.

Consider again the !Kung of Africa, who teach their young by showing them the tradition of their culture *in context,* as opposed to our modern approach of telling our young and old *about* the life of a church out of context. Jerome Bruner and Richard Katz studied the !Kung culture and noticed that all instruction in the ways of the !Kung was immersion of the young in the very life of the community, with constant interaction between young and old. They all play, dance, and sit together, and they participate in hunting activities together. Children are constantly using the rituals, tools, and weapons of the adult !Kung. Says Bruner: "In the end, every man in the culture knows nearly all there is to know about how to get on with life as a man, and every woman as a woman."[78] In our culture, we learn baseball best on the baseball diamond, piano at the keyboard, painting at the canvas, computers at the video monitor, and the gestures of the body of Christ *in* the body of Christ.

75. Belden Lane, *The Solace of Fierce Landscapes: Exploring Desert and Mountain Spirituality* (New York: Oxford University Press, 1998), pp. 8-11.

76. Ibid., p. 8 (quoting Jon Levenson).

77. D. H. Lawrence, "The Spirit of Place," in Armin Arnold, ed. *The Symbolic Meaning* (New York: Viking Press, 1964), pp. 15-31.

78. See Jerome Bruner, *Theory of Instruction* (Cambridge: Harvard University Press, 1966); Richard Katz, *Boiling Energy* (Cambridge: Harvard University Press, 1982).

CHAPTER NINE

Being the Body of Christ, Performing Christly Gestures

In the tender compassion of our God,
the dawn from on high shall break upon us,
to shine on those who dwell in darkness
and the shadow of death,
and to guide our feet into the way of peace.

Luke 1:78-79

It is an early winter morning: the sun is just rising on the eastern horizon, its rays slicing unevenly through the many trees in my backyard, and in the cold house I am tightly holding a hot cup of coffee in my chilled hands. No one else is awake, except for the dog. With lips moving sleepily, I stumble through the words of the Canticle of Zechariah as part of my daily ritual of morning prayer, slowly speaking in hushed tones, "In the tender compassion of our God," and then stopping at the point of asking the Lord to "guide my feet into the way of peace." I rest there before moving on to the prayers of intercession. It is both a call for me to move my feet and my life toward peace and a prayer for someone to aid me in those gestures.

This daily ritual, which I learned when living among the Benedictine monks at St. John's Abbey and St. Benedict's Monastery in central Minnesota, grounds me in the dailiness of the small and large Christly gestures. For example, I know that when I pray the morning prayer, I join a magnificent chorus of other voices praying a similar prayer to God this very morning and evening. Even this short line from the Canticle, or the words at the opening of the daily prayers, "O Lord, open my lips, and my mouth will proclaim your praise," are a reaching out: infused by grace, I am reaching out to take hold of God's gift of grace, while welcoming the assistance of others in making the gestures I perform each day. From moving my lips in a "Good morning" greeting to reaching out to comfort someone who is distraught, this is a way of worshiping God and following Christ in the ways of peace, faith, and love.

In this last chapter I wish to give the reader a narrative description of what a congregation might look, sound, feel, and move like if it were to follow the educational approach I propose. In reaching out to both academic classrooms and family tables, the household of God gathered together for worship and the people doing Christ's work on the city's streets or in rural ministries, I want to make palpable — if not palatable — the "what, when, why, and how" of the life I envision for members of Christ's body who yearn to discover the way they can be that body in their common gestures. Readers may hear echoes of their stories in my own stories of living in a l'Arche community; being an oblate in a Benedictine community; worshiping in Presbyterian, Baptist, Catholic, Episcopal, and Methodist congregations; being part of a Disciples or Kerygma Bible study, or a Narcotics Anonymous (NA) or Alcoholics Anonymous (AA) group; and being part of a midweek dinner or youth group outing. Undoubtedly all these weekend gatherings and tightly run organizations inside or outside the church contribute to the vision I have when I broadly describe a life that is based on our learning and performing the gestures of Christ's body together.

In outlining this vision, I will roughly follow what Jean Vanier has proposed as key elements of a growing community:

> A life of silent prayer, a life of service and above all of listening to the poor, and a community life through which all its members can grow in their own gift. It is by looking at these three elements that a community can evaluate whether it is alive or not.[1]

Building on Vanier's three basic elements, I propose the following areas where we Christians can discover, learn, and live the gestures in the truthful reality that we are members of Christ's body: communal worship; meals and celebrations; prayer; learning and performing our gifts and services; attending the various schools of the Christly gestures; taking gestures to our homes and

1. Jean Vanier, *Community and Growth* (Mahwah, NJ: Paulist Press, 1979), p. 80.

families in the household of God; and listening to and serving the needs of those who are poor or otherwise marginalized in the life of the church and the world.

Worship

I begin with the worship of God on the Sabbath day, when the members of Christ's body come together in the communal bodily gestures of bowing, kneeling, swaying, dancing, and praying to God in Christ.[2] In worshiping God, we stand on our feet — if we are able — to show the solidarity of our convictions. I am intrigued that it is an "unwritten expectation" that we stand for the opening and closing hymns, the confessions, the Lord's Prayer, the Apostles' or Nicene creeds, and for the passing of the peace. In some churches dancing occurs during worship, or individuals stand in solidarity with the preacher, while others make the sign of the cross at the mention of the Holy Trinity, standing and bowing whenever the processional cross comes near them.

Likewise, prayers may be prayed in all kinds of postures: some bow their heads, close their eyes, and fold their hands; some hold hands with others, such as when a congregation prays the Lord's Prayer; still others kneel in front of the pew or their seat, placing their head and hands on the seat in front of them. Positioning our bodies in a gesture to pray is a prayer embodied.

In worship I find that hospitality begins with the work of the greeters or ushers, who welcome members to church. Recently, when I arrived at a church five minutes late, I sat in an unoccupied seat near the back of the sanctuary, only to be "ushered out" of the seat by that morning's usher. She informed me — kindly but sternly — that the seat I had taken was her seat, and she did not help me find another seat. To discern the warmth of a congregation, I also watch for the contact that goes on during the passing of the peace or the time of greeting — to see whether people look each other in the eye and talk directly or whether they look away.

The Eucharist and baptism, the reaffirmation of baptisms and foot washing, the laying on of hands and altar calls — all these serve as great opportunities for members of Christ's body to move, individually and corporately. There are some churches that serve the elements of the Eucharist by intinction, while others come to the pews with heavy trays of bread and the

2. I realize that this could be on a late Saturday afternoon worship, as is the case with some Catholic and Episcopal churches, as well as on Sunday morning.

juice of the vine. Likewise, some baptisms welcome only a few spectators around the font, while others gather everyone together for the baptism in a pool or a river.

All in all, such powerful and purposeful gestures of the body, as directed by the intentions of the mind and the desires of the heart, are meant to both mark us as Christ's own and shape our interior posture so that we may be in a better position to worship and follow Christ. I have discovered that the more physical movement there is in worship and the more we participate with our bodies, minds, and spirits, the better the chances that the very young and those with disabling conditions — and all of us in between — are able to mark the process in which our lives are being made right with God. I remember being told by a mentor that worship is like physical therapy or a massage: our very lives are being straightened out by the Holy Spirit, who transforms our sinner's cramped and crooked posture.

But it isn't only my individual life that needs straightening out, but our gestured lives in the body of Christ. I emphasize the "our" in "Our Father" when I pray the Lord's Prayer; I hang onto the words "We believe" in the Nicene Creed, which remind us that we are all members of Christ's body. Worshiping with my community at St. Benedict's Monastery, I am reminded of the deceased sisters who have been a part of the life of the monastery when their names are mentioned on the anniversaries of their deaths; they are not forgotten because they are now part of the "communion of saints," which we confess that we believe in (Apostles' Creed).

The closing words of the Charge and the Benediction are crucial reminders of what we are to do during the week, now that we have been made right with God in Christ by the blessed infusion of the Holy Spirit: we must go out to serve the Lord in serving the needs of one another. Bowing one more time before the cross, dipping a hand in the baptismal font and crossing ourselves, we are marked as Christ-followers as we leave this service of worship.

Meals and Celebrations

To reinforce what has transpired in worship, we continue to shape and nurture Christly gestures during mealtimes and other celebrations, both immediately following worship and throughout the week, whether in our own homes or with other people in the body of which we are members. Jean Vanier has written that at the heart of a community are forgiveness and celebration, which are two faces of love:

> We celebrate the fact of being together; we give thanks for the gifts we have been given. Celebration nourishes us, restores hope and brings us the strength to live with the suffering and difficulties of everyday life.[3]

Celebrations are ways in which our Christly gestures are nourished and given purposefulness. Vanier says that the goals of a community are evident in the symbolic forms that bring hope and renewed strength and love as we take up the issues that confront our everyday lives.[4]

Our daily meals together are also a daily celebration dependent on gestures: we meet each other around a common table to be nourished physically, emotionally, and spiritually by the food, drink, and conversation. Vanier warns that meals should not be a time for contentious discussion. In point of fact, mealtimes with our enemies may bring about a necessary conversation toward making amends since it is difficult to keep a fight going when the salt or butter is at the other end of the table. Vanier writes:

> Even the simple gesture of passing the potatoes is a natural moment of communication which can bring people out of their isolation. They cannot remain behind the barriers of their depression when they have to ask for salt. The need for food encourages communication.[5]

Vanier is correct in his attack on self-service food, or eating many meals alone, or giving the young people in the house permission to "graze" on breakfast cereals for dinner in the evening. Research continues to show that children and adults alike develop certain social and conversational skills while eating at least one meal together during the day. The mealtime is also a time of remembering the gesture of prayer. I remember only too well rushing into a meal without the prayer, when Parker, then four years old, stopped the table of adults by bellowing, "We've not prayed yet." He was more in tune with the ritual of mealtime prayers than were the adults.

I envision a congregation having meals together at least once a week, either breakfast before worship or a lunch soon after. Or there might be other times during the week that small groups of people in a congregation would gather for a meal, with a specific meeting or an educational event before or afterwards. I know of some individual families who live in the same geographical area and attend the same church who gather together once a week

3. Vanier, p. 200.
4. Ibid., p. 201.
5. Ibid., p. 206.

for a common meal as a pseudo-house-church within a larger congregation.[6] They do this for a variety of reasons: on one hand, it is a time to practice gestures that are common among a group of people, such as the simple gesture of sharing food together; on the other hand, more than simple etiquette is being learned at a common table, because it is a time to share the stories and important issues of our lives in the church.

Prayer

There is much about the life of prayer and practicing the presence of God that is central to the shaping, nurturing, and well-being of a Christian community. For some, prayer is as necessary as bread, water, and shelter: to live is to pray. Prayer is more than a technique, though there are some techniques of prayer that lead us to a way of living our life *as* a prayer. The gestures of prayer take practice and must be repeated often throughout the day, and weekly as a community of Christians in worship. In prayer we open up our lives to that which is holy, seeking to be comforted and renewed by the One who alone hears and knows the ins and outs of our lives. Thus prayer is a communal gesture — taught, learned, performed, and nurtured by the members of Christ's body. We learn gestures of prayer from those who are well-versed in the ways of prayer, with some performed gestures passed down through the centuries, for example, Ignatian prayers and *lectio divina.* After Jesus' disciples asked, "Lord, teach us to pray" (Luke 11:1), he taught them his own prayer, what we call the Lord's Prayer.

Being a Member of Christ's Body

In our baptism we were publicly welcomed and celebrated as we each died to "self" and sin to join Christ's resurrection. We often mark baptism as "Day One" in enabling all those baptized to grow into an understanding of the "divine mystery" that changed their lives irrevocably. Furthermore, baptism celebrates the gifts and services we have been given by the Creator. Each person, regardless of his or her capacity or limitations intellectually, physically, emotionally, or spiritually, is blessed by God in Christ with such gifts for the com-

6. I mean to use "family" broadly, to include people who are not necessarily married, extended family members, people with or without children, people with or without partners.

mon good and further up-building of Christ's body: "We have gifts that differ according to the grace given to us" (Romans 12:6), and "all these gifts are activated by one and the same Spirit, who allots to each one individually just as the Spirit chooses" (1 Cor. 12:11).

I propose that, first, at baptism a person would be assigned a member of the church as an "accompanier," someone who would accompany the newly baptized in his or her life in a congregation. The task of the accompanier would not be that of counselor or spiritual director — or even "best buddy." Rather, the accompanier would metaphorically "walk with" the baptized one, checking in with that person at least once a month to be sure all is well in his or her life, keeping tabs on how well that person is learning the gestured practices and traditions of the church. Each member of a congregation or parish — from priest or pastor to janitor or sexton — would have an accompanier.

Second, part of each person's confirmation would be a time for the congregation to discern what his or her gifts and services will be in the life of the church. I have found in teaching Christian education classes that few have been told by their church that they are to be teachers in the body of Christ. Rather, students have told me that they decided to be teachers themselves, without feedback from the community of Christ in which they were raised. Discerning is an ongoing dialogue between the person and the congregation, a process that includes prayer, much consulting with the elders, family members, and others whose life interests are similar — as well as with those whose are different. I agree with Yoder that our gifts do not necessarily equal our job or career vocation or professional specialization.[7] Yet I am hesitant to say that there is a great disconnect between the charismatically empowered roles we each have in church and our professions. Often the nurse or special educator is a healer in the life of a church, and the art teacher in the public schools is also a teacher in the congregation.

What are the gifts and services? They could be the gifts of ministry, teaching, exhortation, giving, leading, and compassion (Romans 12); or they could be the service of an apostle, a prophet, or a healer (1 Cor. 12). Confirmation — which can come at any age, depending on the life experiences of the person being confirmed — would then be a time when a person's gestured gifts and services to the body of Christ are confirmed, as they are brought even deeper into their dependence on the life of Christ. For example, there are some whom we see through their gestures as healers, teachers, or prophets early on in life. Let us not forget that Jeremiah was a young boy when he became a prophet, chosen by God.

7. Yoder, *Body Politics,* p. 53.

Gestures may take different forms among the gifts and talents. Some may teach with words or writings, while others may use art or dance; some are prophets who lead oppressed people in protest movements against racist policies in a church's polity, for example, expressing themselves in loud demonstrations with a keen sense of massaging the body politic. Others protest with sharp writing or fantastic paintings. For example, I know artists who have sculpted incredibly dramatic images out of the guns gathered during a gun buy-back program. Some — such as physicians — heal the wounds of others; some do so with harp music; or, in the case of counselors, with soothing words to a troubled soul.[8] The person's gestured gifts and services to the good of the Christian community are supported by the entire congregation. I am especially struck by how these gifts will take different forms in a person's life. Consider Sister Margaret van Kempen of St. Benedict's Monastery: a geologist by profession, she is a wonderful painter of butterflies and a textile artist. The art is a gift that came to her later in life, or was always there but never found an avenue for expression — until she became a teacher of it in her spiritual community.

Third, once a person's gifts and services have been identified, it is the responsibility of the church to shape and nurture the gestures that are part of the gifted one for the whole of that person's life. In most churches, one person's gift is shared by others who may have had more time and experience with the gift, those we designated earlier as "master craftspersons." The duty of the master craftsperson is to teach and shape the particular gifts of the young apprentice, much as one would in a professional guild. Each year both the master craftsperson and the apprentice would report to the elders about their progress in nurturing the gift. When the master craftsperson does not have much more to teach the apprentice, the teaching duties would shift to another elder craftsperson. Soon enough, the apprentice will become the master craftsperson of gestures and will assume the responsibility of teaching others the gestures specific to his or her gift.

Fourth, there would also be classes with other apprentices in the church; and, most importantly, there would be gatherings of other master craftspersons and apprentices with different gifts and services — all with the intention of learning to work and live together. The key to all of this "working" is the gift of listening to and comprehending the gestures of others in

8. It is here that Howard Gardner's theory of multiple intelligence is most helpful. Gardner argues that there are various intelligences by which a person knows the world: linguistic; artistic or spatial; physical; musical; mathematical; inter- and intra-personal. Gardner, *Frames of the Mind* (New York: Basic Books, 1985).

sharing the vision of a Christian community. The body of Christ must discern together; they must have a sense of how to share authority in a gathering; and they must supply the overwhelming support that is necessary for each person to grow and be better able to carry responsibility for the up-building of the body.[9]

The goal is for us in the church to be responsible for planning and carrying out the educational progress of each member for his or her entire life. In modern education there is a formal set of expectations of what students will have achieved by the time they graduate from high school. This should also be true in the church: if we are constantly growing in the life of Christ, intentional pilgrimage catechesis should be for the duration of a person's life, with a yearly assessment of what he or she has learned about the gestured ways of Christ. What we have "achieved" in using God's gifts, nurtured by our spiritual communities, is one of the wonders to be celebrated throughout the course of our lives — from birth to death.

Schools of Christly Gestures

Education in the gestures of Christ's body is both social enculturation — the culture in which we live educates us — and an intentional, systematic form of instruction about the *telos,* the narrative, and the technique of the gestures we perform. There are a few characteristics that are important in discussing such "schools," services, and gestures. First, along with shaping and nurturing our gifts from God, there is the task of learning the basic gestures of Christ's body. This can be done in numerous ways (depending on the particulars of a congregation or denomination) but should be tied to the rubrics of the church itself. For example, Bonhoeffer proposes, in *Life Together,* that a community's ministry include various schooled gestures: the ministry of holding one's tongue; the ministry of meekness; the ministry of listening; the ministry of helpfulness; the ministry of proclaiming; and the ministry of authority.[10] In *Body Politics,* Yoder suggests five practices in which God is active in human history: (1) fraternal admonition; (2) the open meeting; (3) the diversification of gifts; (4) baptism; (5) and the Eucharist: "They are actions of God, in and with, through and under what men and women do. Where they are happening, the people of God is real in the world."[11] Jean Vanier suggests loose

9. Vanier, p. 135.

10. Bonhoeffer, *Life Together,* pp. 90-109.

11. Yoder, p. 73.

guidelines for being community: covenant, nourishment, gifts, welcome, meetings, and celebrations.[12] Alongside the rubrics of these three theologians, I would include a school of the Eucharist; a school of Baptism; a school of Prayer; and a school of Mission or Outreach. (Another scenario might be to group the schools according to theological virtues: for example, a school of Charity, a school of Justice, a school of Honesty and Truthfulness, to name but a few). I would also include a school of Common Christly Gestures.

Second, I use the term "school" to designate a place for teachers to teach and students to learn certain skills and disciplines with teachers. In using a schooling approach, I understand that we no longer use age and grade groupings in ecclesial instruction: that is, all education in the church is both intergenerational and integrated — a mixture of old and young, women and men, poor and rich, disabled and non-disabled, and from all racial and ethnic groups. I assume that all members will need to attend my proposed "schools" perhaps twice or more in their lifetimes, because our traditions and rituals grow and are reformulated and refined; for example, what we learned once about the Eucharist may have changed by the time we investigate it again — ten years or more later. I could see portions of a "school" being for members who have spent many years in a church but may want to explore certain beliefs or practices in greater detail as they mature.

Third, I am blending the ages together because experience has shown me that young and old can learn a great deal from one another. Chronological age may not be the best basis on which to decide groupings; age in terms of experience in the life of the church may be more determinative of our abilities to absorb the lessons of these "schools." For example, consider these two biblical admonitions: "When I was a child, I spoke as a child, I thought as a child, I reasoned as a child; when I became an adult, I put an end to childish ways" (1 Cor. 13:11). Or, when speaking to the "young" Corinthian church, Paul says: "And so brothers and sisters, I could not speak to you as spiritual people, but rather as people of the flesh, as infants in Christ. I fed you with milk, not solid food, for you were not ready for solid food. Even now you are still not ready, for you are still of the flesh" (1 Cor. 3:1-3). But consider these words of Jesus, when he was asked who was the greatest in the kingdom of heaven: "He called a child whom he put among them, and said, 'Truly, I tell you, unless you change and become like children, you will never enter the kingdom of heaven. Whoever becomes humble like this child is the greatest in the kingdom of heaven. Whoever welcomes one such child in my name welcomes me'" (Matt. 18:1-4). On the one hand, while we may be chronologi-

12. See Vanier, pp. vi-viii.

cally old, we may be mere infants in the eyes of God when we first join the church; on the other hand, we need to have some aspects of a child's dependency for the entirety of our lives, so that we may receive, with gladness and humility of heart, the kingdom of heaven. Having children in our midst is a good reminder. However, it does not dismiss the idea of two or more levels of experience in each school: one with novices and another with people of greater experience and age.

Fourth, each "school" will cover these aspects of a subject and the accompanying gestures: the theological importance of a subject; the biblical implications; the historical and liturgical aspects; the pastoral and practical implications — all of which are educational, of course. Teachers would identify how each person learns best, and would then teach to that strength rather than forcing everyone to read or write, paint or draw. Some will learn best through art, others through the written word; still others excel and learn best in mathematical or musical settings. And, when teachers include the very young and those with some disabling conditions in the class, there is a good chance that others in the class will be stretched in finding ways to communicate the gospel with them.

Fifth, for those churches following a liturgical-year calendar and a lectionary calendar for the biblical text, I suggest that those holy days, feast days, and lectionary texts be included in the various "schools" — to guide discussion and teach Christly gestures. For example, in the school of the Eucharist, how does the work of St. Benedict or Bonhoeffer influence our understanding of breaking bread together with strangers during the Christmas season? This gives us a richer and deeper understanding of the connections between the Bible's stories, the liturgical year, and the daily issues of the Christian life.

How would these schools work? Here are some examples:

School of the Eucharist

The room looks more like a kitchen than a typical Sunday school classroom. The purpose of this class will be a deeper understanding of the eucharistic practices throughout the story of the church. Consider a year-long study of the Eucharist beginning with lessons on how to bake bread, starting with wheat and yeast; some will discuss the metaphorical use of "bread" in the Bible and the church's history. Studying the biblical texts in these ecclesiological groupings will evoke issues long unheard in the church. Others will teach about the story behind the use of bread at the Last Supper and the story of the loaves and the fishes. Another group will look at the liturgical use of a flat bread — with no leaven — in contrast to a home-baked loaf. Throughout these two- to three-month hands-on sessions, our bodies, minds, and spirits will be engaged, all five senses stimulated in the learning process.

For two to three months after that, the subject of wine would follow a similar approach: discussing and producing wine or grape juice; discovering the biblical references and metaphorical or literal use of "wine" in the Bible and church history; and perhaps sessions of bread tasting and wine tasting. After some months, the sessions would focus on the liturgical and historical roots of the Eucharist in our various denominations and congregations, followed by a focus on the connection between our formation in Christly gestures in the Eucharist and our application of that to the rest of our lives.

School of Common Christly Gestures

This is the other "school" that should be implemented as a core course: a church's membership needs to learn and perform some gestures that are characteristic of being Christ's body on earth. The space for this course would look more like a dance studio than a typical Sunday school classroom: one wall would feature a mirror — and perhaps a dance bar for those unsteady on their feet. There would also be video and taping equipment for those who would choose to videotape their bodily gestures — in order to review them immediately after class. In this school there would be a long list of gestures to be performed, as determined from the Bible: for example, along with the Old Testament's Decalogue and Proverbs, we read in the Beatitudes a long "laundry" list that Jesus gave us, his followers, of things we need to do to live the Jesus-life in the church. Paul, in his letters, gave us a complementary list of gestures that mark us as Christians: "Bless those who persecute you; rejoice with those who rejoice, weep with those who weep; live in harmony; don't be haughty" (Rom. 12:14-16). These common Christian actions and values are gestures that embody all that we believe, think, and desire in our lives; and we will be required to learn them through continual performance throughout our lives.

The Household of God

Outside the intentional catechetical instruction in the way of Christly gestures, there are also the learning and formation that continue in the family's life in the household of God. What we learn as master craftspersons and apprentices, or in the context of the various schools, or in worship — these we apply to our lives as members of God's household. It is imperative that we see the life of a family not as "outside" the church but rather as the church itself, for wherever two or three are gathered in the name of Jesus, he is there in our midst. The ritualistic Christly gestures must be nurtured and further shaped in the context of our family — among the sisters and brothers of God's household — as well as in our jobs, schools, and other activities that crowd our lives.

Welcoming Those on the Church's and World's Borders

Jean Vanier says that "opening to God in adoration and opening to the poor in welcome and service are the two poles of a community's growth, and signs of its health."[13] In working with those who are poor or in distress, it isn't so much to do "charity work" or to "comfort the distressed and distress the comfortable"; it is to practice the gestures of *being with* those who are poor or distressed, listening to their needs rather than telling them what they *should* need; and together building what they need and want as they acquire a new sense of self-confidence in discovering the gifts and services that they — and we — can bring to Christ's body. How far should we go in such gestures? To the ends of the earth and the end of the ages (Matt. 28:20).

This necessary work of Christ's body is not easy; often it is in the eyes of the marginalized that we experience the ways we may have participated in a system that has robbed people of justice, love, and hope in their lives. We may see in the eyes of the poor and disabled not only the weaknesses of others but our own personal weaknesses. For example, it is in my work with people suffering profoundly disabling conditions that I can fully perceive my own mortality, limitations, and vanity. I must learn to truly see what I'm looking at and to have the stamina of character to perform the gesture of seeing this world as *God's* creation and listening to it as if Christ were really among us now. He calls us to stop looking for the Holy Spirit everywhere else but in the eyes of those who are homeless or victims of rape, those in prison or in drug halfway houses. Joan Chittister says, "The Now is holy and full of God and to be savored and suffused with the consciousness of the God of time. . . . God is where I am. . . . God is where you are."[14]

Christ has no hands but our hands in reaching out to those who need assistance, just as we need his hands when we ourselves feel fragile. Outreach

13. Vanier, p. 81.

14. Chittister, *Wisdom Distilled from the Daily,* p. 205.

gestures may be as common and mundane as working at an interfaith shelter or corresponding with a political prisoner in another country. The streets of our modern world make up one of the best classrooms for learning and performing gestures of charity, hospitality, courage and justice, and for speaking truth in love. For example, as my close friend and my daughter and I were getting out of the car on a cold evening, there was a homeless man on the passenger side begging for some money. As I punched quarters into the parking meter, I watched my eight-year-old daughter carefully observing my friend as he engaged in a gentle conversation with the man in need. Convinced that the man was indeed needy, and calling him by his first name, my friend reached into his own pocket and pulled out some money. This gesture of engagement and charity became a fantastic "teaching moment" for my daughter as the three of us discussed for a couple of minutes what had just happened; and she and I have repeated the same gesture on other occasions.

The words of the old hymn may best explain how the worship of God and service to others make a complete circle:

> Called from worship into service
> Forth in your great name we go,
> To the child, the youth, the aged,
> Love in living deeds to show.
> Hope and health, goodwill and comfort,
> Counsel, aid, and peace we give,
> That your children, Lord, in freedom,
> May your mercy know, and live.

In the concluding Canticle of Mary (in the Evening Prayer), we lift up our voices with hers as our souls rejoice in the Lord. I usually mumble this prayer late in the evening, as my eyes droop with sleepiness, and I see a grain of hope in the realization that in our gestures God in Christ continues to be on the side of those who love and fear God in every generation, and God scatters the proud in their conceit while lifting up the lowly. This is the promise God has kept since making it to Abraham and Sarah — and all generations since. The God of Christly gestures reigns in love.

Epilogue

[Jesus said,] "For I have set you an example, that you also should do as I have done to you."

John 13:15

Christians are called to be gesturers of the Word, and that Word is Christ, God's living Word to us: "And the Word became flesh and lived among us, and we have seen his glory, the glory as of a father's only son, full of grace and truth" (John 1:14). Jesus performed many gestures in God's name: he healed the sick, cared for the poor, proclaimed the goodness of God's kingdom in his very being, and enacted it in his charitable gestures. To be in Christ means to be gesturers of the Word of God, the One who not only dwelt among us but continues to dwell among us, emboldening and enabling us to perform the gestures he would offer, that is, caring for the neighbor out of love for God. Taking care of children who are sick because of a contaminated environment, being with those cast as outsiders in society and the church, standing in solidarity with those disabled and those without families, equipping those who are poor, preaching the Good News to those who thirst and hunger for it, showing hospitality to all who are strangers to us — these things are what it means to be doers and gesturers of the Word-become-flesh. The risen Lord is present in these multitudes of gestures of his body in the world.

Given the power of gestured movements — from using our tongues to raising our hands to heaven in worshiping God — let us consider in what other ways congregations are currently performing Christly gestures. I want to suggest ways churches may more intentionally learn and more fully live the gestures of Christ.

A Renewed Appreciation for the Gestures in Worship[1]

The Bible is full of examples of Christly gestures, as well as directions on how to perform them for the good of the body. Paul Connerton demonstrates the significance and power of one such gesture performed in worship by many Roman Catholics (and some Protestants): the gesture of kneeling.

> In rites the body is given the appropriate pose and moves through the prescribed actions. The body is held braced and attentive in standing; the hands are folded and placed as though bound in praying; persons bow down and express their impotence by kneeling; or they may completely abandon the upright posture in the abasement of bodily prostration. The relative sparseness of such repertoires is their source of strength. . . . The subtlety of ordinary language is such that it can suggest or imply finely-graded degrees of subordination, respect, disregard, and contempt. . . . But the limited resources of ritual posture, gesture and movement strip communication clean of many hermeneutic puzzles. One kneels or one does not kneel. To kneel in subordination is not to state subordination, nor is it just to communicate a message of submission. To kneel in subordination is to display it through the visible, present substance of one's body. . . . Such performative doings (gestures) are particularly effective, because unequivocal and materially substantial, ways of "saying"; and the elementariness of the repertoire from which such "sayings" are drawn makes possible at once their performative power.[2]

If kneeling has such a powerful impact on the life of the worshiper, what impact do the other movements of worship have? Liturgy is at the center of church life and the reason we perform gestures: to worship and glorify God. Max Johnson, quoting Vatican II's "Constitution on the Sacred Liturgy," says:

> The liturgy is the summit toward which the activity of the Church is directed; at the same time it is the fountain from which all her power

1. In the following descriptions of gestures in the various parts of congregational or parish life, I am using words with the prefix "re-" on purpose: to show that I am not advocating something new but educating Christians in something quite old.

2. Paul Connerton, *How Societies Remember*, p. 59.

> flows. . . . From the liturgy . . . as from a fountain, grace is channeled into us; and the sanctification of [people] in Christ and the glorification of God, to which all other activities of the Church are directed as toward their goal, are most powerfully achieved.[3]

In the gestures we perform in worshiping God as Christ's body, we discover a sacred place for what Johnson calls our "displaced" lives: "Indeed, the spiritual journey in Christ is a journey of both place and displacement, a journey of death and resurrection, of birthing pangs and the bringing forth of new life, and the paradigm for all this is most certainly baptism."[4] Gestures themselves become markers for the pilgrimage: through them we signal to God and others where we are out of a deep knowing of whose we are.

Consider that we often enter worship in a rushed state of mind, body, and spirit, if not bruised severely by the world that preoccupies our lives. It is a gesture to come into worship, with or without music playing, and before the call to worship to sit down and bow our heads, to let our lives quiet down. When we stand for the call to worship, we change gestures and let everyone know that worship has begun.[5] In the Presbyterian Church (USA), I am struck by the flow of the gestures: the singing of the opening hymn to uttering the prayer of confession; then the audible — if not threatening — silence following the unison prayer; then the release of tension in the minister's declaration of forgiveness; and the invitation to embody the forgiveness with Christ's peace as we share the right hand of fellowship narrated by "the peace of Christ be with you," thus cementing what God has done and is doing in our lives. We then rejoice and praise God for his gift of peace by singing the *Gloria Patri.*

There is a powerful traditional gesture of standing for the reading of Scripture in both the Roman Catholic and Anglican liturgies, connoting reverence for the gospel (some church bodies sing "Alleluia" before Scripture is read, while others make the sign of the cross on their forehead, lips, and heart). Then, before we sit down to hear the Word proclaimed in the sermon, we utter the gestured words, "Praise to you, Lord Jesus Christ." Our worship of God is alive with a rich repertoire of Christly gestures, the grace of which renews and changes our body, mind, and spirit. Liturgy, says Johnson,

3. Maxwell Johnson, *The Rites of Christian Initiation,* p. 365.

4. Ibid., p. 365.

5. I understand that there are those who, for a variety of reasons, are not able to stand. There are other gestures by which they may participate in the movements of worship. For example, some congregations remain seated to be in solidarity with those in wheelchairs. Others in wheelchairs raise their hands to worship God in the opening call to worship.

is a welcome place in our constant experience of displacement, inviting us home always, always back home to reclaim, renew, reaffirm and reappropriate our baptism so that we might learn again to become who we are, the people God has already made us to be in Jesus Christ by water and the Spirit. Not only can we go home again. We must go home again! Our very identity depends upon it.[6]

Reclaiming our Baptismal Vows and Gestures

Baptism is forever; it is more than a casual reminder that we have been saved. Baptism is a watery yet indelible mark on our very lives, a gesture in which the congregation makes clear to everyone that God's grace has been performed and that the baptized one is saved by the blood of the Lamb of God. Martin Luther, when in despair, would trace the sign of the cross on his forehead and say, "I have been baptized." No matter what he experienced or perceived as dangers before him, the sign of his baptism reminded him that God had promised both justification and sanctification.[7]

Baptism is an unofficial beginning of our education in the performance of Christly gestures. It is a sacrament and thereby a gestured ritual that announces to all in the present world and to the communion of saints that we are God's possessions and thus have been given a new name — child of God. This sacramental gesture begins the intentional indoctrination into the myriad gestures we must learn and perform in Christ's body. We are to learn the necessary gestures as we are placed in the world as members of what Max Johnson calls a "community of displaced people, people on a pilgrimage, who belong nowhere except where they are led, a people sure of their identity as the body of Christ."[8]

We perform the gesture of many profound vows at our baptism. The crucial ones in the education of Christians are the ones uttered for the child by parents or guardians and the ones uttered by the adult being baptized, and the gestured utterance of the members of the congregation — that they will raise the newly baptized into what John Calvin would call an "understanding of our baptism." The radical nature of baptism is that the gestured baptismal mark on our life, and the vow that both the baptized and the witnesses have uttered in their oral gestures, can never be rescinded. The gesture marks us

6. Johnson, p. 391.
7. Ibid., p. 390.
8. Ibid.

for eternity. It is important for us congregants to comprehend our lifelong part in teaching the one newly baptized the vast wealth of gestures that will guide her or him on the pilgrimage of this life into eternal life.

We could have a "primer" of gestures, in which we begin with the gesture of prayer, to be followed by instruction in the gestures of worship, including the gestures of the creeds and confessions of the church. But we should never forget to remind those baptized of the gestures performed at their baptism, which have brought them into a baptismal understanding of life in the body of Christ.

Reclaiming Ancient Catechetical Practices and Relearning Gestures of Loving Neighbors and Welcoming Strangers

Having been baptized, we spend the rest of our lives learning and relearning the gestures that mark our being and shape our character in Christ's body. Again, in the ancient practice of catechesis, understood to be a lifelong course of instruction in Christly gestures, we examine our lives time and again. I am advocating that congregations again take an active role in bringing up the people of God to be Christian people. At some time in our lives in Christ's body there should be a process of identifying our gifts and roles. In some denominations vocation is an inner calling of the member, and in others it is an outer calling; nevertheless, there is the need for all members to have their roles and gifts confirmed in Christ's body. Once the church has confirmed a person's vocation, he or she has to be designated a master craftsperson, who then works with five or six others who share the same call (as teachers, apostles, or prophets, for example), or designated as one who is a cheerful giver in Christ's body. Instructions may be weekly or daily, depending on the gestures being learned; but each member will be examined yearly by the elders of the church concerning his or her performance of the gestures learned.

With regard to the relationship between master craftsperson and apprentice, churches should assign master craftspersons and accompaniers who can continually refine the daily gestures performed by apprentices — as well as those specific to the apprentice's vocational calling in the body. Even master craftspersons may be under the tutelage of other master craftspersons. Throughout the course of the church year there will be opportunities to learn other gestured performances of the gospel outside of our vocations. For example, there may be sessions for learning the gestures of the Eucharist or baptism, sessions on the gestures of hospitality and the visitation of the sick, sessions on the gestures of nonviolence for young people. There may be sessions to learn the gestures associated with a holy day or a feast day in the church year. Instructions in the gestures can happen anywhere — in a church sanctuary or at home, in a nursing home or on the city's streets feeding the sick and hungry.

The highlight of a graduate seminar I taught on pilgrimage as Christian education (in which we read pilgrimage narratives ranging from Chaucer's *Canterbury Tales* to Dorothy Day's autobiography) came in the last two days, when we walked almost twenty-eight miles — from Snow Camp to Durham, North Carolina. The purpose of performing this gesture of Christian pilgrimage was to embody the way of a pilgrim, which changed forever how we read pilgrimage narratives. An unforgettable moment came on Franklin Street, the main thoroughfare of Chapel Hill, as we neared the end of our journey. Walking single file, with one pilgrim holding a six-foot cross and leading the way, we encountered three homeless and hungry men on the curb of this crowded college street. In their hands they held a small cardboard box with the words "I'm hungry and could use some money" written crudely on the top and some spare change jingling in the bottom.

The moral imperative that would direct our Christly gestures was simple yet profound: as pilgrims carrying the cross of Christ, we faced the dispossessed and marginalized, the homeless and hungry, with our pockets full of loose change and dollar bills. Looking at each other quickly, feeling frantic and not knowing quite what to do, we nonetheless knew we had to do something. Someone held the cross while the cross-bearer dug in his pocket for money; then the rest of us dug into our pockets and backpacks. "Just as you did it to one of the least of these who are members of my family, you did it to me" (Matt. 25:40) is something I uttered to the pilgrims, and it rang in our ears, pricking our consciences to make the manual gestures of dropping money into the box without questioning those asking for it. "Be doers of the word, not just hearers" made complete sense as we extended our hands — both offering money in a gesture of compassion and also extending friendship and hospitality, shaking the hands of those we were giving to, looking them in the eye, and sharing the peace of Christ with them.

Such is the serendipitous nature of learning in context, as we performed gestures that embodied the Christian virtue of charity: our minds, bodies, and spirits were moved to do the right and good thing in Christ. We learned to present ourselves and welcome others as Christ calls us to show proper honor to all who share our faith, for in the guest and the stranger we welcome Christ himself.[9]

9. *Rule of St. Benedict,* Chapter 53.

Index of Names

Index of Scripture References